RETAIL THERAPY

Retail Therapy

Making strategic relationships work

Rob Jones

with Dan Murphy

© Rob Jones and Dan Murphy 2003

First published 2003 by
PALGRAVE MACMILLAN
Houndmills, Basingstoke, Hampshire RG21 6XS and
175 Fifth Avenue, New York, N.Y. 10010
Companies and representatives throughout the world

PALGRAVE MACMILLAN is the global academic imprint of the Palgrave
Macmillan division of St. Martin's Press, LLC and of Palgrave Macmillan Ltd.
Macmillan® is a registered trademark in the United States, United Kingdom
and other countries. Palgrave is a registered trademark in the European
Union and other countries.

ISBN 1–4039–0171–6

This book is printed on paper suitable for recycling and made from fully
managed and sustained forest sources.

A catalogue record for this book is available from the British Library.

Designed and formatted by
The Ascenders Partnership, Basingstoke

10 9 8 7 6 5 4 3 2 1
12 11 10 09 08 07 06 05 04 03

Printed and bound in Great Britain by
Creative Print and Design (Wales), Ebbw Vale

Contents

Acknowledgements

I would like to thank family and friends who helped with suggestions and proofreading. Thanks to Danny Turner of Astech for letting the book come first. A special thanks to Emma Cahill who was endlessly supportive, enormously helpful and terribly amusing. Thanks also to Dr. Dylan Evans for his input on evolutionary psychology.

Rob Jones

Preface

David Williams

I came to retail relatively late in my business career, and I never had the advantage of being able to read this book as we embarked upon the huge challenge of turning around one of the UK's largest retailers here at First Quench.[1]

Dan Murphy has worked closely with the First Quench management team for the last year or so and recently passed me a draft copy of his and Rob's book. As our turnaround journey was well underway by that time, and because I assumed that the book would be simply another retail 'primer', I put it to one side. A week or so later, I took the book with me on a business trip, and was very pleasantly surprised to find a book which placed in context so many of the initiatives that we had implemented as Private Equity owners of a major UK retailer.

First Quench was acquired by the Principal Finance Group of Nomura[2] in October 2000 who saw the solid cash flows and high asset backing as extremely attractive features of a poorly managed and underperforming business. What I found so engaging about this book was the way it sets out in clear and easy to read language exactly why such multiple retail cashflows are so attractive to private equity investors, and what needs to be done from a 'retail best practice' viewpoint to improve the management and performance of such large retailers.

My own experience of successful business turnarounds, including our journey here at First Quench, has been that they tend to follow a certain pattern. To quote the old phrase, 'Why change a winning formula?'. However, as I have come to understand more about running a large retailer, I have realised that we operate in an extremely complex and

---

1 First Quench owns and operates 2200 off-licences under well-known high street names including Thresher and Victoria Wine. It is one of the UK's largest retailers, and until October 2000 was owned by two UK brewers, who ran it as an outlet for their brands. Under Nomura's ownership the business has grown in value through implementing a series of customer-facing retail initiatives and through a fierce focus on working capital, cashflow, and inventory management.

2 Nomura PFG, now called Terra Firma

competitive environment. Small changes in margin points make a significant difference to our bottom line and 'competitive advantage' is an increasingly elusive concept. Across our national chain of stores and brands there are ever-changing local and regional differences in consumer profile and competition which make it hugely challenging to keep hold of our customers and build loyalty. If I have learned one thing about retail in my time, here it is – that we must never allow ourselves to think we have achieved a 'lock' on our knowledge.

The team here continue to work hard to build clarity and direction around our product ranges, our supply chain, our store proposition and the way we interact with our customers. It is enormously complex and challenging when we consider that we have over 2000 stores, 15,000 employees, 4000 product lines, and hundreds of suppliers. However, as I read through this book many of the issues and concepts we have been thinking about started to fall into place. The sections concerning the way retailers might manage their relationships with customers, suppliers, and people really threw some light onto the big issues that we faced in our early days here at First Quench.

So, if you are expecting just another 'retail primer' from Rob and Dan, please think again. This is a stimulating book that places retail in the wider context of good business practice. It's about business first and retail second. It contains some forthright views on business that many will find uncomfortable but if there is an underlying theme it is that 'there really is a better way out there' ... something I've believed in all my career.

Above all, the book is based on common sense and observed practice ... both traits that the Private Equity investors value and are applying increasingly to the exciting world of retail.

David Williams,
CEO, First Quench Retail Limited
September 2002

Opening remarks

A little background

The way things have turned out, most of the words in this book are mine; the ideas, though, are largely a joint effort. They come from the discussions Dan Murphy and I have been having for several years now about the art and science of retail. It's difficult to say who came up with what because we've talked most of it backwards and forwards so often.

While I've been locked away slaving over a word processor putting the book together, Dan has been running a huge retail project as an independent consultant. While I've been rounding out the theory for the book, he's continued to explore new ideas in a live business and to discover what works in practice.

As well as developing the ideas and contributing an introductory chapter for the book, Dan's also lent a hand with the rough drafts of my chapters. If a juggernaut of a consulting project and the arrival of twin baby girls hadn't coincided with our publishing deadline, you'd probably be reading his words now.

Dan and I met a few years ago, when we worked for the same UK-based management consulting firm. We were both retail specialists, and naturally we tended to end up on the same projects. Most of the time, he was my boss, but like all really good bosses he hardly ever reminded anybody of that fact. The only way you can tell that Dan is in charge is that things tend to run smoothly and everyone seems to know what they're supposed to be doing. He's also been around retail – real retail I mean, not consulting – for two decades. Dan knows shops.

If he and I had only worked in retail, we probably wouldn't have come up with the ideas you'll read here. What really started us thinking was seeing retail from the perspective of management consultancy.

Consultancy is a funny business; some days I think it's more like something the military would come up with than a business idea. Dan and I would be part of a small team metaphorically parachuted into a client's firm. We'd have an objective to achieve and we'd have to familiarise ourselves very quickly with the lie of the land. Sometimes it even felt like we were behind enemy lines.

Then again, maybe it was less like a commando mission and more like entertaining the troops during wartime. We'd be sent in with only four weeks to come up with a script and put on a show.

There's always a lot more going on behind the scenes than meets the eye in consulting. Some companies bring in the consultants to put a little icing on the cake, to help give them a little something extra. The projects *we* worked on, though, tended to be at the other end of the scale. We'd be called in the way a person who's been told they only have a month to live might call in a personal-fitness trainer. Occasionally we felt like a chain-smoking alcoholic was asking us whether we could recommend them a good vitamin supplement.

But that's just one extreme; we encountered the full range of scenarios. Sometimes the clients realised they were in a mess and were receptive to *real* ideas for change and not just placebos. Other times, the problems a business was having would turn out to be nothing more serious than growing pains.

Whatever the condition of the company, the business itself was only ever half the story. Equally important would be the dynamics of the board and the senior managers – what you might call the politics of the situation.

Actually, there's a whole chapter I wrote about the politics of management but you won't find it here; I left it out. I couldn't get the tone right in the end; it always came out either bland or insulting. Talking about politics is like that.

In truth, I think most people are against politics – right up until they need a consensus from a group of opinionated people. Then compromise seems like the most natural and productive thing in the world and doing a deal becomes the only way to make progress. I think maybe if you eliminate politics, you eliminate business too.

Coming at it from the other end of the spectrum, a company that can't keep its staff feeling good is heading for trouble. It's just a question of how far you'll go to keep everyone happy and positive. Taken too far, safeguarding morale can become an end in itself and pointing out that there are real problems becomes an attack on the business.

Fortunately, I've decided to spare you my musings on the subject – at least for now. We'll dip into it in a couple of places, but we'll try to avoid wading out far enough to get into trouble.

So politics don't make it into the book, but they still had a hand in creating it. Boards aren't elected in quite the same way public officials are, but there are some similarities. A lot of directors feel that if they acknowledge every little thing that might need improving they're going to cause a panic and weaken their own position of authority – and with it their ability to fix anything.

So directors rarely want to pull the plaster off the whole way. They want to tackle a problem, not a crisis, and they want to do it by leading a charge not a rout. As consultants, we would never get the chance to really lay all our cards on the table.[1] We always knew a bit more than we were allowed to say.

And maybe there is no way to expose the whole truth *and* do it constructively. Personally, I've always believed that having the full picture helps, but there is a school of thought that says if you paint too dark a picture for people you are adding to their burden rather than helping.

It is true that the only way to repair the structure of a business is by using that structure itself. The same people who carry out the work of the firm, must carry out any repairs on it. Consultancy isn't surgery; it's assisted self-help. As an outsider you can't rush it or force it. Occasionally, it's tempting to try, though. The only clients I've really had a difficult time working for were the ones who used fact-finding consultancy projects to delay the inevitable – putting off any action for another six months, when all along they knew what needed doing. Fortunately, I haven't encountered a firm like that for a little while now.

At any rate, Dan and I have spent a few years flitting about the retail landscape, working on all sorts of projects. We've seen the dirty laundry of quite a few companies but we've never had either the opportunity or the mandate to discuss it all. Well not with the client, at any rate. We talked about it privately between ourselves. Somewhere along the line, it started to make sense to generalise our findings and put it all in a book.

As a matter of principle, I don't know that I agree 'retail is detail', but I think most retailers work outwards *from* the detail. I tend to work in from the big picture. Every client presentation I wrote, I always wanted to get more context into it. What is retail about, what are we trying to achieve, what are the fundamentals? It's not what a client with a hole in his roof wants to hear. It's a discussion best reserved for a book.

By writing it all down, I can leave the specific-and-urgent to one side and consider the general-but-important. I can depersonalise it. Uncovering the problems of a single business implicitly raises the question of who's to blame. If we look at the problems of the whole industry, we're all off the hook. You didn't do it, neither did I. We can concentrate instead on how to fix it.

1　Well Dan did a couple of times, but it's like the story of the emperor's new clothes. That little boy was marched off to the emperor's dungeons where he remains to this day, whatever the fairy-tale writers told you.

So discussing the sector's maladies in a depersonalised way makes sense. I can leave it to you to choose the timing, the manner or the extent of any overhaul you might decide to carry out. You'll know better than any outsider where you stand at the moment. But nevertheless, it's time some of the problems Dan and I have encountered were discussed openly. There must be and there needs to be a suitable forum to have the conversation and an appropriate time to consider a remedy.

Perhaps you don't know it, but every consulting project starts with a little in-joke. At some point in the initial meeting, the client will always tell the consultants that no matter what they might have seen in the past, "this business is unique". For Dan and me it was a source of private amusement, because six weeks later, the chances were that we'd be looking at exactly the same catalogue of problems we always see in a multiple retailer – and for pretty much the same reasons too.

For all I know, retailers all over the world are panicking, saying to themselves, "Why am I the only one going through this?" If that's the case, let me tell you: you're not alone. If you get nothing else from this book, at least you'll see that you're in good company.

But we're not just going to talk about problems; we're going to look at some big ideas. There are always facts you can't get too close to in a consulting project, but at the same time there are others you can't get away from. There's always a problem that needs fixing and anything you say to the client has to have a direct bearing on that. So we've been carrying around our own private version of a Grand Unified Theory of Retailing without having an appropriate venue for sharing it. It's not a quick win; it's about long-term investment in the future.

All in all, a book is much more liberating than a consulting project. We can leave the specifics behind and tackle the big issues for once. We can also spell out what's broken, but in general enough terms that nobody needs to take it personally. We can also, most importantly, have some fun.

Dan and I were never the most sombre of consultants, even when we worked for other people. One client said we reminded him of the two heckling old men in the Muppet Show. But we were still duty bound by the traditions of business conduct. It didn't seem right to have too much fun considering the rates our old employers were charging for our time. That restriction is lifted as an author; in fact it becomes an obligation to make sure you don't get bored or bogged down.

For that reason, I've tackled the themes in this book in just the way I'd want them handled if I were reading it instead of writing it. It's very light on case studies, for instance. Firstly, I think you can summarise someone's business to get any conclusion you want. Secondly, I realised that if I was going to give you the full, warts-and-all version of what we've seen, it wasn't fair to single anyone out. Where I had originally used real, live businesses to illustrate problems I've taken them out again. The names that were in here weren't the worst offenders, but they might have given that impression if they were the only ones mentioned.

Thirdly, I didn't want anything in the book that wasn't either interesting or funny. I don't know if I've been completely successful – it is a book about business strategy after all – but I steered away from bulky case studies, lengthy statistics, and sterile or convoluted business-speak. They hardly make an appearance. I'm not trying to prove any of the ideas here, I'm explaining the way Dan and I see the world in case you find it helpful. With the Internet at your disposal, it's never difficult to lay your hands on plenty of facts and figures if you feel the need, but I haven't included formal research within the book, just the conclusions and the ideas for the future – not to mention my sense of humour. Above all I've tried to make reading this book as painless as possible.

So try to put aside your preconceptions before you start reading. Don't be thrown if you find yourself in unfamiliar territory – there's a business book buried in there somewhere.

Dan pointed out that parts of this book are more like a theme park ride than a work of retail strategy. He's got a point. So, it's only fitting that he takes us through the first few loops and turns – over to Dan.

Dan's introduction

This journey

The majority of this book is about the future. It asks questions about where retail has got stuck and how it might free itself. It offers new ways of looking at old problems and speculates as to where these new insights might take us. But before we look at the future, let's stop and take a look at where we are and how we got here.

The forces that shaped retail, the economy and the views of the average citizens who are our customers, are still at work. If a vision of the future is to offer us something of value, it has to address the reality of our circumstances and relate to our situation.

That's why we need to begin our discussion by turning a critical eye on the past. I'm going to pick out a number of historical trends or events that point the way to the future. At the same time they also shed light on why a book like this is needed – why we need to change.

One of the major factors pushing us to change is the tectonic shift that has occurred in consumer markets in the last decade or so. Retail's response to that shift played a big part in influencing the current structure of retail. Investment in IT and pressure on supplier relationships can both be seen as attempts to adjust to that shift and restore the balance.

As businesses change, they reveal their managers' preferences and their blind spots. The first changes made are always the easy and painless ones; what remains unchanged can tell you a lot about the attitudes of managers and they way they look at the world. We will look at the traditional retail world view – what you might almost call the philosophy of retailing – and the history of thinking that precedes it.

Each of these separate, but intertwined, strands lead us to the present. They explain the repeated experiences Rob and I have had, the recurring problems we've seen, the sense of *déjà vu* we've felt as we examined each new business.

The current state of retail

Let's use the UK as a microcosm for the world. As we move into this new century, retail spending has reached approximately €300 bn, accounting for a full third of all consumer spending, or 20 per cent of total GDP. The top 100 retailers account for about 70 per cent of this spend, the grocers and food retailers comprising about half of the total market.

Some 2.5 m people, 7 per cent of our total workforce, are employed in retail, working in something approaching 320,000 shops. Adam Smith observed that Britain is a nation of shopkeepers[1] but it is an equally good description of a host of developed countries around the world.

Whatever people may think of the retailing or services sector ('teenagers selling hamburgers to each other' as it was once scathingly described), it is no longer the poor relation to the manufacturing sector. All over the world, retail is big business – and no matter where you look it seems prone to the same set of problems.

Common problems

Retailers suffer with overstocks and poor distribution, they run out of best sellers, are trapped into high markdowns, struggle with a lack of accurate management information, endure long planning and delivery lead times, are forced to contend with inaccurate forecasting, underperforming stores and low staff morale and the list goes on.

In the years leading up to this book, these problems were so prevalent and widespread that we thought it strange when we didn't see them. If we were talking to a retailer from any sector we would ask if they were having problems with too many product lines, low sell-through rates, poor sales densities, and a problematic supply chain. They would say something like "How come you know so much about my business? Who has been giving you this confidential information?" That isn't meant to sound like a boast, but rather to make the point that most if not all multiple retailers are afflicted with the same problems.

Rob and I began to wonder if there might be some underlying principles to multiple retailing. We wondered if these principles would shed some light on why the standard set of problems is so difficult to fix. After all, the essence of retail seems so simple. The checklist of important

---

1   Actually, the first person to use the phrase was Josiah Tucker, the Dean of Gloucester, who referred to a 'Nation of Shopkeepers', but nobody remembers him.

things to get right reads: buy a product, mark it up a bit, send it to the shops that can sell it, and wait for the cash to roll in. What can be so tough about that?

IT

Another thread running through Rob's and my experience of working with retailers is the impact of technology. I read a statistic at a Retail Solutions conference a while back that said British retailers had between them spent somewhere between £5bn and £10bn on systems and technology over the last fifteen years, mostly on EpoS,[1] central stock replenishment and integrated management reporting & finance systems. This had been great for the big technology companies,[2] particularly in the late 90s when everyone was clamouring for the latest web-enabled systems. But it didn't seem to have made a lot of difference to retailers' performance.

There are numerous examples of retailers who have 'lost their way' in the retail technology jungle. Two of the most recent high profile examples are Kmart, which spent $millions on Bluelight e-commerce technology and has now turned it all off and renamed its online channel Kmart.com. Whilst no one has suggested that the Bluelight venture was wholly to blame for Kmart's problems, a number of their senior executives agreed that the diversion wasn't particularly helpful. In the UK, Habitat UK has recently posted a pre-tax loss of £2.8m against a £6.7m profit last time. The retailer stated that a group-wide integrated IT system caused disruption and moved internal focus away from sales performance. I can (I'm sorry to say) remember when all planning, forecasting, and replenishment was done using pencil and paper, and I can remember what the average operating ratios around margins, mark-downs, terminal stocks, lead times, and sell-through were in those dark days.

To be honest, one would have to admit that these key ratios haven't changed all that much. They certainly don't show the change one would expect after spending billions on systems designed to streamline supply chains and reduce markdowns to the bare minimum. I even worked with

---

1   Forgive me, all you retailers, but I probably need to explain that EpoS stands for 'Electronic Point of Sale', or 'Tills' (in old money).

2   And for technology-related consultancies, I'm bound to say.

one major retailer who spent over €15 m on integrated systems and struggled for almost two years to get the business to use them. In the end, they decided that the best solution would be to turn it all off and rip it out.

OK, it's a cheap shot to blame the systems. The solution sellers would (rightly) say that the gains have been in competitive performance. They'd point out that whilst retailers may still have similar operating ratios to twenty years ago, any multiple retailer without the basic systems in place would be long dead. That's all true, but the point is this: if the technology hasn't been able to fix these fundamental problems, maybe they aren't 'technology' problems at all.

The customer revolution

There's another important element to consider. Back in 1999, when the ideas for this book were starting to form, we spent a lot of time thinking about the shift in consumer markets. With the advent of an Internet-enabled world, consumers were changing their behaviour. Even to the casual observer of shopping patterns, it was clear that some major shifts were taking place. Consumers were becoming much more informed about what was on offer and much choosier about what they wanted and how they wanted it. The old 'prescriptive' retail model, where retailers simply piled their goods into shops and customers came in droves to buy it, were past. Adair Turner (ex-Director General of the CBI), put it eloquently when he said, "The days when business could continue to survive because customers didn't know their options are long gone".

In many ways, the growth of multiple retailing since the 1970s has brought about a widening of the gap between retailer and consumer. In order to grow larger, retailers also had to grow more impersonal. Multiple retailing depends on standardisation, and its first casualty was the personal touch. The world where the store manager would know his local customers and form long-lasting relationships disappeared. In its place was a world where central buyers spent much of their time negotiating big exciting deals with suppliers in far-flung corners of the world.

EpoS and central sales and stock management software replaced local account management, and those systems often made no provision for storing individual customer details.[1] Customers have become anonymous,

---

1 As I write, the London Times is carrying a piece trumpeting the advent of the latest customer loyalty scheme ('Nectar'). Many retailers defend their commitment to customer loyalty by pointing to investment in similar loyalty schemes, but you have to wonder who is supposed to be loyal to whom.

transient spenders; retailers have paid a price in individuality in order to achieve massive economies of scale in purchasing, distribution, and management reporting. (In the chapter on customers, we'll take a closer look at the implications of that bargain.)

That's not to suggest that a separation between retailer and customer is untenable. It didn't cause a problem so long as customer behaviour was stable and predictable, and retailers could be prescriptive. In the early 80s, the explosive success of clothing store Next was only possible because they were able to fill their stores with orange and green clothing and more or less state, "If you shop with us, this is what you are going to be wearing". And it worked.

By the latter half of the 90s it was becoming ever clearer that better insight into what customers wanted and a greater focus on responding to customer demand were the way forward. The solution providers, whose sales of integrated systems were starting to flag a bit, leapt on the opportunity to market CRM (Customer Relationship Management) systems to retailers. Intuitively, though, retailers understood that building relationships with customers is not about technology, it is about people.

Even if CRM solutions aren't the key to bridging the customer-retailer gap, all of us have some insight into the problem. After all, we are all customers some of the time and we all know the difference between a good relationship and a bad one.

Relationships

Rob and I spent a lot of time thinking about the nature of relationships in multiple retailers. In our role as consultants, we were always talking to people from different disciplines across all manner of retail businesses, and we'd hear about the problems they saw their companies experiencing. What emerged over and over again was that the people who worked in these organisations rarely saw barriers in terms of technology or systems, but rather in the way that various relationships worked, and the tensions that existed between them. Perhaps their managers didn't value or understand them. Maybe they had lost sight of who their customers were or what they wanted. They probably felt they had too many conflicting pressures and performance measures. A typical comment might be, "I am targeted on getting 100 per cent availability on all my best-selling lines, but I get hammered if I go overstocked; the finance guys are only interested in squeezing extra margin out of suppliers but the suppliers say they can't do it". When listing problems – managers, their role, the pressures from other departments – it was always people and relationships that came up.

Time and again in our consulting assignments we stumbled across long-simmering dysfunctions in the internal and external relationships of a business. Things got interesting whenever we tried to use those 'tensions' to explain a company's predicament. The senior management were generally unmoved. A typical view might be, 'Our problems are caused by poor systems – once we get the technology and processes sorted out, things will look up'. You could almost say there was an aversion to talking about how the various relationships worked (or didn't work). It wasn't possible to press the point, no matter how compelling the evidence. When we tried, all we did was damage our rapport with the guys at the top.

Viewing a business in terms of its major relationships seemed full of promise. To us this approach was very revealing, but to the boards we encountered it seemed like a distraction. Inevitably, our clients had some pre-existing views of what a solution might look like and our analysis of the business didn't fit the bill. On a couple of occasions we pushed hard enough to convince a business that they needed someone who understood the *real* issues to take over the assignment.

There was one positive outcome from these setbacks: we had plenty of opportunity to consider these ideas on their merits. Life would certainly have been easier if we'd gone with the flow.

On reflection, I can say that in the majority of consulting assignments that I have been involved with, the problems that exist across the business come from the way that certain key relationships are managed.

After lengthy consideration of the matter, Rob and I distilled the key relationships down to four principal ones. The main content of the book is a discussion of these key relationships. They are the relationships that exist between employees, customers, suppliers and the financial shareholders of the business. Each of these is a complex network of tensions and priorities. The way each functions on its own, and the interplay between them when considering the business as a whole, is the basis for understanding what makes a retail business tick. In the next two chapters we'll get to the bottom of why that should be.

To get John Donne spinning wherever he is resting, one could say that 'no retailer is an island', but rather a 'part of the main' linked to the world *via* these four strategic relationships. Retailers make choices (sometimes explicit, sometimes not) about how they manage each of these relationships, and the relative importance that is given to each. Those decisions shape their future.

Finance-led change

In the last couple of years it has been my great fortune to work with a couple of retailers that had been bought by large investment firms (Homebase, bought by Schroder Ventures, and First Quench[1], bought by Nomura PFG[2]).

While working with Homebase and First Quench, it was fascinating to watch how the balance of the key relationships shifted as a result of new ownership.[3] In the case of First Quench, the business had previously been jointly owned by its two biggest suppliers, Whitbread and Allied Domecq. As a result, buying and stock management was largely defined by the fact that the two owners had large amounts of product to shift coupled with the fact that they owned nearly 3000 drinks stores across the UK. This naturally had a great impact on the product ranges that found their way into the stores, and it would be fair to say that the product ranges offered were not always entirely in line with what the average off-licence customer wanted to buy.

With such a heavy emphasis on the supplier relationship, it was natural that the priorities of the business as a whole had a distinctive bias. With the purchase of the business by Nomura, the weighting of the relationships shifted overnight from supplier to financial shareholder. To an employee standing in the middle of it all, the change could put you in mind of a shift in the earth's crust.[4] The fabric of the business had been built on an almost symbiotic (some have harshly said uncommercial) relationship with the key suppliers, and the shift towards a focus on cashflow, GMROI and range control represented a fundamental upheaval in almost every corner of the business.

It's also fair to say that major financial players like Nomura don't waste time on lost causes. They clearly saw the potential for a multiple retailer with a simple operating model to be highly profitable and to achieve a massive weekly cashflow.

---

1 You may not have heard of First Quench, but it is the large drinks retailer that runs over 2000 off-licenses under names such as Thresher, Victoria Wine, and so on.

2 Schroder Ventures and Nomura PFG have since become Permira and Terra Firma respectively.

3 It is no coincidence that these businesses show immediate improvements in ROI and profit. As I write, I am reading about Homebase's growth in profits from £42 m to £90 m, and a LFL growth of 12 per cent. FQ's figures have been even more impressive.

4 As an aside, some people believe that the periodic shift in the Earth's crust as a result of the 13,000-year cycle of precession is what caused the extinction of the dinosaurs. Perhaps if I tried, I could find some parallels between the extinction of the dinosaurs and the management changes we're discussing, but politeness prevents me from pursuing it.

Working with these guys was a revelation because they didn't approach things as 'dyed in the wool' retailers. They would look at every aspect of the business and ask, "Why does it have to be like this?" That experience led me to re-examine almost every aspect of multiple retailing. It became clear that there were some long-established patterns of retail behaviour that simply didn't hold up under close scrutiny.

The power of what has happened at First Quench (not least the £65 m growth in profits within 12 months of the takeover) illustrated very clearly the fundamental role that these strategic relationships played in the workings of large retailers. Whilst the new owners and the operating board of First Quench may not have explicitly set out with this change of relationship emphasis in mind, that's what happened and the results have been astonishing to say the least.

We can also look at the example of Bhs. As widely reported in the financial press, Philip Green took over this ailing retailer in 2001 and, on a similar timescale to the changes at First Quench, has shifted the emphasis of relationship towards the customer. It is said that every decision that Mr. Green makes starts with the question, "Does this represent a better way of giving our customers what they want?" Whilst his somewhat ebullient[1] management style has its critics (there are no reports of an attempt to focus on the relationship with the employee), there is no doubt that the shift in the customer relationship has reaped significant rewards for Mr Green and Bhs.

There's a point to make at this stage; we're not suggesting that there is a right balance to achieve across these four core relationships. Like any set of relationships, the balance shifts continually, and is best determined by a blend of existing market conditions and the strategy of the particular business at a point in time. The important point is that retailers need to recognise their fundamental importance. The decisions they take that affect the relative priorities between them, whether they are aware of that effect or not, will determine the overall shape and success of the business. In fact retailers ideally should actively invest time and resource in managing these relationships as part of their overall strategy, as it is the performance of these relationships that sets the scene for the performance of their business.

---

[1] Of all the adjectives I have heard used to describe Philip Green, this is the one most likely to get past our publishers and their legal team.

Examples

We can look at examples of what happens when retailers fail to manage, or neglect any of these strategic relationships. M&S is a recent example of what happens when a retailer allows focus to shift away from the customer relationship: a senior Director of M&S was once famously reported as commenting that, "We don't need to talk to our customers, we just deliver the best product ranges to our stores and they come to us." Luc Vandevelde was reported in the press as making rather disparaging remarks about the average British woman shopper and her knowledge and understanding of fashion compared to her French counterpart[1] – beside the point if one is not running a French store and potentially rather damaging.

What happens when retailers focus almost exclusively on a particular relationship and devote a large percentage of their efforts to making it work? Richer Sounds Hi-Fi is an obvious example that springs to mind. In his book *The Richer Way*, Julian Richer explains why his business consistently breaks records for the highest profit per square foot[2] of any retailer on the planet: he focuses on making every customer feel like a million bucks when they come into any of his stores, and rewards for store staff are always built around the number of positive customer feedback comments they get. He says he is consistently astonished that he is paid large sums of money to stand up and talk about the secret of his success, when all his business does is focus on getting the customer relationship absolutely right. Senior Directors from other retailers refuse to accept it. "Go on, tell us the real secret", is what he hears after every seminar he delivers.

Another famous (and by now well worn) example is Zara, part of the global Inditex Group. What is interesting about their approach to supply chain management is that they have succeeded in vertically integrating most of the design, manufacturing, and retailing functions in their supply chain. The result of this has been to remove a lot of the operational disconnects and 'buffer costs' that exist in most other retail supply chains, and has helped them to the enviable position of enjoying 9 per cent like-for-like sales growth and a 35 per cent year-on-year growth in bottom line profits. (Rob talks in more detail about operational inefficiencies in

---

1   Such remarks have become known as 'Ratners' in the UK. Perhaps each country has its own example of a boss who holed his business below the waterline while shooting himself in the foot.

2   Detractors would point to the fact that he sells high-price-point products from small, low-rent shops, but this does not alter the fact that his customer loyalty and following are highly enviable.

his chapter on supplier relationships). Despite the suspicion and inertia in many people's attitudes toward supply chains, Zara is an undeniable example of what can happen when a retailer makes every effort to get it right.

Resistance

I've mentioned how important our consulting experiences were in forming the views you're about to read. I've also mentioned that we've encountered resistance when we've attempted to apply them. It's possible that's left you wondering if this book is going to be a couple of hundred pages of war stories about consulting assignments or grumbling about our setbacks. Whilst some of the seeds of our thinking were undoubtedly sown in the many conversations we had with retail executives who seemed loathe to try anything new, I would prefer to see this book as offering an alternative or complementary piece of thinking that helps to shed some light on some longstanding issues.

There are three major difficulties we've found when trying to engage senior managers in discussions about internal and external relationships (we reached the conclusion that the best way to get around them was to write a book). The first of these problems is time: senior managers in retail (and I guess any other sector) simply don't have enough hours in the day. There isn't time to sit and talk in depth about whether or not the relationships between their employees, customers, suppliers, and so on are functional or dysfunctional: they simply want someone to get on and jolly well fix everything.

Whenever we managed to get a senior Director engaged in the discussion, it always ended up with someone saying, "Look, this is very interesting, but if we sit around all day discussing this stuff we are never going to get the new widget-system implemented, and we do have a business to run".

The second (related) problem is that it all seems a bit wishy-washy. Some people seemed to think we were trying to turn their business into a hippy commune.[1] This sort of thing does seem to put senior people into a bit of a tail spin ("Look here, Perrin, I didn't get where I am today worrying about whether everyone likes each other or not. I'm a hard-nosed business man, like to get things done, don't you know …").

---

1   More than once, starchy Brits asked us if we would be recommending something along the lines of the Wal*Mart company song.

The third – and we think the most fundamental – issue is that it seems to strike at the very heart of long-established behaviour that exists in retail businesses. Whilst the Permiras and the Terra Firmas of this world are less precious about such things ("We don't care how you do it, just make it profitable"), they are not really the people who run retailers day to day. They might own the business, but I've yet to see Guy Hands working behind the counter in my local Thresher wine store. People who have worked in retail for many years and have become directors, have a natural discomfort with the suggestion that some basic problems have existed for years and never been addressed. It is much more palatable to view things in terms of speed and efficiency: "We know we are doing the right things, this new system will allow us to do much more of it, faster, and surely that has to be the answer?" Well, in our experience, it has been shown time and again not to be the answer. The fundamental issues, which few people feel comfortable discussing, are really at the heart of most of the major problems large retailers face.

The standard approach

Now it's time for a change of direction. Let's leave the specifics of retail behind for a while and dip into some history. Let's look at where the conventional modes of management thinking originated. Since we have just been talking about management perceptions, I want to zip back in time and look at the origins of the business mind-set.

I want to say a few words on the subject of systemic thinking. Back in the first half of the seventeenth century, natural scientists were trying to understand how living organisms functioned. The favoured approach was to dissect specimens down to their smallest particles in order to understand how each part worked. In principle, armed with this knowledge, one could reconstruct a picture of how the whole organism operated. This method became known as 'Cartesian' or 'Newtonian' (after René Descartes and Isaac Newton, two fairly bright sparks of the time). For obvious reasons, this sort of approach is referred to as reductionist, but it could also be thought of as 'linear', which is another way of stating that something is just the sum of its parts. Researchers of the age imagined all the tiny pieces of an organism arranged in their proper places, each playing a distinct role, much like the components of a clock. Sadly for these biologists, this approach fell at the first hurdle. Every time they dissected a mouse to try to understand its component parts, the only result was another dead mouse. Descartes was led to conclude that the most important component must be invisible – the animating force of a living creature. In modern times, we've discovered that the secret is neither linear nor invisible, but we'll come to that in a minute.

Despite a number of failures, reductionist thinking is still with us. It has kick-started any number of technologies although it generally runs out of steam before providing a complete picture. Nevertheless, reductionist thinking is intrinsically attractive to business people. There are four main reasons why.

Firstly, it is rule-based, meaning that once we have figured out how one system works, we can then apply these rules to other systems and understand how they work too. This makes tackling new situations easier, faster and simpler to understand – ideal for business people in a perpetual hurry.

Secondly, it is repeatable. When you've broken a system down to its basic constituents, the behaviour of each one is usually very predictable. Desired results are repeatable.

Thirdly, it is scalable. In reductionist thinking large and small are only a matter of scale; a large system is no different in principle to a small one. An elephant is just a mouse only bigger.

And finally, it is objective. The observer stands outside the system, setting aside their own involvement. (A bonus is that one is able to fix a problem without having to admit that one might be part of it.) For those people running large multiple retailers, these features add up to a very attractive approach.

In commerce, of course, nobody calls it reductionism; it's just seen as a natural part of a professional approach or a business-like attitude. It is one of the many things managers absorb as part of their development.

But reductionism will only get you so far. In the last few decades in particular, scientific thinking has moved towards a more holistic model. The systems that have always given scientists the most trouble are ones where there are lots of components and each is capable of influencing lots of others. We are just now starting to understand these so-called complex systems. Biology is the source of many of them; for example, to appreciate a creature's behaviour you really have to see it as part of a larger eco-system.

Sometimes the most notable properties of a system are a feature of the way the components are connected; the details of the individual components themselves can be almost irrelevant. The Internet, for instance, is all about connections; hardly anyone (except the manu-facturers) cares which models of computer were used to build it.

This is the third way of looking at systems I mentioned. With complex systems, examining one piece at a time can be misleading, because the connections contribute so much to the overall behaviour. Socially, we don't even question the role of interconnectedness.[1] It is probably true to say that we all accept deep down that what makes the world go round are the interlocking relationships between all the individuals and communities.

So what has this all got to do with the way retail businesses work?

Well, for a start you can see a business as a complex system, which spells trouble for a reductionist approach. Secondly, you can see a single business as part of an even larger complex system, in which case ignoring everything outside the boundaries of the business will also cause problems.

As consultants, we often found ourselves carrying out assignments that involved a thing called 'process mapping', which is part of a wider school of thought known as 'business process reengineering'.[2] This involves breaking down everything that happens in a business into its smallest component processes, and analysing how each of these works. By carefully redefining each of these 'EBPs'[3], and then working out how we could automate them using systems and technology, the business can be reconstructed, gleaming and supremely efficient, with lightning fast processes and no wasted effort (and usually fewer of those pesky people). Without going into the gory details of whether or not this actually works in practice, the point is this: there's an obvious parallel between this approach and the way that Newton and Descartes attempted to understand the natural world. Process Engineering is a way of trying to understand how a business works by analysing the smallest component parts and then trying to fit them all together in a simple, mechanistic way.

Incidentally, another problem with process engineering is that it takes a 'snapshot' of a business and attempts to rebuild the company from the picture captured at that instant. The logical disconnect here is that retailers (like any other business) are always changing. The balance between the four key relationships is continually shifting. Perhaps, if we want a better understanding of our business, we should think of ourselves as directors making a movie rather than photographers capturing a scene.

---

1   For more on these ideas, try the works of Fritjof Capra and Margaret Wheatley.

2   This approach to understanding how business works took the world by storm in 1993 when Hammer and Champy published their book *Reengineering the Corporation*.

3   Being consultants, it is a legal requirement that these 'Elementary Business Processes' are referred to using a TLA (Three Letter Acronym) .

Come to think of it, that's what people who run businesses call themselves, so maybe we are halfway there already.

At any rate, the problem with reductionist process mapping, as with reductionist biology, is that the pieces of a complex system don't operate in isolation from the world around them. Customers and people (whoops, I forgot for a moment there that they are the same thing) tend to be unpredictable, and sometimes even illogical. They also react to each other in sophisticated ways, and their responses normally depend on the personalities and relationships that surround them. It's all very well mapping out the process for distributing stock to stores based purely on the basis of last week's sales, but what if the Store or Area Manager is screaming down the phone that they need more of this or more of that? And where does it leave us if we determine that the process for selecting suppliers should be based purely on gross margins, flexibility of supply and lead times, but the buyer has longstanding relationships with a number of suppliers who fail to meet some or all of these requirements?

Time and again, carefully designed processes crumble when confronted with the way that people really work together – that is, the way they interact with those around them and the tensions that exist between them.

We said at the start of the chapter that the pattern of change in business gives insights into the thinking of its managers. It stands to reason that important relationships have been neglected if the leading tool for business re-engineering takes no account of them.

An overview of retail

Retailers traditionally divide up their business into departments or functions and place a board director in charge of each of these (Buying, Marketing, Finance, Logistics, Store Operations, HR and so on). The daily dynamics of most large multiple retailers are influenced by the tensions (and disagreements) between these functions. However, if we pull back and view the retail model as a whole (let's imagine that we are high above the business looking down), we can see that it is a complex network of interactions both internal (between the various functions) and more importantly external, with suppliers, customers and shareholders. We can see the flow of goods from the manufacturers/suppliers through the retail distribution network down to the local consumer markets. We can also imagine the flow of information back up the supply chain; information about what did and didn't sell forms a much larger and more complex picture viewed from up here. The line between the suppliers, customers and the retailer becomes very blurred from such a height. In today's retail markets with direct supplier deliveries, outsourced distribution, multiple channels to the customer and vertical integration, the divisions between these previously separate parts of the system seem too arbitrary to be relevant.

A more accurate description of a multiple retail model is as part of a complex system incorporating everything from the original manufacture of a product to its final sale to the consumer. Everyone along the way has an interest in what happens and everyone in the chain benefits from making the end-to-end model more efficient.

Just going back to the subject of systems thinking for a moment, there are some things that we know about the behaviour of systems or environments that can shed some light on our observations and understanding of what happens in larger systems such as consumer markets. The main thing we know from scientific observations is that there is a tendency towards disorder in any system, that is the longer we leave things the more fragmented (and even unpredictably chaotic) they become.[1]

If we think of a retail supply chain just in terms of a network of connections and feedback loops (incorporating the supply of goods, retail buying and distribution and the consumer markets), we can look to see where the growth in disorder is occurring. Fifteen years ago, consumer markets were relatively well ordered, demand was relatively stable and predictable. Retailers knew with some confidence that they could order products on reasonably long lead times and when the goods arrived in the stores the customers would buy them; it's what I've referred to as 'prescriptive' retailing. The situation was characterised by stability and predictability.

Taking advantage of this stability, retailers started to build massive economies of scale into their 'upstream' operations (that is, from supplier to retailer), opting for large order quantities, long planning lead times and sophisticated supply chain management systems which managed the planning and ordering of product ranges. As long as the consumer market remained reasonably stable, these economies of scale delivered some great results for retailers in the 1980s and early 90s.

---

1   This is described in the second law of thermodynamics, or the law of 'increasing entropy'. Two centuries of study have gone into understanding the basis for this law, but the matter is not settled yet. We'll take the prudent course and just accept that it's a fact: the disorder in a closed system can only increase (though you can move it around a fair bit).

Explaining the customer shift

Then something began to happen to global consumer markets in 1989/1990. Consumers started to become less predictable, fussier, less loyal and shopping trends became increasingly unstable. Ranges that retailers had previously delivered to the stores stopped selling; competition increased as niche retailers started springing up, stealing customer spend from the large retailers, and the big multiples started to feel the pain of large overstocks and the margin erosion forced on them by the need to mark-down unsold stock.

There have been many studies of the changing nature of global consumer markets since the early 90s and they all point towards the disintegration of previously homogeneous and stable demand patterns. With the wealth that was created in the boom years of the 80s, people were travelling more and becoming exposed to a multitude of culturally diverse influences around food, fashion, music and so on. The average customer's expectation of choice exploded, putting ever greater pressure on retailers to provide more diversity in their range assortments. This was not easy because the huge economies of scale retailers relied on were based on stability. Their supply chains were like super-tankers: able to transport enormous volumes efficiently, but not designed for rapid changes in direction.

When we look back to those years, we see the fall of the Berlin Wall; the Romanian revolution; Tianenmen Square; the release of Nelson Mandela; the downfall of Margaret Thatcher; and many other examples of global iconoclasm. All of these events fundamentally rocked our socio-economic psyche. One of the effects was that consumers started to wonder about the benefits of prescriptive retail marketing. Anything was possible; the old order *could* be challenged. To be glib, a world that could kick Ceausescu out of office should surely be a world where customers could buy what they wanted in their local shops.

And of course, consumers always had enormous power to affect big business, but in the past they either hadn't realised it or hadn't known what to do with it. Combine this explosion of consumer power with the growth of communication technology, mobile phones, e-mail, and the web, and we can see how people started to realise the power of the individual in global communities.

Unfortunately, multiple retailers were in the middle of a massive and hugely expensive implementation of integrated or ERP[1] systems designed

---

1   Enterprise Resource Planning (ERP) systems were designed to hardwire all the various business functions (including supplier management) into a single model of systems and process. The main

to maximise the economies of scale underpinning their efficiency and profitability. The growth in consumer unpredictability clashed horribly with the inflexibility of upstream streamlining in systems and process. It has been this fundamental disconnect between the two halves of the system that has been at the root of most multiple retailers' problems over the last ten years or so.

The pre-history of retailing

We've talked about recent developments in retail, shifts in the zeitgeist, the lineage of business thinking; let's complete the preparation for the rest of the book with a whirlwind journey through the history of retailing itself.

Customers often have a jaundiced view of retailers. From their side of the counter what they see is that retailers sell goods for twice what they paid for them and frequently add very little in the way of value or service. Whenever I tell non-retailers about the mark-ups that retailers put on goods, they look quite shocked and mutter about going direct to source to buy their chickens, or beans, or socks or whatever. Of course, that's not a practical way to come by the myriad goods each of us takes for granted. And, really, that's original basis of the value added by retailing: it beats the alternative.

When markets first started springing up, some say in the Fertile Crescent, or Mesopotamia, others suggest Egypt or Africa, they formed where travelling groups of people found that their routes intersected; these intersections became the hubs of the old trade routes. People brought jewels and spices from the East and exchanged them for food and cattle on their way West. These were the ancestors of modern day consumer markets and the ancient birthplace of the retail industry.

Merchants would set up their stalls and sell their wares. They would sell products they'd bought elsewhere, or more often products that they had produced themselves (pots, food, leather goods and so on). The original economies were based on the barter system where goods were paid for with other goods. Naturally, this was prohibitively awkward much of the time (it was a bit tricky carrying the three hundred loaves

---

problem was that these systems required the design of a single 'best practice' way of doing things, which was then hard-coded into the retail operating model. When retailers attempted to add new capabilities in recognition of their increasingly demanding customers, the problems started. A good example of this is the home delivery process used by large department stores who (until recently) could deliver your new fridge to your home, but only while you were out at work.

of bread needed to buy an emerald ring, never mind the unlikely prospect of finding a jeweller who was that hungry). A mechanism was needed for breaking the exchange into two halves, allowing goods to be acquired or passed on in separate deals. That intermediate mechanism for exchange was of course money.

With the introduction of money, anyone could exchange cash for whatsoever their hearts desired. Markets became dramatically more efficient, which encouraged much greater volumes of trade and a corresponding increase in the variety of the goods available. Flourishing trade brought increasingly exotic products to market, and so began the shopper's love affair with novelty and variety. Over the centuries, merchants travelled further and further afield to find new goods and bring them back to their local markets.

Money was not just an intermediate stage in the exchange of goods, it was a means of storing wealth. The growth of the merchant classes in the eleventh and twelfth centuries was made possible because money allowed traders to amass, gather up and transport their personal fortune from place to place. Merchants became more adept at managing their cost of sourcing or production and setting their prices wisely – the result being that they could often sell their products for significantly more than they spent on them. Since the invention of currency, merchants of every stripe have devoted their ingenuity to widening that gap and increasing their profit.

One wrinkle was that the manufacturers of products, say cloth or bread, were keen to sell their entire daily or weekly production in one go as soon as it became available. That way their funds could be ploughed straight back into more raw materials. It was usually difficult to find local consumers who wanted to buy whole consignments at a time. Enter the retailer.

The word 'retail' originates from a French-Italian word *retailler* meaning someone who cuts off or shreds a small piece from something. The retailer would buy the entire production volume (a hundred loaves or a complete roasted pig) and by cutting bits off, or 'retailing', for the general public, he could devote his time to selling at a profit, rather than actually producing anything. Of course, this is a symbiotic relationship; the producer needs the retailer and *vice versa*, because they both want to use their time and resources to do what each does best – which in turn brings everyone the maximum economic benefit.

Over time, these merchants or retailers worked out that if people were coming to them to buy their bread, they might be able to sell them some cakes as well. Thus began the art of *Range Assortment Planning*. The retailer and customer both knew that the customer wanted a variety of goods for his family's everyday life and would be glad of some help in obtaining them conveniently – they would even pay something for that service. What's more, if the retailer could provide a good selection of these products, the customer would be likely to buy all his daily needs from that retailer, rather than trudge around from one to the other to find what he wanted.[1]

There were a couple of key refinements that helped along this process of selecting and offering for sale. The first was that the presentation of goods should be attractive and inspire the customer to buy things that he would not otherwise have thought of (*visual merchandising*). The second was that it really helped if the retailer knew what it was the customer would be most likely to need. Of course, the most obvious way of finding this out was to talk to the customers[2] and ask them what they would like to buy. Over time, the general trend has been for retailers to get better and better at predicting what their customers will want.

As an aside, another view of retail is that essentially it's the act of choosing for the customer a subset of the world's goods. The selection needs to be both broad enough to satisfy the customer's needs and narrow enough to make shopping simple and practical. There's a parallel here with the art world. As the concept of art has broadened to include photography or gallery installations, the artist is not necessarily directly creating anything; instead their role is to select some feature or view of the world and call it to attention. In a sense, all they do is decide where to place the frame. That makes award-winning photography sound simplistic when clearly it's not. But it's the same with retail; a retail offer is an artfully chosen selection of the world's bounty with a shop window framing it. That said, it's not a good idea to dwell on the artistic aspect of range planning; as we'll see in later chapters, too much art and not enough science can cost a retailer dearly.

Relating

At any rate, as retailers got better at understanding their customers, the relationship developed into a two-way conversation. Retailers would set

---

1 It's this basic need for one-stop convenience that has allowed a modern Wal*Mart or Sainsburys to replace the local butcher, baker, and candlestick maker.

2 Christopher Locke *et al.* make some great points about 'Markets as conversations' in their book *The Cluetrain Manifesto*, which is a fantastic read.

out their stall to show the latest range of products they had obtained from their suppliers and the customers would select from that, all the time giving the retailer more information about what they really wanted, what they didn't like, and how they felt about the process of purchasing. All this enabled the retailer to go back to the producers and wholesalers and ask for slightly different selections based upon his customer's requirements.

At some point here, the retailer would have started getting a bit smarter about 'association' or 'solution' selling and the art of 'trading up'. This is the scenario where a customer who regularly buys five loaves of bread is asked by the retailer, "How about if I could get you a nice carved bread bin for your house, so you can put all that bread in it?" The retailer has moved beyond the essential transaction (selling a loaf of bread) and really started to consider the problems and needs of the customer, and how these could be resolved. At this point, the relationship moves from being transactional and takes on a new form in which value is being added. The value comes as a result of the parties starting to consider what the other might want out of the relationship. It becomes a question of 'helping me to help you' and frequently the value added carries almost no cost to the one providing it – carrying the right product being no more costly, in principle, than carrying the wrong one. This will be a recurring theme in later chapters.

Becoming one with your market

It's evident to most of us that for a retailer to build a successful business, he must build successful relationships with his customers, and this means opening up and responding to the consumer market in an active way. I find this notion easier to think about using analogies to a number of other learning processes.

When we first learn to drive, ride a bike, ski or sail we have to invent for ourselves, usually through trial and error, an extensive set of rules that tell us how to react. They are of the form 'if this happens then you do that'. To start with, this is quite clumsy; the child riding a bike for the first time will lurch from side to side very noticeably because it takes a while after the 'external event' (say, the bike veering to the left) to recollect the appropriate rule and apply it. The 'internal reaction' (say, moving the handlebars to the right) only happens after a delay and a bit of thought.

The same applies to clutch control when learning to drive a manual car, or when learning to ski. In fact it's true of everything else that involves an activity requiring continuous reaction (or more accurately response) to external events. Over time, however, these responses to events start to operate through the subconscious, and they become much smoother. We still do the left-right event-response thing on our bike, but it happens so automatically that it is unnoticeable and we can ride down rocky mountainsides with confidence. Some people describe this as 'forming a relationship' with your environment, where the actor and the environment become as one. Some ski instructors talk about 'feeling the mountain through your boots'. I like to think about this in terms of moving from a 'reactive' state to a 'responsive' state, where our actions are not simply mechanical reactions to external events, but instead are involved and subjective 'responses' which strengthen our sense of 'being part of the system'.[1]

Operating in consumer markets involves a similar scenario, except that the external events (millions of customers making millions of buying decisions) are even more complex and unpredictable. One would imagine that the role of the subconscious, or the 'relationship with the environment', would be even more vital here; the mechanistic, rule-based model would be even more clumsy and inappropriate. And yet this is exactly what large retailers do: they buy their ranges months ahead of time, they decide where it is all going to go, and they set their course. There is very little steering or responsiveness in the model. It's like a mountain biker whose handlebars have seized; once he has set off down the mountain, he has to hope that the direction he started in is the right one and that nothing knocks him off course along the way. There is no 'relationship' between the rider and his environment, unless he comes off and head meets mountain.

Handing over

We are a long way off from that ideal of responsiveness to customer behaviour, but in later chapters of the book we will see how to bring the retailer much closer together with the other parties in its major relationships.

We have spent some time looking at where retail came from, the thinking it has adopted, the external events that have affected it and the improvements it needs to make. It is now time to consider the options available to us if we wish to redesign our business in light of these facts.

For the remainder of our journey, I'll hand you back to Rob.

---

1   This concept is described perfectly by Fritjof Capra in his book *The Web of Life*.

CHAPTER 1

Balancing the tension between competing business aims

This journey

I'm going to start each chapter with a section like this one. The idea is to give you some travel information and some clues about our route. Otherwise, there's a risk you'll find yourself in the middle of some discussion of game theory and conclude you've picked up the wrong book by mistake.

This chapter, for instance, is going to take a fairly high-level look at how you might approach the design of a retail business. But, like much of this book, we're not going to jump right in; we're going to take the scenic route.

Before we get to business design, we'll tackle design in general and the design of big, complicated things in particular. We're going to look at the basic structure of organisations and even take a quick look at the natural world in case there are any useful lessons to be learned.

While a better understanding of retail is always lurking behind the scenes, the aim is also to have a little fun along the way and fire your imagination whenever possible.

Though the scenery may threaten to obscure our view of the destination on a couple of occasions, by the end of the chapter we'll have uncovered the topics that we'll be spending the rest of the book considering.

Relying on instinct

The history of physics in the twentieth century suggests that we don't have much natural intuition about the very large, the very small or the very fast. Quantum mechanics, for instance, seems preposterously unconvincing. Einstein felt sure it couldn't be right. In fact, if it weren't for the fact that its predictions are totally dead-on accurate, hardly anyone would give it a moment's consideration.

The lore of risk suggests we also have no real feel for the unlikely. We get confused between how unpleasant something is and how improbable.

Radioactivity, because it works invisibly to cause harm, is much more worrying to people than deadly threats a million times more likely. The illusion of control also affects our judgement. If humans had a good appreciation of risk, nervous fliers would be a lot more anxious about the drive to the airport than the flight.

Twenty-first century biology is demonstrating another serious shortfall in our intuition. We have absolutely no grasp of very complex systems. Many natural systems with large numbers of moving parts are still a complete mystery to us. Worse still, we have a reductionist tendency to focus on the components in a system rather than the connections.

The human brain is mainly neurons. They're not the simplest structures in the world, but they are essentially sensitive switches. If you wire them together just right, you get something that can speak Mandarin or crack The Times crossword. If you do it wrongly – and there are many more wrong ways than right – you get a bunch of switches. We just aren't any good at seeing how you can make something intelligent from a collection of mindless parts, or for that matter how to make something that's alive from a lot of dead chemicals.

Yet, that's what business is all about. It's not about each of us running mini-companies, all doing their own scaled-down versions of the whole. The capabilities of a large organisation are partitioned and distributed in weird and wonderful ways and no one person knows how it all gets done.

Darwin spotted a way round the incomprehensibility of complex systems. You don't need to understand how a complex system works; you just need to be able to spot when it does a good job. Evolution works by rewarding favourable outcomes. Like a good delegator, it doesn't specify *how* things get done, just that they happen.

Rewarding favourable outcomes makes it sound benign. Really what evolution does is keep the numbers up and kill off anything that doesn't perform. There is an argument to be made that it's the only way to 'design' anything really complex.

When you see the growth of a business, you know there's more going on than the unrolling of the business plan, more than just adherence to a single scheme or vision, however much its managers may wish otherwise. Businesses grow organically[1] – each part changing, adapting and frequently expanding. But how can you tell whether what you're seeing is evolution or an uncoordinated growth, like cancer?

---

1   Whatever that means. 'Not solely under guidance from the centre' is one possible definition. The business uses of technical terms are often rather inscrutable. A quantum change, for instance, could be described as the smallest change you can possibly make. It's used popularly to mean a really big change.

Complex systems

It's only in the last hundred years or so that people have begun to design their own complex systems. Humans have been putting together communities and economies for quite a while, but historically they've either tended to be about everyone doing what they want, or more commonly everyone doing what the guy in charge tells them to. Co-ordinating people without dominating them is a relatively recent invention.

The first of those two, the scenario where everyone looks out for themselves, has some advantages. Morale is good, people show initiative and broadly speaking they co-operate. You can think of this model as being like the social structure of a village (minus the wealthy landowner). Unfortunately a village is a difficult thing to steer.

As soon as you want to get some useful work out of people you find you have to switch to the command-and-control approach. The transition is not usually a smooth one. The cultural change-management process traditionally begins with the order to 'start kicking ass and taking down names'. And that pretty much puts paid to the feel-good side of things.

It echoes quantum physics; the workable solution is not the appealing one. Command-and-control is unpalatable and outdated. Unfortunately, it is the fastest, simplest and frequently the cheapest method of achieving results. In contrast, organising the empowered citizens of the village model is, for the most part, like herding cats.

Management seers have lately begun to look to the natural sciences for assistance. Some, in fact, have observed the happy-and-creative village model and said, "Why steer?" If people are co-operating efficiently, why try to set a direction? You might stifle their creativity. From a personal point of view, I would love to work in a business based on that concept. I suspect it would work. I just can't imagine anyone getting permission from whoever's in charge to try it.

If you've ever heard of Heisenberg's uncertainty principle, you might have noticed that there's a similar trade-off operating in the workplace: you can have creative productivity or you can have control, but the more you have of one the less you can have of the other. The open-source software[1] 'movement' is dramatic evidence of this.

---

1 See *The Cathedral and the Bazaar* by Eric S. Raymond. If you're a traditional manager this is your worst nightmare. Someone let the 'nerds' work without supervision for a few minutes and they built the Internet – a global information repository with the potential to rewire the way planet Earth works. This was done in spite of managers, not because of them. What do you suppose they'll do for an encore?

Intriguing though the idea is of turning your workforce into something reminiscent of ball lightning (all incandescent brightness and sudden lane changes) you're probably saddled with some predetermined goals. If you're running a company the chances are that you didn't get that gig without making a few commitments about what you planned to do with the top spot. It's your job to ensure that the cat-herd follows the five-year plan.

Mother Nature is still the only real complex systems expert; is there another way of following her examples that would allow us a bit more control? Mother Nature does seem to get all sorts of useful work out of complex systems. Animals aren't just bags of squabbling cells. The billions of semi-autonomous cells in a cheetah seem to divvy up the work well enough to produce an animal able to break the national speed limit. Nature evolves its solutions; can we?

Interestingly, our bodies use a mechanism just like evolution to achieve a number of aims. It relies on something called apoptosis, which might well hold the secrets to curing cancer and arresting ageing. The basic idea is very simple. Take a large number of cells and set them a task. Allow them to vary a bit in their approach and then kill any that run into problems. It's even used as a tool for construction, killing cells that aren't in the right place. It's like the aphorism that suggests sculpting is just a matter of removing all the clay that isn't part of the design.

In fact the killing is achieved by instructing unwanted cells to commit suicide. It's the ultimate in tough management. There's no system of rewards or incentives, no disciplinary meetings, counselling or feedback. It's all a bit like the British Army of yore. Your service revolver is laid out for you and the Officers' Mess is instructed to set one less place at dinner.

Achieving compliance so heavy-handedly is a wasteful process. And reminiscent though it is of the management style of some movie villains, it relies for its effectiveness on components that are much more plentiful and disposable than employees.

Self-managing workforce

If we don't want to dominate the workforce, we can't allow them free rein and we can't find a workable evolutionary approach to organisation, is there another solution?

Perhaps, with careful recruitment, the organisation could be filled with what one might call management-tolerant employees? Wherever possible they would show initiative, but it wouldn't make them any less responsive to top-down directives. They would need to be bright enough and enthusiastic enough to work independently, but disciplined enough to follow any guidelines they were given.

Perhaps we could even make it the responsibility of the individual to link their day-to-day decision-making to the high-level strategies of the business.

Consultancies sometimes use this approach. They recruit bright, capable and very low-maintenance graduates and encourage them to find their own way. There is a part of me that finds the idea slightly unfair. It pushes responsibility for motivation and leadership back on to the employee. It becomes each person's obligation to manage themselves. It seems like cheating. More importantly, does it work?

Well, I started in Retail straight from University. I was older than most graduates, but I went through a revelation that I'm sure was not unique. After a few months I began to notice that I was quite a bit brighter than, those around me. I don't for a minute suggest that I was more useful to the business, just academically brighter. The sky, I therefore deduced, was the limit. Surrounded by people who were basically average I felt sure I would shine.

The second revelation came a year or two later, as I pondered some of the mysterious ways in which management moved. The fact that I was bright was an irrelevance. Of course bright people could achieve amazing things when they set their minds to it, but retail – and business in general – is not full of academic over-achievers or brilliant minds. It's full of ordinary people. That's not to disparage them. If it makes it sound less deprecatory, swap the word ordinary for normal. We all like to think we're normal, right?

A national retailer might employ ten thousand people, the majority on unspectacular salaries. It's just not possible to beat the average ten thousand times in a row, especially if you're not offering to make anybody rich. The companies taking the self-managing workforce tack recruit only junior employees who are potential senior managers. Mass retail doesn't have that luxury. The challenge of retail management is to get the job done using regular people.

It's like a make-at-home project on a kid's TV show. You have to limit your specifications to what's available and practical. Of course you can make a model rocket fly using a gallon of NASA-quality hydrazine, but can you get it to work using compressed air or elastic bands?

Round-up of the options

So, let's review what we've said about business design. Businesses are undeniably complex (in the sciencey sense of the word). They frequently comprise thousands of agents acting in loose concert. Command-and-control is unappealing to the employee, and wasteful of initiative. It also seems a little unimaginative. But we don't seem much better off trying to use an evolutionary method for building businesses.

Evolution is the only approach with a track record in co-opting complex systems to do useful work – and yet evolution is all about duplication and variability of designs and taking the very long view. It is slow and, in a sense, it is massively wasteful. Like quantum mechanics, if it didn't work so well, it would hardly have anything else to recommend it. At its core it is a process of endless iterative 'weeding'. It doesn't 'deliver' within our timescales or our budget.

Organisations grow and change, but we can't perfect them by aggressively pruning the workforce. And we can't allow growth to be uncontrolled. We can't improve the organisation by a wholesale upgrade of the staff. We are left with a method of advancement that is uniquely and originally human: creative, planned design.

We need to *design in* initiative alongside alignment to the strategy. We need enough discipline to get the job done and enough freedom to motivate and empower the workforce.

How do we create the structure for a business? Where do we start? How do we know when we are doing well? The place to start is with constraints.

Universal good or bad

I want to digress for a moment before I talk about constraints. I want to talk about the image problem some management terms have.

There are a number of words in common business usage that have acquired an absolute rather than a relative value. 'Proactive' is a good example. From the way it's used, you'd deduce that 'proactive' is always good and 'reactive' is bad. You'd conclude that 'flexible' is always a good thing as well. 'Constraints' on the other hand seem undesirable.

I recall having an argument with a group buyer about the need for price flexibility in the run-up to Christmas. We were operating from two different sets of assumptions without realising it – in effect we were talking two different languages.

He felt we needed the 'flexibility' to drop the price quickly if trading was slow. I questioned why he would want to do such a thing. I may have even referred to it as 'losing our nerve'. I might have suggested that putting in place a system for conveying our mistakes to the market more quickly was a bad idea. His argument continually returned to the fact that he was only asking for more flexibility. What could be bad about that?

As a general principle, I would say you haven't fully appreciated the benefits of an approach until you can give an example of where it is inappropriate. Being flexible, can be what you might call 'a bad thing' when you're working in areas in which decisions take a while to pay off. Most management styles work better once people have settled down and got used to them. People don't want 'mercurial' from a boss, they want 'consistent'. Being the same person after lunch as you were in the morning helps people work out what you want from them. You know this to be true if you remember the days when managers could go out and get drunk at lunchtime.[1]

Reactive management also gets a bad press. In the aforementioned argument I think I tried at one point to 'get clever'.[2] I pointed out that dropping the price in response to slow trading was in fact 'reactive' management, and surely only 'proactive' management was 'good'. The underlying point is a good one (although it's even better if you can avoid sounding snide). Understanding when 'proactive' management is inappropriate is an important step in using it effectively.

Back to constraints

Constraints and limitations certainly sound like bad things. Why would we be glad of constraints? The answer is that without them the whole infinite world of possibilities is open to you for consideration and comparison. In today's hectic world, who has time for tasks that take an infinite amount of time? The answer is no-one.[3]

Constraints are also assumptions, so of course great care is required in handling them. When designing a business we want to cut the range

---

1   Ahh, the Eighties! Getting drunk on business was called 'hospitality' in those days. Now it's called 'networking' and is altogether more restrained.

2   These days Dan usually spots the signs and bundles me out of a meeting before I get to that point. He's got some theory that there's no point in winning one little battle if it loses you the war. But who worries about that sort of thing in the middle of a good argument?

3   Although I'll accept 'the Civil Service' for half marks.

of possible solutions – what I'm afraid I'm going to call 'the design space' – down to manageable proportions.

We already have two constraints. We need to achieve the financial returns we've committed to. We also need to do it without replacing our staff with the content of McKinsey's graduate intake programme.

This is not about making a list, though. The first step in business design is in seeing how the constraints fit together to block out large volumes of the possible design space. These constraints put large parts of the map in shadow; whatever's left is where we build.

We can also approach this design work by thinking in terms of organisational capabilities and the resources that support them. We have commitments on what we must achieve – this tells us a lot about what our organisational capabilities need to be. We have constraints on the resources we must use. Often these constraints will be about time or money.

Effectiveness, efficiency and risk

The relationship between resources and capabilities is our efficiency – the ratio of what we get out to what we put in. It should always be as high as we have time to make it.

The organisational capabilities themselves are our effectiveness. They should be as high as our strategy requires and no higher. No higher, that is, unless our efficiency is infinite. If it's anything less than infinite, that means the extra, surplus effectiveness cost us something, which, since we don't need it, is a bad thing.

You can already see, I hope, that confusing efficiency and effectiveness is just going to cause a lot of problems. The likelihood is that you've known that for a while. Even so, in my experience, if you want to talk to people in business about the distinction, you have to spend a couple of minutes defining your terms. That doesn't suggest to me that it's a daily topic of conversation.

The efficiency/effectiveness distinction is also worth making because of two, totally contradictory, trends. The first is just the tendency to think that if something is worth doing, it's worth doing well. I say 'trend', it's an aphorism and we probably come across it many times before we started our first jobs. There's nothing wrong with it in a business context, provided that we apply it to efficiency and not effectiveness. See the foregoing. So in my revisionist future, parents nag their children that 'if something's worth doing, it's worth doing *efficiently*'.

Gunning for Pareto

The second trend is something I'm considering starting a crusade against. You may know it as the Pareto principle, the 80–20 rule or just the idea of diminishing returns. Eighty per cent of the benefit comes from 20 per cent of whatever it is we're talking about. Now I'm not disputing that it's true – well actually, I am disputing it. But whether it's true or not, it's what we do about it that's relevant.

The idea behind 80–20ing something (it's a verb now) is the suspicion we all have that, in business, most of the time we're doing triage. We're trying to do as much good in as short a time as possible. Giving someone a haircut can wait until after you've restarted their heart. Or in the true spirit of 80–20, you never get to the haircut, because there's another patient about to expire. We know this to be true because retail is tough, manly work with no time for finesse. Firefighters don't redecorate, they put the fire out and then they move on – to put another fire out.

But hold on, we've had a hundred years to get retail organised, why is there no time for finesse? The only acceptable answer is 'because we don't need finesse'. If finesse were important, we should have found a way to include it in the price. Well, my conviction is that most of the time it *is* important.

We're not fire-fighters because that's our role, we're fire-fighters only because we screw up. Most of the time, we should be following a plan, not reacting to an emergency. And to those who don't think that's possible, I tend to ask: "How much of your week do you spend planning for contingencies?" We're coming on to contingencies in a minute. They're the third side of the triangle of design. But for most of us, contingencies are what happen when the plan goes wrong. We frequently tackle them in the flesh and not in the imagination.

Consider customer service. Is that an 80–20 situation? In fact, it's not. Every last percentage point of good customer service you can persuade your staff to give is an important differentiator and a competitive edge you have over your competition.

What about, to pick an example at random, stock management? How valuable is getting the last couple of per cent right? Well, if you turn over a billion a year with gross margin around a third, then one per cent of your stock is worth sixty-six million at cost. I feel sheepish every time I lose even a few million in stock.

Have a run-through of your business. Find a process where it's really not worth getting things more than 80 or 90 per cent right. They are not easy to find and yet everyone knows the 80–20 rule. It's an idea that succeeded so well that it's a menace. It's even used as a smokescreen: it looks like I'm only doing a half-arsed job, but I say the phrase '80–20', and behold, now I'm working smarter not harder. And despite the fact it has limited application (unlike efficiency and effectiveness), I find I never have to explain to anyone what 80–20 means.

A word about out-sourcing

While I'm on this particular high-horse, the other side of the coin is out-sourcing. Everyone's out-sourcing things. Everyone thinks they're surrounded by 80–20 processes. When they realise very few processes are 80–20, I think they also realise that out-sourcing brings at least as many problems as it solves. Out-sourcing, in most cases, should be *more* difficult than doing it yourself but also more efficient. Why more difficult? Because you are using resources that reside in an external organisation to perform part of your company's internal processes. Co-ordinating across organisational boundaries is always tricky. Here are five reasons to out-source:

1. Because we don't have a good enough credit rating to get the capital to set it up ourselves.
2. Because we didn't plan far enough ahead to allow time to do it ourselves.
3. Because we don't think our management of those resources would be as competent as an outside party.
4. Because we are focusing on 'core activities'.
5. Because it's a new/problem area for us.

You can tell by my phrasing, I suspect, that I consider the first three reasons legit and the latter two rather dubious.

Morale and confidence are important in a lot of situations, but I think boards need to be honest among themselves. You can't make everything sound like a victory and if you can, you shouldn't. Out-sourcing things you never plan to get 100 per cent right makes sense. Out-sourcing something you hope one day to perfect is a courageous choice. While it's out-sourced, it's more difficult to develop internal competence in that area and getting something exactly right is difficult enough without splitting the process across two businesses.

The simple summary of the 80-20/out-sourcing rant is to get very clear on the level of effectiveness required. High effectiveness nearly always costs a lot – in time, money, effort – but if it's something your business needs to be good at, you don't have a choice.

For a retail business there are a couple of hundred high-effectiveness requirements around the store. How often is a stock-out acceptable? How important is it that the till software works? Can we skip the occasional electricity payment and work in the dark? Not to be flippant, but there are a lot of processes behind running a store that just have to be spot-on the whole time.

Stock availability is a good example. I was very surprised when I first learned that gaining a few percent of stock availability was worth the company-wide upheaval and expense of an automated replenishment system.

Choose your capabilities

That's enough about 80–20. But hold on to the distinction between effectiveness and efficiency. We were thinking about business design and it's probably time to actually tell you something useful, so here goes.

Effectiveness is about organisational capabilities and organisational capabilities are externally-directed things. Efficiency is about the level of resources required to support a given set of capabilities. It's internal.

There are some nuances to this, but the general idea is that the capabilities your organisation needs depend on the outside world. Providing those capabilities efficiently depends on factors within the business.

Hey wait a minute, what about strategy? I thought the board decided on our capabilities. What do they do if it's not that? Good point. What the board do is to select a balance of capabilities that they think will play well in the current and future climate. You people reading this are business-types, so here's a golf analogy. The board decide how to play the shot, but what they can't do is move the tee, the hole, the trees or the sand. The geometry and conditions of the course are non-negotiable, they are external and they define the capabilities required for success.

The strategy is needed because of three factors:

- Although the course defines the capabilities it doesn't always spell them out. Realising what is required can take some work.
- There is more than one set of capabilities that will work. In many cases there are an infinite number of ways to proceed – a continuum. One set of capabilities needs to be selected.

- Horrifying though the thought is, there is sometimes a gap between what gets written in the business plan and what happens in reality. If we imagine that there is a word 'achievability[1]', then it needs to be a feature of any strategy.

As we shall see later, these external conditions are not immutable for all time, just as fixed costs are not fixed forever. Businesses don't *have* to accept them, but it's a lot less work to adapt to a market than to create it.

There are always ways to change the external landscape if you are determined enough (let's forget the golf analogy at this point, shall we?). But a business doesn't have to be completely original; it just needs to be completely profitable.

For the most part, we will allow current and projected external conditions to define our operating criteria. At the same time, we should bear in mind that you can't stay in the lead by copying the guy in front. In later chapters we will look at some untapped opportunities for re-shaping the trading landscape.

Attitudes to risk

We are going to move on to think about risk and contingency in our organisational capabilities, but we're going to take a roundabout route. Before we say any more about what our organisational goals should be, we'll just have a quick look at the way we express them.

Modern business thinking has certainly been influenced by sports and the military. Hopefully, we are all aware that the world has moved on, and metaphorical language in which we 'kill the competition' or 'seduce the customer' says a lot more about us than it does about our business. Even so, there's still a sense that 'we need to get out there and give 110 per cent' and other such well-meaning nonsense.

Too much 'can do' cheerleading affects our ability to handle risk, probability and contingency. Imaginary conversation:

> "Jenkins, what are your sales looking like for the year?"
> "Good, Mr Prenderghast. I think we'll hit our targets with no trouble."
> "You *think* you'll hit your targets?"
> "I mean I'm sure we will. We'll definitely hit them."

---

1 Well, it's in the dictionary, so I suppose it's a word. Although put-off-able is more useful and I don't see that anywhere.

Obviously, I'm exaggerating to make a point, the logical conclusion to which is that all employees face front and yell "Sir, yes sir!" in reply to questions. But like a lot of things you'll read here, there's some truth to it.

This isn't just about over-zealous language; it's about attitude and it raises an issue about the importance of morale. There's a risk that safeguarding morale can get in the way of accurately measuring progress. Before we get back to organisational goal setting, I'm going to spend some time thinking about morale and credibility.

Morale *versus* morology

As professional managers, you will no doubt have read somewhere that motivation is important. As human beings, you'll also be familiar with that moment after the alarm goes off in the morning, but before you swing your legs out of bed. What goes through your mind at that moment? When I'm in a real routine, I'll tend to get up on autopilot. The norm, however, is a momentary mental debate about whether there really is a pressing need to leave a warm bed. Perhaps it's Saturday[1], or I've retired? Perhaps I'm rich enough already.

There are a few thousand of these moments in the working day. They're not full-blown existentialist debates, for the most part, but each one provides us with an opportunity to really go for it or to take a breather. Motivation makes all the difference.

And this fact is not lost on managers, and yes, even politicians. Whatever the whys and wherefores of a plan, if people are unhappy about it, it will probably fail. Conversely, the right attitude can make any plan succeed. Correct?

Well, the UK had that debate recently when it had to decide how to handle a succession of 'scares' over contaminated or unsafe food – BSE, foot and mouth, salmonella, GM crops. The government felt it was important to keep everyone calm while they figured out what to do. That sounds so reasonable, doesn't it? But how do you keep people calm? You tell them that there's nothing wrong, nothing to worry about. This strategy works fine up to the point when the newspapers report a death from something you've designated 'harmless'. Panic ensues and in order to

---

1   As you know, Saturday is often the most important day of the week for retail. It's vital, therefore, that operations get a clear run at it without any interference from head office. Which is why non-operational staff get the weekend off. Did I get that right?

restore calm you have to really emphatically state that there's nothing to worry about. Which works up until the facts blow a hole in it again.

I'm hardly an expert on genetics, but I dare say I've earned the right to snort derisively from time to time during Jurassic Park. I don't actually think that current GM crops are anything to worry about. We've eaten crops deliberately mutated by radiation for some time now; it's just that most people don't know it. GM seems to me to be an improvement on that. But the public uproar would tend to suggest I'm wrong.

The big problem with GM crops is that the government says they're safe. And recent experience has shown that when the government says something is safe to eat it turns out to be dangerous. So we have something with no known harmful effects, which no-one will touch, because of a credibility problem.

I said earlier, you can't make everything sound like a victory, and if you can you shouldn't. Good morale requires that you find the up-side to a situation and highlight it. I would urge you, though, to consider when telling the bleak, unpalatable truth might be the wisest course.

If, for instance, you happen to be a senior US politician, or a TV evangelist, there is hard evidence to suggest that 'fessing up and saying you're sorry works a lot better than denying everything and getting caught. And anyway, in my experience, people already know the truth. Secretaries, mail-room guys, chauffeurs and anyone with the word 'assistant' in their title know everything they want to know about your company. Looking them in the eye and making a statement that's not quite factually accurate isn't the morale-booster you might hope it is.

And can I make a personal request? I'd like to see a big company fire someone senior and admit they were fired. We all know that 'leaving to pursue outside interests and spend more time with the family' is a polite fiction. It would restore my faith to see an official announcement that said, "John Smith leaves the business this week. The board discovered that for all his assurances that everything was fine, his department were miserable and demotivated and things would only have got worse. It turns out he was a bit of a bully, actually, and by continuing to employ him the company would have tacitly signalled our acceptance of that – as though only senior managers had the right to expect courteous treatment."

Obviously, this person would sue you if you made a statement like that. But then again, in the kind of atmosphere you'd create, you'd have thirty-five witnesses volunteering to back your version. It was just a thought.

Subjectivity is just as real

George Soros, who periodically seems to be making something of a success of himself, talks about the reflexivity of the market. What he appears to mean by that is the tendency for people's opinions to influence the outcome of a situation.

Most scientific disciplines have a twelve-foot high security fence between what they believe and what they can prove. The two are separate and distinct, and everyone works hard to keep them that way. T.S. Kuhn[1] points out that actually we tend to fit the evidence to our view of the world, rather than *vice versa*, but even so – you wouldn't expect the evidence to alter just because you changed your opinion. The stock market possesses 'reflexivity' because that's exactly what *does* happen.

A company literally can't borrow money unless enough people think it's a good idea. We can pretend that such a situation is objective by talking about a credit-rating, rather than a belief, but the e-commerce boom demonstrated neatly that conventional objective measures couldn't stand in the way of mass opinion.

On the other hand, the markets aren't *just* opinion. If your market capitalisation drops below the net value of your assets, someone will buy your business – if only to sell the bits; opinion is no longer a factor. So it's clear that the market has both a subjective and an objective component.[2] Both are important, just as they are in business.

It's a balancing act for senior managers. Keeping confidence high is just as important as keeping the business solvent in many cases. In fact, you can think of it as a sort of emotional solvency. If everyone thinks the business is finished, then it's finished.

But that's lack of faith. There's a vital distinction here. Too little faith will damage the prospects of any enterprise. On the other hand, diminishing returns apply – a business's prospects don't keep improving the more confident its employees are. Sooner or later, it just starts to seem like delusion.

How does this affect risk? Well, when we start to believe that confidence will lower our risks then we are in danger of losing our objectivity.

Thinking about airlines – should all Catholic passengers be given last

---

1   In case you've ever wondered where the popularity of the word paradigm came from, it's from this guy.

2   I suppose you could view technical analysis as the belief that investor sentiment will dominate and fundamental analysis as the belief that it won't.

rites before boarding? No. On the other hand, should airlines remove the oxygen masks, escape slides and lifebelts because that's just defeatist thinking? No, again. You can plan for problems without increasing their likelihood. In fact, you might even decrease their likelihood with good planning.

This takes us back to that imaginary conversation about sales:

"You *think* you'll hit your targets?"
"We think there's about a 90 per cent chance of it. We've also got some good sale-or-return deals to be on the safe side, and a promotion ready to run if we dip below 85 per cent of target."

I like this second version a lot more than the gung-ho happy-talk of the previous one. We just need to be clear that preparing for failure is not to be confused with accepting failure.

How much certainty do you want?

If we take the matter of contingency planning to heart, we need to go beyond the idea of doing something or not doing it as though it's a binary thing. Whatever preparations we make, we can only ever improve our chances; we can't guarantee success. All pep-talk aside, nothing is ever a sure thing.

Risk management books contain terms like 'sovereign risk', the risk that a government becomes a bad debtor. A world that needs a word for that situation is a world that needs to think about contingencies.

When considering business design and choosing our organisational capabilities, we need to consider the cost of failure *versus* the rewards of success for any single capability. With what level of reliability do we wish to do something?

We touched on this when I was trying persuade you that Mr Pareto is welcome as a guest, but shouldn't be considered a permanent resident. To clarify the importance of risk, consider two industries: airlines (again) and pizzas. Both of them make deliveries, and in both cases the clock is running. Consider two questions: how important is it that the delivery arrives on time and how important is it that the delivery arrives at all?

In both cases you choose your organisational capabilities, so that your timescales for delivery fall within a suitable window. But how many exceptions do we allow ourselves? How much effort do we put into mitigating the risk of missing our targets?

Well, I've certainly been delayed when I've travelled by plane – so much so that I'm tempted to write that I've *usually* been delayed – and I've also had to wait for pizzas. Curiously, the former happens more than the latter. But one company, Dominos, decided they could differentiate themselves from the competition by guaranteeing their ability to hit that particular target.

> **Excerpt from Dominos FAQ**
> *8. What happened to the 30-minute guarantee?*
> The company's 30-minute guarantee has been replaced with a re-emphasis on product quality as demonstrated in the 'Made Fresh, Arrives Fresh' guarantee.
> *9. Where can I get Dominos' logo wear?*

On the other hand, I'm not even aware that airlines consider an apology for a delay mandatory. I think they find delays so costly that they consider they've been punished enough without grovelling to the passenger. If they could afford to guarantee 'no delays', you can bet they would.

But Dominos for a number of years did offer a guarantee: delivery in thirty minutes or it's free. They don't have that guarantee any more, though. It was causing too many traffic accidents. This will be a big theme in later chapters, but you have to be careful what you pressurise your people to do for you, because there's always a danger that they were listening. You can imagine that to the directors of Dominos, injuries and car crashes were the last things on their mind. I'm sure they were horrified to find that some employees were endangering lives just to get a pizza across town. In the case of Dominos, they were able to fix things – they abolished the thirty-minute guarantee.

Airlines face a different problem – it's clearly accepted that some passengers will be delayed from time to time – but how acceptable is it if they never arrive at all? Billions are spent on mitigating that particular risk.

We rather unfairly demand that airlines are much safer than any other forms of transport. Or to put it another way, a fatal car crash will only make the national news if it involves a celebrity, a plane crash will not only appear on the news, it will dominate it. Airlines strive for safety and the public demands it. It is not the organisational capability that is at issue – the ability to fly people around the globe – it is the reliability with which it can be done that we notice.

So, when your business selects its organisational capabilities, it will need to think about the level of reliability required. As the airline example hopefully illustrates, often it is the reliability level that requires the investment and the effort and not the capability itself.

It is here that I begin to have sympathy with the thinking behind 80–20 – except that the diminishing returns in many capabilities don't kick in at 20 per cent or even 90 per cent. It's when we strive for perfection that we really start to run up a bill. It can cost a lot of money to move from 99.8 per cent reliability to 99.9 per cent. Being clear on the level of reliability required is often vital to the economics of your business. Which is why a good understanding of acceptable risk is important. It's also why the gung-ho hyperbole I mentioned can be a bad thing. We have to have a business culture that permits us to talk sensibly about risk.

Counting the full cost

Let's think about the costs of achieving reliability, against the costs of failure.

If there's a quick way of describing what accounting is about, I'd say it was 'figuring out what things really cost'. I don't suppose many people would agree with that definition, but for me the interesting thing – and I think it is interesting – about depreciation, accruals, amortisation and the design of a chart of accounts is that they can help you understand the resources that were used to achieve a particular income. In effect, they can help you measure the financial efficiency of each revenue stream.

It's an idea that can be reapplied endlessly. We're going to cover KPIs (Key Performance Indicators) in some detail in the finance chapter, but often they are nothing more than attempts to add in indirect, but relevant, costs when calculating profit.

Counting the cost of failure gets more and more difficult the more that human behaviour and/or the future becomes a factor, but it's worth attempting. When thinking about reliability levels one really needs to have a broad definition of the costs. In the case where you don't have an item in stock, the accounting costs associated with that failure are zero. But you'll want to consider opportunity costs as well. Lost sales are easily quantifiable, if you're an organisation that receives customer orders. If you're a self-serve operation, like most stores, you may know very little about your lost sales.

What about the repeat sales you might jeopardise as well? Quantifying the damage done to your relationship with the customer is in another league of difficult. But, just because you can't measure those effects, doesn't mean they're not there.

For many questions about the costs of failure, you'll have to be satisfied with recognising the problem and estimating its extent. For certain capabilities, you might be able to run store trials. The aim, of course, is to find the point at which extra reliability costs more than it generates in sales. Benchmarking against your competitors might also give you a few extra points on the graph to help you choose the optimum trade-off.

I don't have very many wise words to say about finding the perfect solution, beyond pointing out the general lie of the land. But we will have quite a number of useful things to say about how customers interpret reliability levels and some ways to mitigate against damage to that relationship.

Errors in perception

The final point to make about the risk aspect of the effectiveness-efficiency-risk triangle is that not only are there reliability questions about your capabilities, there are reliability questions about your interpretation of the external constraints.

As we mentioned earlier, one of the reasons we need a strategy-minded board is so that they can 'take a view'. For all but the largest companies, the economy and the trading climate are givens – they are not something that can be directly influenced. Since these external conditions define the kinds of businesses that will be successful, it is vital to perceive them clearly. There will always be an element of risk in an activity like that. The design of the business will need to take account of this second source of risk. By building in a margin of extra efficiency a business can obtain a little protection against the effects of misreading the market – a cushion against demand that is lower than expected. Effectively, the business can be designed to 'run lean' if needs be.

So risk affects both effectiveness and efficiency. When applied to effectiveness it gives us the concept of a reliability level. When applied to efficiency it gives us a safety margin.

Now it's time to consider what the external factors shaping our business might actually be.

External design factors

For a couple of minutes, once, I nearly became a medical physicist. I'm always impressed by any medical technology that doesn't appear to be an offshoot of carpentry.

These days the field boasts quite a number of imaging technologies that don't involve making any new holes. Most people know what an x-ray photo looks like and they've at least heard of CAT scans. MRI scanners – which used to be called NMR scanners[1] – use magnets instead of x-rays and do a much better job of imaging what you might call the squishier parts of the body. There are also PET scanners and exotic things like Neutron Boron Capture. Each one shows you a different aspect of the body's composition.

As a business-designer you also have a number of imaging techniques you can apply to a business, each of which will highlight different sorts of structures.

Imagine what the geographical layout of your business would be like if you could view the distribution of the following:

- Current assets – stock, debtors, and so on
- Fixed assets
- Sales and purchasing or cashflow
- Expenses and cost
- Capital expenditure
- Head count
- Average wage
- Staff turnover
- Shrinkage

It would also be fascinating to see in what way these measures vary over time. You may track many of them by department or location already. Though, I don't know that many companies display them as pictures, let alone time-based animations. Let's consider what a couple of them might show us.

Imagine the sales/purchasing view. It's pretty easy to imagine what that view looks like. If you've got centralised purchasing and a store-based

---

1   The official story is that the name was changed because NMR stands for Nuclear Magnetic Resonance, and the word nuclear frightens the bejeesus out of people. I don't buy it, personally, because all medical technology frightens people. I tend to think it was the similarity in pronunciation between the acronym NMR and the word 'enema' that caused the problem. I don't have to spell out the scope for gaffes and subsequent bad publicity there.

retail operation, all the (non-consumable) buying gets done at head-office and all the sales happen in the shops.

A picture of the business in sales/purchasing terms would show a river of money flowing in through the stores and, somewhat diminished, out to the various suppliers.

Contrast this with cashflow. What will the differences be? For many retailers there'll be a roughly fifty-fifty split between sales revenue in cash and the amount that comes by way of merchant services. (In either case, retailers who don't involve themselves with consumer credit don't usually have much in the way of debtors to worry about.) The credit/debit card companies make their payments daily or weekly. Occasionally, there might also be a huge gulp of cash flowing in from debt, equity or loans. There may also be occasional inflows, perhaps once or twice a year, from suppliers in the form of rebates. These sums can be quite sizeable.

On the outflow side the largest sums will be supplier payments. Then there are wages, taxes and dividends. Occupancy costs these days are pretty high as well – now that it's unfashionable to own property. There's also capital expenditure and then the myriad of expense items that make up the various cost centres of your business.

This cashflow picture shows all the important external links:

- Customers
- Suppliers
- Employees
- Shareholders
- Other creditors
- Taxes
- Property
- Investments

It seems pretty obvious that a business that makes best use of these links, maximising the inflow and minimising the outflow, will prosper.

We're going to use that cashflow picture to arrive at a picture of the external constraints on the business. There are a couple of points to make, though, before we consider that we have identified the important considerations. First is the discretionary or interactive element.

It is difficult to imagine that the tax situation of an individual company provokes the government to alter its assessment rules very frequently. From the point of view of the retailer, tax liability is not interactive. That's not to say tax liability is fixed, but the rules which govern that liability are fixed. This is in contrast, say, to the relationship with the customer, which very much depends on the retailer's actions.

So, tax efficiency is something that influences business decisions, but it is usually considered after the operational decisions have been made.

A business will have other long-term financing options than just the equity market. However, since the shareholders own the business it is difficult to envisage a situation where the interests of, say, the bond market were both in conflict and of greater importance than the wishes of the shareholders. For this reason, other long-term-debt providers can generally be considered grouped in with the shareholders.

Short-term creditors, on the other hand are chiefly suppliers, who already appear on our list.

Besides suppliers of product, retailers will often have a number of consumables suppliers as well as various service partners. They should be considered, of course, but in general they are too small a factor to be worth including when revising the top-level design of a retail business. In addition, a fair amount of what is said on the subject of suppliers (of goods for resale) will apply to these other companies.

The final entry on the previous list that needs tackling is investments. Since they are solely under the control of the business, they can't be considered an external design constraint.

The important external factors

That leaves us with:

- Customer
- Shareholder
- Employee
- Supplier

These are the four external interfaces of a retail business which determine its success. They are each amenable to negotiation and relationship-building. Each has the discretion to contribute or withhold something vital to the business. And each can be won over with the right approach.

The rest of the book considers a unified way in which that might be done.

What was that all about?

- Effectiveness is about capabilities; efficiency is about the resources consumed by those capabilities.
- Effectiveness will be planned based on the external climate; efficiency will be as high as we can make it.
- Risk affects the economics of the business. Required level of reliability will be a big driver of cost.
- Organisation capabilities need to be designed with the customer, the shareholders, the employees and the suppliers in mind.

CHAPTER 2

Planning strategic relationships

This journey

Because relationships are at the heart of this book, we're going to spend some time thinking about how to manage them. Is there really such a thing as a business relationship or is that just a figure of speech? Maybe relationships are things to leave behind when we set off for the office. And what about relationships between businesses?

And if there really are business relationships, should they be managed using emotions or logic? We're going to think about whether being tough is the same thing as being business-like. We're going to think about whether there's a link between co-operation and being weak.

The answers to these questions have a bearing on everything from supplier negotiations to employee discipline. Our route might seem roundabout at times, but our destination is very close to home.

In order find our answers, we're going to clear away some of the myths and propaganda around both good and bad emotions. In order to do that, we'll need to understand a bit more about where they come from and the jobs they evolved to handle.

We want to arrive at a view of what constitutes appropriate business behaviour and to understand the consequences of different approaches to emotion in business.

As before, we're also going to discuss a couple of examples from nature, where the mechanisms explored in this chapter have been in use for millennia.[1]

Finally, we come in for a landing by considering what this tells us about the nature of strategic relationships in retail and the most productive way to approach them.

---

1 I'm thinking once you know these ideas work in practice, you might be prepared to believe they also work in theory.

What is a strategic relationship?

In the last chapter we suggested that the design of a business would depend on four key external groups:

- Customers
- Financiers (shareholders and others)
- Employees
- Suppliers

These are the four strategic partnerships discussed throughout the rest of the book and they are the four points of the compass you can see on the first page.

Clearly, if they constrain the shape of the business, they can be considered strategic. But why am I referring to them all as relationships?

In the previous chapter, we excluded taxation as a primary shaping element of the business because it was nothing more than a set of rules. The way in which a business interacts with the four groups above, is much more complicated and does not follow simple rules.

Consider a single one of the groups, say suppliers. The way a business's suppliers react to new initiatives will depend on the history of their dealings with one another. There is no way to erase the past and start with a clean slate. Even when switching to a new supplier, both parties' previous trading relationships will condition expectations.

To use a venerable old analogy, it is a little like a chess game. The rules themselves are not overly complex, but each move depends on those that preceded it. The way in which each choice compounds the complexity of the situation means that there are billions of possible chess games.

When both parties have a range of options and when each action is influenced by those that went before, we can say that we have a relationship. Contrast that with the way one might talk about a tax 'position'. In the four key relationships, each side influences the other.

Let's just check our thinking, though. Are all four really relationships?

Because buyer and account manager sit down and talk about last year, this year and next year, it is fairly obvious that a relationship exists. What about shareholders?

Well, to give you another of my unpopular definitions, one way of describing the chairman's job is 'having lunch with the investors'. It is an important part of a chairman's role to make sure that there is a relationship and that it is a reasonably amicable one.

What of employees? Well, the popularity of the phrase 'employee relations' should make it clear that there is a relationship there.

Excerpt from Cadbury Report on corporate governance – the role of the chairman.

"The chairman's role in securing good corporate governance is crucial. Chairmen are primarily responsible for the working of the board, for its balance of membership subject to board and shareholders' approval, for ensuring that all relevant issues are on the agenda, and for ensuring that all directors, executive and non-executive alike, are enabled and encouraged to play their full part in its activities. Chairmen should be able to stand sufficiently back from the day-to-day running of the business to ensure that their boards are in full control of the company's affairs and alert to their obligations to their shareholders."

No specific mention of lunches but I think it's implied.

When we talk about staff being loyal to a business there are two possible interpretations of what's going on. We are either referring to a relationship the staff have with the business itself, or senior managers are calling upon junior employees to be loyal to them personally. Very few exhortations are phrased according to that second option (or, I suspect, would succeed if they were). Staff are being loyal to the web of relationships they have *with each other* – the structure, history and values of that web.

Finally customers – is there a relationship there? Well, if one hundredth of the hype around 'customer-facing' businesses is true, then that's *all* anyone in business ever thinks of: the relationship with the customer.[1] This is perhaps the most elusive of the four, because it is both the most prominent and widely recognised strategic relationship and at the same time the most misunderstood.

Having established that the way a business interacts with each of the key groups is a relationship, we can begin to consider the nature of these relationships.

Emotion has no place in business

Ideally, serious management books would never explain things in terms of Star Trek. Sadly, that's not the case here. Maybe you can trust me that I *could* cover what I want to say by talking entirely about game theory,

---

1   We also talk about customer loyalty a great deal, but often it just seems to mean inertia or habit. By strengthening that relationship we'll see how to achieve real loyalty.

but it would take longer, seem more like being back at college and we'd still end up at the same place.

I'm talking about the shows from the sixties, here, with Spock and Kirk. Remember Spock always wanted to leave emotion out of any decision and follow the dictates of logic? Remember that more often than not, Kirk did something illogical which worked out pretty well? We've been playing with this idea since Mary Shelley wrote Frankenstein – wondering about the source of inspiration and whether the world is really a rational place. The Kirk–Spock debate is about whether there's more to the world than mechanical, clockwork logic – whether there's a vital spark, a soul to things which we ignore to our cost.

The portrayal always suggested that Spock was at a disadvantage because his world of logic was limited; he was missing the bigger picture. Kirk was harnessing the human ability to make leaps, to play hunches, to jump ahead of the plodding logician though flashes of inspiration. Isn't that what you miss if you're too logical?

Well, I have to say I think it's nonsense. There is nothing illogical about emotion; it usually makes perfect sense.

If Spock were really the big, analytical thinker he was made out to be, he'd have considered a scenario like the following one.

Imaginary supplier scenario

As a retailer, imagine you get an offer of some great deal from a supplier based in some distant part of the world. He will supply you with some product, let's called them Thingies, at 30 per cent below the going rate. Thingies are a big Christmas item and in short supply, so you sign him up.

You do all your other Christmas forecasting and realise you can really make a killing on Thingies – you order plenty and buy less of everything else accordingly.

Delivery is now due and you get a phone call from the supplier, you can hear loud bangs in the background and he explains that there's been a revolution and currently there is no government in his country. However, he will still ship you the order, but instead of 30 per cent below the going rate, he wants 30 per cent above.

Now you're stuck. There are no Thingies to be had elsewhere, you've got window posters and ad campaigns and point of sale all trumpeting your stocks of Thingies. You've also got nothing else to put in their place. You tell him you'll call him back and you do some quick sums.

If you pay him, you'll still make 2 per cent margin, whereas if you don't you'll make nothing. Unhappy, but resigned, you make the call.

The delivery arrives, Christmas sales go well and you pocket the meagre margin. Then the phone rings again. It's that supplier. Good news, order is restored in his country and the government are forcing everyone to honour any new contracts in an effort to restore international trade. Your supplier has a huge shipment of next year's big seller, Hoozits, available at a bargain price. Do you take him up on it?

Now, presumably, Mr Spock would say there is an excellent chance of enforcing the new contract, the deal is a good one and grudges are a regrettable human emotion which should play no part in logical decision-making.

Maybe Kirk (were he a retailer not a starship captain) would go for it too. Or maybe he'd say, "I don't trust them, Spock".

What would you do?

If you're logical about it, and make each decision on a case-by-case basis, you leave yourself open to a gradual erosion of benefits when dealing with an unscrupulous partner. They can chisel away at a deal and providing you still get some small benefit, you won't call it all off, despite the fact you were originally promised a much better arrangement.

Think about another situation, the Cold War.[1] How do you stop the Soviets wiping out America? (In this scenario you play the Americans, the Soviets are the bad guys.) Up until the Soviets have launched their missiles, all you can do is threaten them. Once they have launched it's too late. You could still wipe them out, but why bother? Would you do it anyway out of spite?

One way out of this dilemma is to build a doomsday device. You set up your missiles to *automatically* launch if you are attacked. The Soviets have only one course of action – don't attack.

How is that relevant? It is relevant because emotions like anger, the need for revenge, even spite, play the role of the doomsday device. If your intellect is allowing you to get beaten up regularly, your emotions can kick in to fix things.

It is an observed fact that the notion of honour seems to be held in

---

1   The film Doctor Strangelove uses this idea, and the book *The Language Instinct* by Steven Pinker goes into more detail about the concepts involved and a lot of other interesting things besides. If you have young children you will probably find it a fascinating read because it explains how babies learn language.

the highest esteem in countries with weak justice systems. Where law and order is not enforced, people seek alternatives. The principle of a vendetta, for instance, is a doomsday ploy which says 'harm my family and we will strike back whatever the cost.' It is the 'whatever the cost' part that is important. If the threat is 'harm my family and we will strike back unless it makes no sense' it doesn't work.

Senseless vendettas are senseless for good reason.[1] It is the guarantee to pursue the matter long after there is any benefit to be gained which makes the whole thing unpalatable to any would-be aggressor.

It is the same situation as with the supplier above. An emotional doomsday device which kicks in and exacts retribution will ensure a much higher rate of success in negotiations than a so-called 'logical stance'. If the supplier knows you will never deal with him again if he cheats you, no matter what future fabulous deals he offers, he may decide not to risk it. But you have to convince him you mean it. Emotions can help persuade others that you do mean it, by taking away your choice in the matter.

So, Star Trek has it back to front. Although the human race may be increasing its *capacity* for logic, that doesn't imply we are becoming less emotional. The whole point of the more negative emotions is that they can override logic. Otherwise they can't help us out of a tight spot. If we learn to control them, they will lose their power to protect us.

This was, for me, a startling idea. It changed the way I thought about the role of emotion in business. Emotion no longer seemed inappropriate; it seemed sophisticated, even Machiavellian.

Of course in order to get the most from our intelligence, emotions must know their place. If emotion is forever in the driving seat, we might as well have not come down from the trees. We just have to be aware that if emotion is kept on too short a leash, the threat of reprisals loses its credibility – which is the point of the negative emotions in the first place. But should that be a concern? Do we need that protective mechanism?

I said originally that honour and vendettas tend to thrive where the system of public justice is weak. On a smaller scale, it's worth bearing in mind in business. If we decide we want to keep the negative emotions under control in the workplace, then we have to ensure that the rules governing conduct, disputes and appeals are fair and effective.

---

1   Although, I admit, that sentence makes no sense.

Sometimes angry, never kind

The point of the last section was to establish that negative or destructive emotions are a sophisticated evolutionary defence-mechanism, which will remain relevant and useful as long as people are allowed to take advantage of each other.

What of the positive emotions? What about trust, friendliness, loyalty and so on? Ironically, they may be seen as having even less of a place in business than their negative counterparts. And it won't surprise you to learn that they too are sophisticated and effective, despite their soft-hearted connotations.

Have a look at the following qualities/adjectives and think about which ones you actively encourage at work and which you don't:

- Tough
- Forgiving
- Pushy
- Helpful
- Aggressive
- Patient

Try this sentence, "Gentlemen, we need to go after this opportunity aggressively. We're going to get some flack and we're just going to have to be tough. If we're to make the most of our chances we'll need to get a little bit pushy."

That sounded 'businessy'. I actually can't think of an imaginary speech that sounds appropriate for the workplace and which exhorts colleagues to be forgiving, helpful and patient. Only by using the words facilitate instead of help, broad-shouldered instead of forgiving and tolerant instead of patient might it be possible – even then it would be a pretty wimpy sounding speech. Clearly we feel the need to disguise the positive emotions if we are to smuggle them into work with us.

By the way, this isn't about how we should all hug one another and live in hippy harmony, it's just about questioning our assumptions about emotions in business.

Many businesses believe a little aggression is a good thing, but why exactly? Why are softer emotions seen as unbusiness-like, or worse still uncommercial?[1] Why are there no business euphemisms for aggressive,

---

1 'Uncommercial' has to be the ultimate retail put-down. If you are on the receiving end of this jibe, it's probably because you have spent more time at University than your detractor. I'd suggest claiming your idea is 'strategic' – an area where book-learning is less of a handicap.

fierce, killer, attack and so on? Those terms are used freely while their softer counterparts must be renamed. (Remember, I'm not helping you, I'm 'supporting' you.)

It's because secretly (or perhaps not so secretly in some cases) we believe that generosity is a luxury, something which 'in an ideal world' we'd see everyday, but 'when the chips are down'[1] we must put aside. Like bonuses, positive emotions are about sharing the good times, and just like bonuses they disappear when times get hard.

Interestingly, the same sentiment has pervaded evolutionary biology in the past. Nature – 'red in tooth and claw' – is expedient. Nature does whatever works and has no time for sentiment. So it was puzzling to biologists to see what appeared to be altruistic behaviour in the animal kingdom.

By altruism, we're not talking about helping out close relatives. As Richard Dawkins has pointed out, that's just your genes talking. Genes look out for their own survival. They want[2] to keep anyone who carries them alive – be that you or your brother. No, we're talking about co-operation between unrelated creatures.

It can also be tricky to put your finger on what altruism is. If we define it as any selfless act that helps others we have to rule out any not-so-selfless act for which you get a reciprocal benefit later. For the purposes of our discussion it's important that we don't exclude a later payback, because that later payback is exactly what we're interested in.

Turning it around the other way, although helpful acts of martyrdom are altruistic, we're not interested in anything that extreme either. Imagine during a famine you have some food and your neighbour doesn't. You could eat it yourself, give it to him or share. We're interested in whether sharing is a good or bad idea compared with eating it yourself. Giving it away and dying is just, as we say in the trade, 'uncommercial'.

A zero-sum world?

Wherever you are in the world and whatever the prevailing system of beliefs, you'll have been exposed to a certain amount of high-minded, spiritual encouragement to help your fellow man and to think charitably.

---

1 Here's a problem with sports metaphors: you end up mixing them. What do you do when the chips are down? You play hardball. What kind of casino would allow that?

2 Of course genes don't actually 'want' anything. I'm cutting a few corners with the language because it's not the genetics that are the point here. Just don't show this section to any of my old lecturers.

And since you're in business, you'll have been exposed to a certain amount of 'zero-sum' thinking that says grab what you can.

Zero-sum is the technical term for 'there's only so much to go round'. The idea is that if I have more, everyone else has less and *vice versa*. Any simple situation is usually zero-sum – dividing up a cake, sharing out winnings and so on. In a zero-sum situation we are all competitors.

There are a lot of situations, though, that aren't zero-sum. In 'real life' things are usually a lot less straightforward. The idea of hypothetically dividing up a cake is a good example. When have you ever divided up a cake except between family or friends – there's always some ongoing relationship with most of them. And when has there ever been nothing else to eat? In real life, there are always little deals and gambits in play. "Here, have mine. I'm not hungry", you say to someone you're trying to win over. Or, "Swap you my icing for your cake", you say to someone with a sweet tooth. Any time people have slightly different requirements there's scope to do a deal and get away from zero-sum.

Often people think they need to 'align goals' in order to co-operate with others. But what's even better is if you can find a single outcome that fits both sets of (dissimilar) goals. Then, both parties think they've won.

We touched on reflexivity in the last chapter. If keeping people happy is important, the game changes. Maybe the rule is that the party is over early if there's a squabble – in which case you need to be careful how vigorously you try to grab all the cake, you might spoil it for everyone – yourself included.

If this book is about just one thing, then it's about how very little in business is zero-sum – there's nearly always an alternative that's win-win.[1]

But first we need to decide whether win-win is just a poor substitute for being able to grab everything in sight. Is co-operation a fallback option when direct acquisition is blocked? Or is it worth a try even when it's not forced on you?

Co-operative critters

That's why the animal kingdom is so interesting. Our friends, the animals, will have already sorted these things out in the perpetual field-test that is evolution. We need to be just a tiny bit cautious, for evolution is always tinkering with new designs, many of which will fizzle out. But the idea

---

1   I'm sure it's a common phrase, but in case you don't know, win-win is like the 'I'll have the cake you have the icing example'. Both parties do better than if everything is just split down the middle.

is that if we see long-lived and stable forms of co-operation then they must be advantageous – because making a grab for whatever you can is the easy thing in the world. If co-operation endures it must be better than the alternative.

And if we discover animals co-operating, we know it won't be because of the teachings of Buddha, Mohammed or Jesus – it will be simple practicality.

One example makes this point particularly well because it concerns one of the least traditionally Christian members of the animal kingdom, the vampire bat.

Vampire bats drink the blood of cattle and even occasionally humans. Not only does this not do their chosen meal much good, they quite often pass on rabies into the bargain. So, it's safe to say these creatures are not nature's social workers.

Vampire bats also have a fatal vulnerability.[1] They can only last thirty or forty hours without food then they die. Given that they sneak about in the middle of the night, their mealtimes are somewhat restricted. A human being can go a fortnight with only water to drink and the only risk they run is they might be asked to do a photo-shoot for Vogue afterwards. But skipping meals is deadly for the bats.

How do the bats cope when they can't find a cow to suck on? They scrounge. They beg another bat to share some of its meal with them. What's to stop one bat cadging free meals the whole time? Well there's a catch. If you expect favours from others you have to be prepared to be generous yourself. A bat that refuses to share and yet expects assistance will be ostracised. The community won't tolerate freeloaders.

The same thing applies to Emperor penguins huddling in the deep-freeze-come-wind-tunnel that is the Antarctic. They gather together, regardless of bloodlines, and take it in turns to be in the cosy middle of the huddle. It's −50°C and the wind can blow at an astonishing hundred and fifty miles an hour; there's every incentive to avoid your turn on the outside – but the penguins play by the rules.

One might say, well they're genetically programmed to behave that way. But if it were just that, then soon enough a mutant penguin would arise who stayed in the middle the whole time. Such a penguin would find it easy to prosper and have lots of young. After a while, there would be a shortage of non-mutants to stand on the outside. Plus, those that did would hardly ever get a turn in the middle and they'd perish. The

---

1 If you thought it was holy water or crosses you should be ashamed of yourself.

remaining huddle of selfish mutants would die out or start co-operating. When we look at the Antarctic, we only see the descendants of those huddles where co-operation took hold.

Collaboration: for the birds?

So critters sometimes co-operate. The two examples above represent the most precarious of co-operative situations – ones where everyone is competing for exactly the same thing and it's in short supply. And yet, rather surprisingly, stable co-operation exists.

Co-operation is much easier to arrange in the situation we mentioned earlier, where different parties want different things – note: I said *easier* to arrange not *easy*.

Nature just overflows with co-operation between species. There's nothing sissy or soft-hearted about it; it makes sense to cooperate.

We've probably all seen little birds keeping big savannah animals picked clean of insects, or evil looking fish getting their teeth cleaned by tasty little shrimp, which they never eat. There are millions of examples. If you count the cells in a human body, only 10 per cent are human, the rest are bacteria.[1] We need the bugs to help us digest our meals; in exchange the bugs never have to look for food.

Maybe this seems a little abstract. What is good for a bacterium is a long way from what is good for a retailer. Perhaps you're not convinced that an ecosystem full of ingenious and mutually beneficial co-operation says anything about the world of business.

The prisoner's dilemma

Forgive me if you know all about this game already, but the idea is classic and simple. Two criminals are arrested and interviewed separately. Both are offered immunity for incriminating the other. The possible outcomes are:

- Neither prisoner talks, both get reduced sentences because of lack of evidence.
- One prisoner talks and is released, the other gets a full sentence.
- Both prisoners incriminate the other and get full sentences.

---

1   Just in case it isn't obvious how that's possible, the bacterial cells are much, much smaller than the human cells. They mainly live in our gut.

Put yourself in the position of one of the prisoners and devise your strategy. Is it better to be trusting or to be ruthless?

A man called Robert Axelrod, who is actually a political scientist by training, held a tournament to settle that question.[1] Repeated games of prisoner's dilemma would be played between pairs of computer programs. Experts and luminaries in various fields were invited to write programs for the tournament. Each program would contain the rules, strategy and cunning that its designer thought would allow it to prevail against the competition.

Biologists, political theorists, psychologists and economists were each invited to try their hand. Considerable effort went into designing the most deceitful and sly program – one which would outsmart the others. Figuring out when to turn nasty was the trick.

Which program won? The simplest, as it turned out. This program had one simple rule which allowed it to beat the scheming and ingenious opponents it faced. It always started out by co-operating with its partner (by opting not to incriminate them). However, if it was betrayed it would return the favour on the next encounter. In fact, apart from the co-operative start, it would always just copy what its partner did in the previous turn. When faced with a trusting opponent, it would co-operate; a ruthless opponent would see its ruthlessness mirrored.

It coped well with both trusting and treacherous opponents, and even got on fine when it came up against a copy of itself.

Remember when we talked about emotions? Well the wisdom of this winning strategy can be found in the emotions of hospitality and forgiveness, as well as the angry reaction we have to betrayal.

Try though they might, scheming strategists couldn't find a way to consistently take advantage of this simple program, even once they knew the rule it was using.

Again, we are looking at identical parties in direct competition, the most difficult situation in which to establish co-operation, and yet there is a simple formula for achieving it. In the world of business, where no two business models are identical, there are infinite opportunities for co-operative partnerships – no matter that on the face of it everyone is trying to make profit at another's expense.

This thinking will be particularly important when we consider suppliers. On the face of it, the more concessions you can extract from your suppliers, the better off you are. In practice, you want different

---

1 The book he wrote about it is called *The Evolution of Co-operation*.

things – there is often no reason why both parties can't have what they want.

I've been at pains to make a case that the positive emotions have more place in every aspect of business than is generally accepted. They are not about weakness, they are about establishing a basis for co-operation and co-operation is something that can make life better for all parties concerned. The world is not zero-sum; the size of the cake we are dividing up is not fixed. With ingenuity and collaboration, we can all of us have a bigger slice.

Good manners

Under what circumstances, then, should you forget co-operation and just grab what you can? You may wish to hold me to something I said a while back: don't trust statements of universal good. Any attribute, behaviour or attitude will be harmful in certain situations and helpful in others. There are no absolutes. So when is co-operation bad?

Well, depending on what we mean by 'bad' you might say co-operation is bad when it leads to cartels. Or maybe one might say that Enron and their auditors, Andersen, co-operated *too* much.[1] But that is just a way of saying co-operation doesn't do any favours for those on the *outside*.

A better answer, setting aside morality and considering only strategy, would be to say co-operation works best when there are repeat encounters or ongoing interaction between the parties. If you know you will never see the other party again, the penalties for a grab-what-you-can approach may not apply.

We see this in urban life. Queue jumping, pushing past others, a general lack of courtesy are traits encouraged by the law of averages, which says you will never meet those you upset again in a city of millions. In a small community, it is difficult to imagine that sort of behaviour giving any kind of advantage – you would quickly fall out of favour with your neighbours. It is only a virtually limitless supply of new neighbours which allows a totally selfish attitude to prosper for long.

If you firmly believe that there's always another customer, always

---

1 I'm writing this in late July 2002 and Andersen appear to be circling the drain. A friend of mine who claims to be in the know says that when the full story comes out we'll see that the audit rules were followed to the letter and the Department of Justice indictment was a ploy to deflect attention from the administration's Enron connections. We'll see. I'd only just finished absorbing a case study holding-up Enron as a paragon when they collapsed. It's enough to undermine your faith in management books.

another supplier, always someone willing to be a new employee than you don't need to read the rest of this book. I suppose you might still want to glance at the chapter on shareholders, but the other relationships described will seem like a lot of unnecessary effort. If, on the other hand, you suspect that view would eventually wreck your business, then I agree. Please keep reading.

High transit locations

One example of a 'no consequences' trading environment, where there's always another customer to replace the disgruntled ones who just left, is the high transit location. Major railway stations or hub airports, for instance, can often support one or two stores or cafés that do everything wrong and still thrive – with fat margins too. I spent a few months looking into a UK motorway service area company once. In 1999, with sales in the hundreds of millions, they had no way to transmit EPOS data back to head-office. They replenished stock manually, by spotting gaps in the stock room and phoning in an order to a direct-delivery supplier. If they hadn't had a virtual monopoly they would have been out of business in a week. I suggested some changes which would bring them up to about 1990 in terms of IT sophistication and very probably double their profits. To say they were complacent is to massively overstate the urgency they showed with regard to the project.

Success a speciality

Taking a step back and looking at civilisation as a whole, there is something that many of us forget. Specialisation is an act of trust. By training for a single job, say accountancy, you trust that there will be a need for your skills and a fair wage in return. It's a fairly safe bet in a large enough society. But if we go far enough back, the idea of anyone limiting themselves to a narrow range of specialist skills would have been a novelty.

Devoting yourself to one narrow skill brings you many advantages in your chosen field and many disadvantages outside it. A potter will have a wheel and tools and, after a time, considerable expertise. But while he was acquiring that skill he wasn't planting a crop or putting a roof on his house.

Any division of labour requires a network of trust, because we still need all of those other skills despite the fact we choose not to acquire them ourselves.

I happen to know a man who is a great expert on ladybirds and in this field he has made quite a name for himself. If the BBC want to do a story about why there are so many, or perhaps so few, ladybirds, naturally they call him. But one might consider how big a society needs to be to permit such specialisation.

My various sojourns into the world of science have made me aware that all but a tiny part of it works by extreme specialisation. I recently read a paper on the cycling of lemming population levels in the tundra.[1] It struck me at the time, that if you made counting rats in the arctic your speciality, you'd stand a greater chance of becoming a world authority than if you fancied being a restaurant critic.

Specialisation, more often that not, benefits the individual. Diversity and co-operation among the specialists benefits the community. As a race we prosper because, whatever the job, one of us will be good at it.

The point is that complex webs of obligation and co-operation are the norm for our species. We are made that way and it has stood us in good stead. Businesses also specialise. Is there any reason, then, to suppose that co-operation between businesses, even competing businesses, is anything but good sense? Is there any evidence that trusting others and building relationships is in any sense uncommercial? I don't believe there is, but I think we often act as though there is.

Altruism is good business

In case you're starting to get a little anxious, wondering when we're going to get back to retail, let's return to those four relationships we isolated in the last chapter. Let's consider the common ailments for each of them.

For no particular reason, let's start with suppliers. Supply chains are a single logical entity, but for various good reasons they are hardly ever a single *corporate* entity. They can work very well if the various parts collaborate. Supply-chain theorists have been bashing on about that for years, but mostly it has fallen on deaf ears. We're going to consider how the psychology of the retailer-supplier relationship obstructs collaboration and what we might do about it.

Shareholders: the relationship between most retailers and their share-holders is a very strange one. Often neither side fully trusts the other and both sides feel misunderstood. We'll have a look at some approaches to healing the rift and the benefits that can bring.

---

1 Welcome to my life!

Employees: Boy, is that ever a source of untapped potential! If you're a director of a large company you'd really be amazed how many of your employees hate you. They don't know you of course, but a lot of them hate you anyway. One reason for that is that we've never really been clear on what the relationship between employer and employee is supposed to be. We've each got our own version and we each feel it's not being honoured. We need to examine the 'implied social contract'. What is it that each party expects from the relationship? Are they getting it? Any company that heals this relationship can pull ahead of the competition and just keep on accelerating.

And finally, customers: this relationship will probably provide the most controversial discussion. Despite the hundreds of books written about brands, I believe retailers have still not got clear in their minds what a retail brand is. Understanding retail brands will shed a lot of light on why those pesky customers are always getting upset and how to stop it happening.

Hopefully, you can see how treating each of those *interfaces* as a relationship and making that relationship work can unlock considerable benefit.

Can you also see why getting those relationships right is so important that it should define the shape of the business? In a sense, a retail business is nothing more than a way of allowing those four relationships to cross-link with each other.

Remember when we said that aligning *goals* isn't the secret to co-operation, it's finding a single outcome that satisfies different sets of goals?[1] Well that's what the structure of a retail business is for. If a single business structure can satisfy the goals of those four external parties, then it's a good design.

We can satisfy each of those relationships to a different extent, of course. We might even give them priorities (although I wouldn't recommend thinking of it in those terms). What would a business look like that used this ranking of importance for its external partners?

1. Shareholders
2. Suppliers
3. Customers
4. Employees

Well, actually I consider the above to be the priorities in many retail businesses. In order to keep the City or Wall Street happy, retailers

---

1   I don't mean to patronise, but reading that sentence a couple of times might be a good idea.

believe they must provide steady short-term growth. To achieve that they find the easiest approach is to sell the same products using improved supplier terms. Employees don't usually feature. Even though most retailers treat their suppliers in a highly adversarial way, the relationship with them dominates their short-term planning. The frostiness of the relationship does nothing to detract from its dominance.

The big question when considering whether suppliers come above or below customers is this: *Would you rather have a pound from a customer or a pound from a supplier?* Please examine the extent to which you chase retrospective payments from suppliers and the way you run price promotions before you answer on behalf of your business.

Even without striving to understand those four relationships any better than we do, there are still ways in which we could change the ranking.

Sometimes businesses go bust by delivering excellent service. This happens at the top end of the hotel industry more than in retail, but full credit to those who take this route. If you're going to wreck a business, it's a nobler path than many.

Other businesses put the employee at the top. Again, we need to look outside retail to see it happen often – strong unions, for instance, can bring about this inversion of the usual priorities. Sometimes the result is happy workers; sometimes it's commercial suicide. An instance of the latter is the UK newspaper industry in the 1980s when manual typesetting was retained purely to provide employment for manual typesetters – a job which could be done better by a machine. As you'll see, I believe retailers need to be a lot *less* heartless towards their employees – but that's not the same thing as keeping them in a role once it ceases to benefit the business.

I've even worked with a business that put suppliers' interests before that of shareholders, if you can picture such a thing. The shareholders also owned the retailer's largest supplier. The supplier was their core business and they wanted it to appear healthy at all costs. One ploy was to have the retailer buy more stock from the supplier than they could sell. The sales problems of the manufacturer were shifted to the retailer. The group could then appear to address the problem by selling off the unsuccessful retail business. Even while criticising the board's judgement, I had to admire their creativity.

Strategy

We'll take another look at the question of priorities when we encounter shareholders again in the final major chapter.

In the meantime, we have seen that adjusting the relative priorities of our strategic relationships gives us a lot of options for organisational structure – even if we do nothing to improve or better understand those relationships.

Improving the condition of any of those relationships would clearly offer enormous benefits.

Deciding the right way to manage each relationship and to balance them against one another is the most important and most strategic decision in retail business design. The next four chapters will examine the nature of each relationship in turn.

What was that all about?

- Emotions can be highly effective in business.
- Negative emotions are in no sense more appropriate to business than positive ones.
- Co-operation and trust are not a weakness or a luxury, they are the foundation of productivity.
- Fixing the four key relationships and striking a balance between them is the secret to retail design.

CHAPTER 3

Customers and the true nature of the retail brand

This journey

Have you every tried to define 'retail brand' for yourself? I'm calling it a retail brand (like Wal-Mart) to distinguish it from a product brand (like Coke). Once upon a time, retail brands were nothing more than the owner's name over the door and maybe a description of the products – Olsen's Mercantile, for instance. Retail has advanced enormously since then and so have brands. This chapter is about what they've become.

First of all we're going to look at *how* modern retail brands came about. Then we're going to zip back and think about why they're even possible, why they work. That will enable us to finish the chapter with some thoughts about what we're doing wrong (without realising it).

The function of a *product* brand is to sit half way between the product and the customer, to intermediate, to sum up and package the product.

Retail brands sit half way between the stores and the customer. In order to think about what that means we are going to spend some time far off the beaten track of marketing. We're going to have a look at the foundations on which marketing is built. We're going to do a little bit of retail archaeology. We're going to see what lies beneath our modern use of brands.

The relationship between a large retailer and their customers is not some completely new sort of relationship – and it's not simply goods and money changing hands either. It's a trading relationship built on top of relationships that went before.

Human beings have been relying on each other for so long that the mechanisms of managing trading relationships have shaped our brains.

In other words, don't expect to spend the next few pages discussing Heinz and Procter & Gamble. Our route will be much odder than that.

The evolution of retail

Let's think about that example proto-store, Olsen's Mercantile. If you owned a store that was at some isolated spot in the Old West of America, the chances were that you tried to be a general store. "If we don't stock it, we can't sell it", is one of the oldest maxims in retail. You can still hear it cited in even the most modern, the most specialised, of retailers.

The old SKU reduction chestnut

Any time you bonus employees on sales, but not on costs, they will try to fill your stores up with products. They will even consider they are doing you a favour, because "If we don't stock it, we can't sell it". Unfortunately, as the choices for the customer multiply and begin to confuse, the stores become dumping grounds for slower and slower selling lines. The trick is to remember what problem we are trying to solve for the customer. The chances are it will include either convenience, which requires a slim range that's fast to shop – or helping them choose a product that's perfect for them, which requires a deeper range, but lots of assistance in navigating through it. That assistance comes from getting both the assortment and the merchandising right. Too many SKUs (Stock-Keeping Units = products) detract first from convenience and, unchecked, then from clarity of layout. I'm inclined to say, "They won't buy it, if they don't know it's there".

Why did we ever move away from general or department stores? Surely, the more products you stock, the more customers you can sell things to. Plus, as you get bigger more economies of scale will kick in, until your range is not just vast but cheap too. Well, Wal-Mart do a pretty good job of making that point. Once a general store is out in front of the competition, their size makes them a 'destination' – somewhere people make a special trip to visit.

In the UK, the large-format supermarkets are spreading further and further into general merchandise – clothes, TVs and computers, music and videos and the rest – while taking more and more business away from the high street.

Once a general store becomes a destination, it gets easier to successfully add new product ranges. Customers drop in for your core range, which gives you a chance to dazzle them with your new lines. If the process is working properly, as new product areas take off they become the core ranges for an ever-expanding set of customers.

One limitation of this super-shop approach is that it works best in 'green field' situations. In 2000, I drove across the American Midwest, through states like Iowa, Missouri, Kansas and Mississippi. With all due respect to the locals, there's not much there for the urban tourist. At a mall in Missouri I asked someone, "What is there to do round here?"

They looked thoughtful and replied, "You like cows?" and after a pause, "Otherwise, you're out of luck".

The deadpan humour business seemed to be faring a lot better than the retail sector. I drove through town after town where the little main street at the centre had died – shops were boarded up and it was often difficult to tell, at a casual glance, if the remainder were still trading.

The plains are flat for hundreds of miles and the next town along looks pretty much the same to the untrained eye. Into this, Wal-Mart would drop a whole-mall-in-a-store. At a stroke they would multiply the retail space of the town by a factor of ten. And with their huge economies of scale already in place, they can pitch their prices lower than an Englishman can believe. One minute a town has no retail, the next it's all Wal-Mart.

Response to competition

Wal-Mart can move into virgin retail territory with an overwhelming show of force. That's not an option open to most multiples. In fact, many risk-averse retailers wouldn't do it even if they could, because virgin territory means unproven demand. There were many who considered it a dangerous gamble for Wal-Mart to invest heavily in provincial towns three hundred miles from nowhere.

A more typical situation, for most retailers, is to take an established retail centre and add their shop to the mix.

Many urban shopping centres grew up around a single big department store, or maybe an old market. Not only am I old enough to remember when an album was also called an LP, I also remember when I used to buy them at a department store because we didn't have a specialist record store. And the reason we didn't have a branch of one of the big multiple record stores,[1] was that in the UK they hadn't been invented yet.

My local department store tried to be all things to all people. In those days they even sold books. Albums and books are two product groups that require you to sit on an awful lot of inventory in order to be credible – and customers still pester you to order more. How is a department store to beat a specialist bookstore that opens up next door with a much larger

---

1   Three years into this decade and I still don't know what it's called. Did the noughties follow the nineties? The phrase hasn't caught on. Same problem with record stores. They don't sell records anymore (or if they do, it's just for DJs) but Music and Video Store is not a phrase a self-respecting teenager would use – not even to please the middle-aged marketing guys who came up with it.

range? Or a record store? Or a store selling sports equipment? Or toys? In most product areas, a specialist store can snatch the business out from under a nearby general store.

And it's not just in terms of range that the specialist store can dominate; a sports store can recruit and dress its staff with sports in mind because it only has one product area to consider. In a department store, the polo-shirted jock from the sports counter won't impress someone who has come in to buy a suit or a diamond.[1]

The hows and whys of specialising

Let's introduce a couple of terms to make this easier to talk about. First let's think about 'co-ordinating'. I'm going to use the word to mean the extent to which the product range has been used to determine the store fit, choice of staff, merchandising colour-scheme, and general flavour of the store. A saddle and tack store with straw on the floor and merchandise arrayed in wooden stalls, sold by jodhpured assistants, is strongly co-ordinated with its range. The same merchandise sold from pegboard and racking, surrounded by vinyl flooring, is not.

Secondly, let's talk about focus. I'll use this to mean the degree of specialisation of the range. A convenience store often covers a broad range of products, but with little choice in each area: it's not focused. The narrower (= fewer *categories* of product) and deeper (= more products in each category) a store range becomes, the more focus it has. Of course, for focus to make any sense, the remaining categories need to be linked by some common theme – as in sports shoes, sportswear and sports equipment.

Generally speaking, the co-ordination of the store is increased at the same time as the focus of the range. You can't very easily make your store more co-ordinated if it lacks focus – you have no product theme to tie into. On the other hand, you *could* try to sell premium fine-fragrance from standard metal shelving if you want – it's a free country.[2]

So, wily retailer that you are, you have realised that you can take business away from the general stores by focusing – to give your range

---

1 It's one of those little ironies that in certain product sectors the people who can afford the product would never have a job selling it. You might want to be as musically hip as the guy in the record store, but you're never going to envy the salesman who tells you Ferraris are the only cars to drive but owns a Ford.

2 Well not really. The fragrance houses would probably refuse to supply you. Though they don't use the words, they usually insist on minimum levels of focus and co-ordination for their products.

real credibility – and then co-ordinating – to give it the right ambience and even more credibility.

Your increased focus means that you don't cover so many product categories, so in theory there are fewer customers who will be interested in your store. The plan is that you will get a bigger share of a smaller segment of customers. The percentage of people in your area interested in your focused offer will fall, but your ability to draw in and sell to those that remain will increase. Obviously, the latter effect needs to outweigh the former if you are to prosper.

This is the opposite of SKU proliferation, by the way, which nearly always allows the range to creep into new areas, while muddying the old ones.

Specialisation[1] is about getting a better grip on a smaller prize. If you've come across the 22 Immutable Laws of Marketing,[2] I'm talking about their Law of Sacrifice. The great example they give is that Burger King, rather than trying to steal back the family market from McDonalds, should roll with the punch and make their restaurants the grown-up choice. They'd let go of part of the market, but they'd have something extra to offer the remainder; after all, most people aren't wild about restaurants run by clowns and they don't actually want to eat with young children running around, not even their own.

A stronger response to stronger competition

Problem: you find that you've become one of three record stores on the High Street. You're not competing against stores trying to sell tumble-dryers and hip-hop from the same sales floor, you're up against similarly focused, similarly co-ordinated competition. What now?

The next stage in co-ordination is qualitative rather than quantitative. You add personality. By focusing just on music, you limited your potential customer numbers, but you hoped to *own* the music-buying segment of the populace. Bringing personality to your efforts at co-ordination does the same thing – some customers will be slightly put off, while the remainder will feel even more at home.

---

1 A point Dan suggested I clear up: I don't mean specialist in the sense of 'only of interest to the connoisseur', I mean it as in 'being very good at a select few things'. He and I have seen a couple of businesses where buyers, who are really passionate about their products, begin to forget that very few of their customers have the same level of expert knowledge as they do.

2 By Al Ries and Jack Trout.

Maybe you decide to make yours a young and brutally hip record store. You might intentionally make the store an uncomfortable place for middle-aged customers, because you know the last thing that credibility-conscious fourteen-year-olds want is to find themselves shopping alongside their parents. As far as older patrons are concerned, your store has become too loud, too garish; they can't find the easy listening or classical sections and the industrial theme makes it look less like a store and more like an oil-rig. That should keep the kids happy.

Alternatively, you could play the traditional card. Your store has royal-blue carpeting and wooden fixtures, and familiar classical themes playing quietly throughout the day. The counter staff are over thirty and none of them have any piercings, tattoos or creative facial hair. You feel you could ask them for an Enya CD without whispering and would receive a civil response.

But we need to be careful when adding personality because we know that every time we subdivide the market in order to appeal to a portion of it, we give up potential customers. That's not something a retailer does unless they have to; so retailers tend to increase their focus and co-ordination only in response to increased competition.

In many cases, though, as specialisation and competition increase, a retail centre's gravity – its ability to draw in customers – will increase. Frequently there will be more customers to go round.

It's worth mentioning, too, that companies like Wal-Mart and the giant destination supermarkets can't really play this game. Almost any attempt to add real personality will upset someone and their business model is based on spreading their net as wide as possible. Even pointing out how cheap their products are risks upsetting snobs, so they end up making slightly bland motherhood statements about 'good' food and great 'value'.

Motherhood statements

In case you're not familiar with the term, a motherhood statement is one that everyone is in favour of 'like motherhood and apple pie'. When Dan and I were apprentice consultants we uttered our share of them. The trick is to use judgmental language while avoiding specifics, for instance: "We need to greatly reduce waste and inefficiency in order to unlock the potential of this business". Waste = bad, unlocked potential = good; no-one can argue with that. Businesses that only want the *appearance* of change tend to get along very well with consultants who only give the *impression* that they have a plan. It's a lucrative and terrifically unfulfilling way to earn a living. These days Dan and I have sworn to use our powers for good.

Empirical marketing

The idea of retail brand personality is borrowed from the product brands. Excuse me for saying so, but retailers can be terrible luddites and reactionaries. Often the manufacturing and supply sector have to push the innovative ideas until retail belatedly hops on the bandwagon. Sophisticated product brands have been around for over a century now and it was the pioneers of product brands who first started experimenting with what we now call the 'image' of a product. They found that a product and its image need not have a lot in common on the face of it.

Marketeers realised that you could sell almost any product as the finishing touch to a much broader suite of choices, which between them made up an aspirational lifestyle. If yours was the deodorant Hollywood movie stars preferred or the gin the Prince Regent requested in his aperitif, you had elevated yourself above the undignified scrapping about product features and value for money. And so much the better if the product *was* peripheral to the lifestyle; you might not be able to emulate Princess Grace's choice in dresses, but you could probably afford her toothpaste.

This sort of marketing also works when the explosion of product features has gone beyond what the average customer can process. The car, for instance, spends most of its TV airtime acting as a sort of fairy godmother – changing people's lives and making dreams come true. If you pay close attention you may occasionally hear a mutter about 'bhp' or 'mpg', but most ad agencies would consider it absurdly quaint to drag the actual specifications of a vehicle into the discussion. It would also ruin the art-house-movie feel and with it any chance of winning an industry award.

The marvellous Audi UK TV ads of a few years ago featured a brash, successful young man test-driving an Audi. It is clear to us by the end of the ad that someone so lacking in refinement shouldn't own an Audi, they should follow the herd and buy a BMW. I can't recall a clearer example of selling a product purely on the basis of the social group you wish to associate yourself with (or perhaps distance yourself from).

Product marketeers have been tinkering around in this area for a while now. Perhaps you recall a couple of chapters back when we talked about evolution? Evolution is a scheme for getting desirable results from a complex system, but those results are not accompanied by explanations. You don't know why it works, just that it does.

If you'll excuse me sounding sciencey, I'll refer to such a process as empirical – as in, results get the final word, not theory.

My belief is that an empirical and evolutionary process is at work in the most advanced forms of marketing. Year after year, client companies review the successfulness of their ad campaigns and marketing plans. If sales are stagnating then they put their account out to tender.

Of all the techniques that sounded great, only the ones that work endure. Yes, there is constant innovation, but at the same time the core of tried-and-trusted tactics consolidates. That core is made up of tactics which engage and influence customers, regardless of whether we really understand why.

Building product brands that incorporate personality and values seems to work. The ideas also seem to translate well to retail brands. This sort of branding has proven itself effective, but has it ever really been explained?

It's time now to think about why brands with personalities seem to possess a mysterious alchemy which allows them to capture our attention.

Which brand came first?

Even though product brands came first, retail brands are in a sense more fundamental. The few marketing books that cover retail brands talk about extending the idea of brands to cover chain stores. That's getting it back to front. In fact, it is much more of a stretch to imbue a hair dye or a chocolate bar with personality and values than it is a store full of employees (who *do* after all have personalities and values).

Retailers always had the store experience with which to create their brand. It happened whether they set out to build a brand or not, whether they studied marketing or not. It was only when they started to care what that brand was that they began to take an interest in marketing.

Stores can build brands more readily than products can because the store experience has so many more dimensions and so much more texture. There is *décor*, there are staff with whom we can interact and argue or flirt, there are signs and posters. A customer might spend twenty minutes wandering round a store, the whole time examining, exploring, being interested. It's very difficult for a product, a packet of something, to create that sort of experience.

Each time a customer returns to a store, the experience contributes to an overall impression. That overall impression forms the store's brand. It can be added to through advertising, but it exists, for good or bad, through the interactive act of shopping.

Product marketeers, on the other hand, have to create brands from scratch and they have to make extensive use of advertising to do so. Product marketeers were forced to invent a whole new discipline to create what retailers could achieve just through serving customers. And so it is the product marketeers who coined the terms and wrote the books. But don't let the lack of scholarship fool you; there's an awful lot to retail brands.

Principals and agents

Store brands, as we've said, started out with just the owner's name and maybe the type of merchandise – Boots the Chemists, for instance. Even if there's only one store, we understand that the guy with his name above the door might not be the one who serves us. He will have staff who handle a lot of the work – but he *is* assumed to be there behind the scenes, making the important decisions.

In fact there are nuances to the concept of a 'shop assistant' that would probably be tricky to explain, if we didn't intuitively grasp them already. We don't need to have it explained to us that sales assistants aren't speaking for themselves; they're speaking on behalf of the person in charge. We understand intuitively that they're acting as representatives.

We might expect a certain amount of initiative from sales assistants, but we'll definitely expect the same set of policies to apply whichever face we find ourselves looking at. When it comes to decisions about credit or returns or special orders, we won't expect the assistant to just take a view, we'll expect that the owner's policy applies regardless of which human being we deal with when we go to the store.

Does it sound like I'm labouring a trivial point? It's important to grasp that although the idea of a 'representative' is instinctively understood, that doesn't mean it's a simple concept. If you wanted to be melodramatic, you could say it's like some retail version of demonic possession. When the representative speaks, it's with the voice of the owner.

This sort of representation has a long and distinguished history. Societies have employed ambassadors, viceroys and plenipotentiaries for centuries. These people could be sent to negotiate a deal on behalf of their leader and it was accepted that the outcome was the same as when dealing directly with the head honcho. It was also implicitly assumed that the deal made by the plenipotentiary would be honoured by his boss.

The origin of knacks

This is where we're going to jump off into the history of trading relationships. Have faith; it all comes back to a discussion of retail in the end.

It should be no surprise that for human beings some kinds of mental activity come easier than others. We're pretty good all-rounders in a lot of ways, so much so that it's tempting to think of our brains as being general-purpose computers. Just like a computer, our brains can tackle accounting, graphics, games, and a million other things. But some of these mental challenges are more of a struggle than others.

Why do we find some mental challenges much easier than others? It's often because some problems *are* easier. But there are a number of very difficult problems that humans find easy. Why? It's because we've seen them before. I don't mean as individuals, I mean our species has seen them before. And as a species we've figured out a way of handling them.

In fact the computer analogy is a good one. The PC I'm writing this on does indeed have a general-purpose processor that does most of the 'thinking'. But it also has a graphics card with its own processor and a sound card with another one. A graphics card processor is great at the calculations needed to do graphics, and bad at many of the other kinds. The same is true of the sound card. They take some of the workload off the central chip and they get those jobs done faster because they're purpose-built for that role.

Even though it's not immediately obvious, our brains have some special-purpose 'modules' as well. They exist because our species encountered the same challenges sufficiently often that it was worthwhile having a special part of our brain to handle them.

This is just like a mechanic getting a tool custom-made. It's a waste of time and resources if it only gets used once in a blue moon, but if it will make an everyday task easier it may be a good investment.

You can think of having a mental module for something as being just like having a 'knack' for something. Since we all have these modules, most of the time we don't think anything of our special abilities.

There's a little bit of a 'black-box' element to these modules. We encounter a problem we have a module for, the module cracks the problem, we go on to the next thing – but often we don't know how we arrived at the answer. The answers just come to us.

That gives us our first clue to understanding brands. Brands work without the customer needing to go on a course first. They obviously rely on something innate for their success. If you're trying to understand innate mental features, these modules are a good place to start looking.

The first module

The idea of mental modules started with the linguist Noam Chomsky. He proposed a module for language. After that idea had sunk in, it occurred to people that there might be other modules too.

Up until Chomsky came along, people just assumed that we learned to talk the same way we learned to drive or cook or tie a shoelace. It was seen as some combination of trial-and-error, practice, instruction, clever guesses and feedback. Chomsky came up with his own estimate of how long it would take us to learn our first language if that's all we were doing. He reckoned it would take us more or less forever. Most children just don't have enough information to go on. So how do we learn to speak?

Chomsky figured out that our brains have a module pre-programmed with a lot of templates for language. We learn language a bit like the way a doctor diagnoses a disease. A doctor starts with a list of possible ailments; it's not infinite, just long. She asks questions to narrow down the list, until she's figured out which specific ailment she's dealing with.

The language module in your brain works the same way. There are various standard questions that need answering. Does the pitch of the voice change the meaning of a word (it does in Mandarin Chinese)? Does word order affect meaning or just add emphasis (it's the former in English but the latter in Latin)? Vocabulary is memorised, but other features, like the way English speakers put 's' on the end of a plural can be handled by rules rather than memorised for every word. We only memorise the exceptions.

The machinery to do all this is already present in our minds. We used to think that languages were like recipes; they could include any ingredients cooked in any way. We now know they are like restaurant menus. You've got a certain number of choices for starter, for main course, for dessert, for drinks. Children are born with a copy of the language menu in their heads, they just need to work backwards and figure out which options apply. That's how we can learn to speak before we die of old age; it's still a staggering achievement, but without a specialist language module it would be impossible.

Other modules

What other modules do we have? Well, there are a number of likely candidates to do with social interaction. Back in the days when our ancestors lived on the African plains, we relied on co-operation for our survival. A lone human is easy prey for all manner of predators; thirty humans working together can handle almost anything.

Humans went through a long period where we either figured out how to keep a social group together or we perished. It's unsurprising then, that we evolved some mental gadgets to help us. Many people think we have a module that helps us figure out what people are thinking by looking at their expressions, their body language and so forth. Most of us can tell when we've upset someone, even if they don't say it. That sort of intuitive ability would help you avoid being abandoned to the lions by your pals.

You remember in school when you had to write a book report, but you hadn't bothered to read the book? One way out of this was to go to the bookshop and buy a summary. Haven't read Hamlet? Buy a pack of prompt cards containing key themes, important quotes, summaries of the story. Well some people think we've also got a few of those in our heads. Not for Shakespeare, of course, but for other subjects like physics and psychology.

Scientists refer to our in-built primer on psychology as 'folk psychology'. Instinctively, unless we are taught otherwise, we assume that people are motivated by desires and beliefs. In academia, there are other views. Pavlov and his famous dogs[1] illustrated the role of conditioning, stimulus and response. But when you look at what people who've never learned any psychology assume, it's always the same: desires and beliefs, because they are relying on their in-built primer.

Our branding module

As you may have guessed, I'm going to suggest that brands tap into one or more pre-existing modules. They work without explanation and on most people, because we've had these modules since before the first cities were built.

The modules that relate to brands are the ones involved in co-operation. We've said in earlier chapters that co-operation enhances overall productivity and that it's a 'good thing', but for a crucial period

---

1 Everyone has heard of Pavlov's dogs and I think many people picture a dog-owner who was fascinated by his beloved pets. I'm sorry if I gross anyone out, but you might like to know that these were lab dogs. He would perform all manner of operations and surgical 'modifications' on them. For the famous salivating experiment they had tubes sewn into their cheeks so he could measure saliva flow. Nobel-prize winner yes, dog-lover no.

in our evolution it wasn't an optional extra, it was all that stood between us and annihilation.

We've all seen buddy movies about soldiers sent to the front line. We know that you have to be able to trust the other guys in your unit with your life if you're all to survive. Well, for the human race, hundreds of thousands of years were spent on the front line, and throughout all we had to rely on was the rest of our unit. If you 'just weren't a team-player' you got sent on your own personal outward-bound course – complete with man-eating predators.

Trust and co-operation are the keys to the kind of tight-knit co-ordination and mutual reliance an environment like that demanded. There is just one little wrinkle: what if someone in the group is hoping for a free ride?

When a group works well together that benefits all the group's members. There's always a temptation, though, to enjoy the benefits of the group without contributing. This, apparently, is still the favourite topic of conversation in the few remaining hunter-gatherer communities in the world. It's not unheard of as a topic for office-based chat either.

The solution to the question of 'free riding' uncovers one of the most fascinating mental modules, and one we are particularly interested in; it handles what you might call 'social accounting'.

We sub-consciously keep track of our obligations: who helps us, who we help, who contributes to the group, and who lives off the group. We did it a hundred thousand years ago and we do it now. It's part of our mental machinery. There's recent evidence to suggest we even have an urge to blow the whistle on cheats – whether we get any personal gain or not.

The more complicated our social environment gets, the more important it is to be on the lookout for cheats. Complicated social environments usually result from taking on tasks that require a lot of co-ordination. Hunting animals that are bigger and more dangerous than a lone human is a good example. Does the guy who organised the hunt deserve more credit (and more food)? Do the beaters deserve the same as the guys with spears? Because of the way the animals choose to run, maybe some hunters don't get a chance to kill anything. Should they be penalised because they didn't do anything useful? Maybe that's not their fault?

We bicker constantly over this stuff, because unless we get the balance right and soothe as many grievances as possible, the group breaks down. It often falls to the 'head guy' to pass judgement and come up with compromises.

Groups

Another feature of hunter-gatherer societies, like the ones our ancestors used to belong to, is that they trade between groups whenever practical.

There are lots of reasons for this. Trade is just a way of reallocating resources so that everyone's happier. I have lots of food, but no animal hides, you've got the opposite problem. Let's trade.

But even if a deal isn't possible, broadly speaking hunter-gatherer groups tend to help each other out. If they catch more food than they can eat, rather than let it spoil, they'll organise a feast and invite the neighbours. It's generosity, but it's good business too. You've obligated those neighbours to help you when you're in need. It's almost like taking out insurance against future disasters.

Just like the problem of individual free riders, whole groups might attend lots of feasts and never throw one themselves. What's to stop them? That's where reputation comes in.

Not only do we keep track of the trading relationships, partnerships and friendships we are involved with, we also gossip about reputation. Some scientists think that gossiping about reputation is what made language such a success, that it's why it caught on. That seems a little far-fetched, but there's no denying that reputation is fundamental to all forms of relationships, especially trading relationships where credit is involved.

People make a fuss about credit-checking these days, but imagine what it was like before currency. If you can agree with your trading partner on a swap, you can do a deal. But what if he wants what you can spare, but he has nothing to offer in exchange? Small groups would encounter this problem with monotonous regularity. You either abandon the deal, or you show some trust – you let him owe you one. Imagine how much more attention we would pay to who our customers were if instead of money they gave us IOUs.

Groups trading with one another is probably where the idea of representatives comes in. Particularly when relationships sour, you send an ambassador (who might just be expendable) not your leader (who would make a nice hostage) to do the negotiating.

Adam Smith[1] said that economic advance requires cheap transportation and cheap communication. When sending a message

---

1   All management books should try to quote Adam Smith or Einstein. That's one taken care of. I'm still scouring the biographies hoping that Einstein said something interesting about shopping.

means sending a person, they're kind of the same thing. If you can't get used to dealing with representatives and messengers, you're not going to get the Adam Smith go-ahead to found a civilisation.

We monitor our dealings with groups in the same way we do with individuals. We keep track of whether our relationship with them is in debit or credit. And just as with individuals, we combine personal experience with the reputation we've heard on the grapevine. In the case of the group, we can also add a third kind of experience: personal contact with a representative.

You can think of the guy who arrives from the neighbouring group as a representative of the leader or as just a member of the group. In a sense it doesn't matter, because we tend to assume all groups have leaders and all leaders speak for their groups (more on this later). Either way, we're going to treat his behaviour as a sample of what we can expect from his group. Let's put the various ideas together and review them.

We started with the idea of a 'social accounting' module that tracks our personal relationships in terms of credits and debits, favours performed and received. We said that the constant tracking it performs means that we are automatically on the lookout for cheats or parasites.

This social accounting module was extended, when we began using language, to include reputation as well as our direct experiences. Reputation is a big breakthrough in the war on cheating. Even if an individual can get away with cheating another, the victim can tell the world and the cheat will be treated with suspicion afterwards.

Finally there's our ability to deal with groups. We can store all sorts of information about a group. Almost anything we can store about an individual we can store about a group – even things that don't seem appropriate. That's where racial stereotypes come from. Our anachronistic group-profiling module is still active, still amassing group-level data long after it ceases to make sense. Picture, as you read this, the appearance of the typical Frenchman or German or American. It's nonsense to think such a thing exists, but I bet your brain happily conjured up an image for you nonetheless.

The reputations of groups

It's in the nature of credit ratings and reputations that we focus on the negatives – particularly in a society where honouring obligations is vital to survival. If anyone transgresses they can expect the offence to be added to the list of complaints against their whole group. A community can rapidly get a bad name.[1]

You can see from this that the human race had business relationships before it had anything we would recognise as businesses. Mentally, we have a 'group level' entity a little like our concept of a person. We automatically use this 'group' concept to store all sorts of info about a community – trustworthiness, previous dealings, even physical descriptions. We think about our community and we think about other people's communities. It's the way we're made.[2] When we get to talking about employees, we'll see how the modern company has become our community.

Retail brands take our ability to profile a group of people and apply it to a business, specifically to the people who deal with customers. Retail brands are based on the same mental schemes as the community relations of old.

Marketeers didn't need to invent the basis for a retail brand; they merely stumbled across the mental machinery for it and figured out how to get it operational. The surprising thing is that there's very little evidence that they really understood what they were doing.

Relationship auto-tracking

To shed some light on why brands hold our attention, consider what happens when you want to do business with a bank. The first thing you need to do is open an account with them. Somewhere in the bank's records a space is created and tagged with your details, where all the history of your transactions with them will be stored.

These days, that will not only permit you to use their various services, it will also allow them to get a lock on you with their direct marketing radar. Expect to get cross-sold and traded-up and have your details passed around until your bank statements become little nuggets of information to be panned from a river of financial junk mail.

Something similar happens in the opposite direction. Marketeers are always competing for what they call 'mindspace'. The more businesses

---

1   Something about rotten apples and barrels.

2   Could this be why so many people watch soap operas? These days, when many of us urban-dwellers don't know our next-door neighbours, we still feel the need to be involved in a community. With a soap opera we can give the part of our brain that tracks relationships and reputations something to work on, but without the need to worry about our own status in the group.

that clamour for the public's attention, the more adept we all get at screening out what doesn't interest us.

The history of marketing has been an arms race, where every advance required a response from the competition and the battleground was the public's attention. A hundred years of 'Over here!' and 'No, over here!' has made consumers difficult to engage. Just as we know not to make eye contact with charity reps at the mall – at least not after the first hundred times or so – we know not to let our attention be snagged by every shiny object or loud noise.

I was in an electronics store the other day that had a TV showing a video loop that called out, "Excuse me? Hello?" and a moment later, "I said excuuuse me?" in just the way someone might if you'd dropped your hat. Everywhere there are marketing people racking their brains for new tricks to get and hold our attention. They're always looking for unused channels in the consumer airwaves on which they can broadcast their message.

If it were allowed, I'm sure people selling time-share apartments would dress as police and 'arrest' potential customers before escorting them in handcuffs to a half-hour presentation on Florida holiday homes.

Brands were just one attempt to hook the attention of the paying public and keep them coming back for more – they turned out to be an attempt that worked.

Brands work by engaging the social accounting module. The goal is to have the customer treat the company as though it were a community, a neighbouring group with which there is a trading relationship.

Consistency is very important, because the company is trying to slot neatly into the mental space available for a single group with a single leader. Somehow, a disparate group of employees at a myriad of locations must appear to be members of a single group, a single retail tribe. Dressing staff alike and decorating stores alike help foster that impression.

Once the company has passed inspection (albeit sub-consciously) as a single group, the social accounting module opens a mental account for that business.

Instead of trying to keep separate in our minds which encounters with which staff in which stores we are happy with, we merely have to add each new encounter to the single mental account marked 'Woolworths' or 'McDonald's'.

The mental machinery for managing obligations tracks who owes whom. It tells you whether you are in a position to call in a favour, or *vice versa*. It's also more or less automatic. Once the tracking mechanism is set in motion we pay a certain amount of attention to the relationship whether we mean to or not. It's a little like those radio tags they staple onto elephants or polar bears. From that moment on, their movements are monitored.

Cheats

We are all of us attuned to 'fairness' and 'cheating'. A study was carried out on people's ability to solve logic puzzles. There were a number of statements of the sort 'If A implies B but not C, then ...' and so on. People were asked to say whether the statements were logically valid or not. Then they re-phrased the same questions to use entitlement, such as whether a person qualified for a special offer or not. 'If you get a free drink when ordering a main course but not a dessert, then ...' People were significantly better at identifying cheats or determining what was owed to them than they were at solving the logic puzzles, and yet the logical relationships in both sets of questions were identical. We can't help it; we're always working out whether we're getting what we're entitled to.

(For more, see the work of Cosmides & Tooby)

A business disguised as a village

So how do we persuade customers to open a mental account for our business? Mental accounts are kept for both individuals and for groups and the two overlap in a lot of ways. One important first step is to make it obvious to the customer that your business really is a single group or community. Uniforms and colour schemes are a good first step. Consistency in appearance is something customers can store in the mental space reserved for 'physical description'. A consistent look encountered on many occasions makes an impression.

It also helps if customers can remember which store they've wandered into, of course. If your stores are consistent and distinctive too, you are helping the customer to make another entry in the group-level record for your business.

This is just like the prerequisites for discrimination. The easier it is to identify members of the group – say through common appearance – the stronger the group profile.

Of course, the original point of these mental accounts was to track and assess trading relationships. The customer is noting whether your reputation is good or bad, based on their experiences and on hearsay.

They are also sub-consciously working out who is obligated to whom. Ideally, the customer will feel that you have done more for them than you had to. Your business becomes the 'community' they most like to visit when they want something.

Adding it up

We've covered a lot of ground and encountered some strange ideas. Have we come up with anything useful? What have we achieved with all that talk about mental accounts for groups and auto-tracking of obligations? Well, there are two conclusions I hope we've arrived at.

First: the mental machinery that tracks reputation and obligation can be engaged by clever marketeers. Strong branding and consistency encourage a customer to maintain a mental group profile for a retailer, complete with personality and appearance – just the way we might have a view of what the archetypal Frenchman or Scot looks like. Once customers have set up a mental account for a brand they are more involved with and more receptive to that brand. This is what marketeers want.

Second point: that mental machinery exists to monitor the status of a trading relationship. It tells us who to trust and whether they are treating us properly. The reason we pay attention to a brand's marketing message is that we are figuring out how we feel about the people behind it. That means we are constantly judging the relationship – and judging it according to an ancient set of rules. This is something that retail marketeers didn't plan on and often don't appreciate.

Show me how it breaks

Medical researchers know that you can learn a lot about how something works by seeing the sorts of ways in which it goes wrong. There is a vogue, currently, for something called knockout mice.[1] These are mice with a specific gene missing. With ten thousand genes operating at any one time, it's pretty tricky to figure out what each one does. But if you

---

1   I haven't been able to come up with a really good solid pun here. I was thinking something about 'knockout', as in 'great looking', along the lines of 'so called because of their movie-star looks'. But that seemed weak, so maybe it should be something about boxing. If there's ever a second edition we'll make sure there's a good snappy quip in here.

delete one of them and the resultant mouse has wavy blue lines all over it, then you've got something to work with.[1]

We can do something similar with the mental machinery behind brands. We can look at situations in which things break down and we can examine the symptoms.

Let's start with a store-based situation. A customer goes into one of your stores and complains to an assistant (call her Betty) that he was sold the wrong product. Betty learns that young Andy, who only works Saturdays, was to blame. How does she handle things?

It might seem sensible to explain that Andy, because he is both new and part-time, is not as experienced as he might be. Betty can suggest that she take over and personally resolve the matter.

The customer is only partly mollified. He explains that he has been shopping with Fictional Stores (your business) for years and wants an apology. Betty is confused. Who exactly is supposed to apologise? Andy? He won't be in until Saturday. Since she was at the seaside that day visiting her sister, she is hardly to blame. She doesn't recruit or train staff either. So, instead she explains again about Andy's regrettable inexperience and reiterates her offer of assistance. What more can she do?

Strangely, the more Betty stresses Andy's lack of training, and incidentally his youth, the more the customer becomes annoyed. In the end he declares that he will write to Mr Fictional himself to complain. Why is he so annoyed? Is he just awkward by nature?

If we think purely in terms of giving the customer good service, this turn of events is a little difficult to fathom. Betty was concerned, professional and polite. She explained how such a thing had happened and made it clear it would be rectified without quibble or delay. What else could anyone want?

But think about relationships. The customer didn't come in to deal with Andy (the new guy), or Betty (the old hand), he just came in to deal with a representative of Fictional Stores. He doesn't make much of a distinction between the Fictional store he visits when he's at his local high street or the one at the big regional shopping centre (and that's as the marketing team want it). Both stores have the same name, uniforms, products, *décor* and prices. It's all interchangeable.

From his point of view what happened is this. First Fictional Stores sold him the wrong product. Then they seemed to partly disown the

---

1   The chances are you've deleted the gene for 'vertical hold'.

representative who did it. He wanted an apology and what he got was an explanation.

The customer wants the brand representative to talk about the brand in the first person plural: 'we did this' and 'we did that'. They should be saying, 'We are sorry for our blunder'. The customer wants to talk to a representative of the group, but Betty isn't acting like one. She's not speaking for the group ('we'), she's talking about herself ('I') and about Andy – like it's relevant which representative did what. Is she implying it's not a single unified group? If it's not a single group then who has the customer been dealing with all these years?

The logical alternative is that every store and in fact every sales assistant be considered by the customer as a different relationship. But one of the most important opportunities of multiple retailing is to have one big, solid relationship with the customer and not hundreds of small, transient ones. Consistent branding sets up the idea that all employees are interchangeable representatives for the same relationship.

Branded retailing relies on the ease with which we can accept the idea of relationships conducted *via* representatives. Without that, we wouldn't be able to lump all our various experiences of the brand together and treat them as one. There would be no customer loyalty, there would only be habit and the search for a bargain.

Betty's explanation attacks the basis on which the relationship with the brand was founded. She asks the customer to stop thinking of assistants as representatives and start thinking of them as individuals. Is it clear why that's bad?

Ambiguous representation

Betty's explanation got the customer wondering, 'Are they saying they dress a person up in their uniform and send them out to interact with customers, but this person doesn't really speak for Fictional Stores at all?'

The explanation makes it sound almost like Andy is a kind of impostor. It also calls into doubt Betty's status. She isn't personally apologising for the gaffe, she's acting as though it's nothing to do with her. So is she really representing the store or is she just some sort of concerned third party who happens to wear their uniform?

Lots of effort has gone into creating the impression that Fictional Stores is a single group of people, with one set of policies. The ostensibly rational response the customer has received is causing the impression of a unified group to crumble in front of his eyes.

It's a bit like the Prime Minister saying, "Oh, you don't want to listen to the Foreign Minister, he's useless." Is this one company or a disorganised rabble who coincidentally dress alike? The customer feels misled.

Betty has undermined Andy's and her own status as representatives. Who is left as a legitimate voice for Fictional Stores? Who is the one person who can't wriggle away and say they aren't responsible for the actions of the group's representatives? That would be Mr Fictional. Sadly for the customer, Mr Fictional is ninety-two and the company is run by an executive board – who would also say, if asked, that they weren't around on Saturday.

But wouldn't a conscientious board still feel responsible? Well, they might review their polices on training and the supervision of junior staff if they felt there really was a problem. Would they apologise? Much more likely they would describe the incident as 'regrettable' and say they were making sure it wouldn't happen again. After all, it wasn't their fault; it was Andy's.

Talk to the owner

Isn't it strange that the customer doesn't want Andy to apologise? Andy is irrelevant. The customer wants the people he thought he was dealing with when he was talking to Andy to apologise: the group, the brand, the community whose corporate name and uniform he is familiar with.

I'm not just making this up. Think about your own experience and your own behaviour. You want the manager to apologise. If you're still not satisfied, you want someone more senior to make amends. Ultimately, you want to speak to whoever runs the business. The one thing you're not really bothered about is having any more to do with the person who upset you in the first place.

If you think of the brand as a single (albeit imaginary) person, then sales assistants are just representatives, ambassadors, for that imaginary person. When 'the brand' upsets a customer 'the brand' must apologise, sympathise, accept responsibility and make amends. It can't just denounce the employee who did it. That just weakens the brand and raises questions about all that unified marketing-speak over the years.

Can you send an ambassador to a neighbouring country to insult their ruler and, when a declaration of war arrives, explain that the ambassador is new to the job?

It doesn't matter whether 'the brand' makes the mistake when acting through Andy and apologises when acting through Betty. They are both just representatives and we have already discussed how good human beings are at distinguishing between the spokesperson and the person they speak for.

The customer wants to hear, "Fictional Stores value your custom. We are sorry we acted this way and we want to make things right."

If you want to claim that you sent a rogue ambassador, you'd better make sure the next one you send has all their credentials in order. You'd also better clear up how you came to have a rogue ambassador in the first place. A breach of trust has occurred, and concern and reassurance are called for.

In the case of Andy, the novice assistant, the customer has been told not to set too much store by him as a brand representative. The customer is also aware that Andy's presence is condoned and tolerated. Andy will be on the sales floor again this Saturday. How can the customer feel their problem is being taken seriously when the situation that led to it is considered part of the store's normal operation?

Groups have leaders

We've gone into some detail in order to make a case that the way we think of a unified group, or community, is really just an extension of the way we think about an individual. Because of that, we find it easier and more comfortable if there is a real person behind the group, responsible for it all. We latch on to the idea that Richard Branson runs Virgin. If Virgin offends us badly enough we want Sir Richard to apologise. We are a little shaky with the idea of a group with no leader – just a board.

You see this not just in the way customers think about companies, but in the way business people and journalists view things. Enormous emphasis is always placed on the man[1] at the top. The CEO's name becomes synonymous with the company. We greatly exaggerate the head guy's involvement in the running of the business because that's how we like to think. We need to believe that someone, somewhere is responsible for it all – not just accountable, but actually responsible.

You remember when we discussed how your brain probably contains

---

1   It's still a man at the top. When I get a minute, I'm going to investigate how many women hold board level positions in the UK. Then I'm going to deduct HR directors from that and see who's left. I think we can all agree, it's not going to look much like sexual equality. In the UK the Sex Discrimination Act became law in 1975. I'm not convinced that there's been a quarter century of progress since then.

primers on physics and psychology? Because they're not always the same as what the academics come up with, they're called 'folk physics' and 'folk psychology'. Well, in a sense we also have an in-built 'folk sociology'. It tells us that wherever there's a group there's a leader. It was always true 'in the old days' if for no other reason than groups always need an ultimate spokesperson to settle the really bad disputes.

The fact is that our folk sociology is out of date. These days, lots of organisations have decentralised or committee-based power. But some anachronistic part of our brains keeps trying to spot the leader.

A good way to think about brands, then, is as imaginary owners. In this day and age, there are still a few owner-driver businesses. By and large, though, anonymous boards rule the world. Consciously, most of us are clear on that. Subconsciously, it doesn't sit well. Even the most rational of us often act like there's a single person responsible for every group.

When the integrity of a group seems to be in question (such as in the Betty scenario) we revert to the more fundamental concept of an individual and demand to see the person in charge. It was always thus.

Emotional labour

How are you feeling? You've covered some decidedly non-retail terrain to get here. There's been talk of primitive civilisations and the evolution of the human brain including special-purpose modules. It probably had a public-service television feel to it – like those programmes presented by bearded academics with wild hair talking about 'early man' in hushed tones. Then, suddenly, we're dragging those ideas into the mall, the High Street and the brightly lit world of twenty-first century marketing. It's quite a journey.

Does anyone out there remember Erich von Däniken? His television shows would take you to an archaeological site and show you a cave painting of someone wearing robes and a head-dress, only he would tell you why he thought it was really a space-suit. If you're feeling that something of that sort has gone on here, then please take a moment to pause and reflect.

Hang around in stores and listen to customers squabble with staff for a while. Listen to what upsets customers and try to fit it to a logical framework. Customers are forever getting what they say they want but still acting difficult. In short, they act exactly like people do in relationships where the other person is only going through the motions.

Scenario: your partner cooks you a special meal for your anniversary but you arrive home four hours late. To use a phrase of Dan's, there are likely to be some very tightly-folded arms in the ensuing conversation. Yes, dinner is spoiled, but much worse is what your lateness says about your attitude. Do you even care about the relationship? How would your partner feel if all you seemed prepared to talk about was the food? Once you've offered to pay for a meal at an expensive restaurant you consider the matter settled and yet, for some reason, on they grumble.

Have you come across the term 'emotional labour'? One sociology dictionary gives this definition:

> As used by Arlie Russell Hochschild, emotional labour refers to paid work requiring the worker to maintain observable facial and bodily displays with the intention of creating particular emotional feelings in clients.

It is used to describe the effort your waitress needs to put in to make it seem like she's pleased to see you, to make it seem like she cares your soup is cold, to look concerned that the fish has lots of bones. Because, you see, the awful truth is that she doesn't care. Her feet hurt and she's tired of smiling at people who complain. Her job involves emotional labour.

If you think about our discussions of brand representatives, you can see that emotional labour is exactly what's missing from many customer/staff interactions. Being a representative for someone means putting your feelings aside and playing a role. That role-playing is what's required to sustain the retail brand illusion when tempers flare.

Branding under fire

Armed with this theory of retail branding we can explore some of the situations where the relationship with the customer breaks down. With a better understanding of what's going on, we should be able to figure out how to fix things.

It seems clear we should ban phrases like, "I wouldn't know about that", when talking to customers. Individual ignorance is permissible, of course, but your sales staff aren't acting as individuals, they're transacting the latest instalment in the customer's relationship with the brand. Picture resolving that argument with your partner by saying, "I didn't remember it was our anniversary"[1], or worse still, "Who are you again?"

---

1   'Pulling a Reagan' – to claim that you have no knowledge of that at this time. Might keep you out of jail, but it's certainly not going to impress anyone.

It's all about maintaining the illusion that there's a relationship going on – because from the customer's side of things there is. Ignorance of what your own people have been up to is not something you want to broadcast. It's an excuse, sure, but only in the same way, "I'm not very good at my job", is an excuse.

In most multiple retailers, enormous effort has been expended drawing the customer into a relationship with the brand. It is imperative that store staff do not push in the opposite direction, by stressing their individuality, autonomy and general independence from the brand.

Continuity is the key. In the earlier scenario Betty needs to apologise. She needs to do so only in her capacity as representative, but if she doesn't do so the rhythm of the relationship is broken. If you do something wrong, then you must apologise. You can't skip over that step or ignore it – it's what comes next – unless you want the relationship to suffer.

It's extremely difficult for someone like Betty to preserve this fiction of continuity for the customer. Firstly, she doesn't know the customer's name. Logically, the customer knows this, of course, but he doesn't wish to be reminded that he's still an anonymous stranger after all these years.

Betty also needs to have the problem explained to her, even though one of her colleagues was the cause of it. Despite the customer's long familiarity with the brand, the stores, the products and all the chatty, intimate advertising, he is a complete stranger to Betty. This creates quite a challenge if the customer is not have his nose rubbed in these facts.

A word about asymmetry

First, though, here's some advice for anyone wondering how to add 'the wow factor' to their stores: don't bother. Why not? Because bad things make a bigger impact than good. Remember we are talking about a relationship here and relationships are based on trust. Anything that undermines trust is headline news, whereas most attempts to 'wow' someone are far less gripping.

Imagine you have the worst meal of your life in a restaurant. The food was cold and tasted bad, the cutlery and tablecloth were dirty and the waiter banged into your chair every time he walked past. Then imagine that along with your bill, the manager had personally written you a poem about how much he hoped you'd had a nice evening. Wow factors are icing on the cake. If there's no cake, icing isn't going to disguise that fact.

For most shoppers, most visits to a store contain a number of unpleasant experiences. There will be queuing, there may be problems finding the right product, it may be out of stock. The store may be unpleasantly crowded and the staff unhelpful. On the other hand, considerable effort will have gone into laying out and decorating the store as well as selecting and merchandising the range. The negatives interfere with what is probably a good solid offer.

All that most shoppers want is for you to minimise, and ideally eliminate, the unpleasant things that happen to them while they are in your shop. If you succeed in that goal, then you can go on to 'wow' them, but woe betide you if you are still screwing up the basics when you turn your attention to embellishments.

What's more, it's overwhelmingly likely that you *are* still screwing up the basics. It's just so difficult to get everything right. Consider queuing. Hundreds of millions are spent on various attempts to delight us with marvellous new products, but we still have to queue to pay for them.

First you must cater to the target customer who can't stand your stores, then you can think about how to take your loyal fans from happy to delighted. First get to the point where none of your target customers hate your store, then figure out how to get them to love it.[1]

One of the big objections, when I preach 'eliminate the negatives' to people, is that great customer service makes such a difference. People see it as a 'wow factor' that can make up for all sorts of negatives, even fundamental ones.

Maybe you can see from our discussion why I don't consider that a valid criticism. The reason is that we're not talking about a 'wow factor': the provision of good customer service; what we're nearly always talking about is the avoidance of bad customer service. Maintaining the customer's relationship with the brand is so difficult that almost every interaction with the customer does it some damage.

To a shopper who considers himself your loyal customer anything less than warm, knowledgeable attentiveness is a negative. Efficient and polite service should be enough, but it isn't. And hence even the best efforts at customer service can be mildly negative. Which is why customer service is a key differentiator. It's not a wow factor that outweighs all else; it's a jarring negative upon which any improvement is a welcome relief.

---

1   In my case, I'd like a parking space that's bigger than my car and the ability to pay promptly for my goods. I don't want anyone spending money on wowing me until those two are sorted.

Playing a role

So focus on eliminating the negatives. The glaring negative of customer service can be addressed by explaining to the sales staff that they are there purely as representatives of a brand. They are playing a role. Any emotions they display, any apologies they make, are on behalf of the brand.

Not only will this help them understand what they should be doing, but it should remove some of the stigma attached to serving customers. A sales assistant saying, "I'm most terribly sorry", isn't humbling themselves any more than an actor would be reading the same line. When we see Julia Roberts tell Richard Gere she loves him, it's because it says so in the script she has memorised. She's not obligated to marry him after the movie is over.

Soldiers sometimes understand this stuff. "It's not me you're saluting, it's the uniform". The same thing needs to be explained to sales staff. Once they understand it better, they may start to enjoy it more. "You should have seen the performance I gave today – Oscar material".

And let's be clear, I'm not saying lie or deceive the customer. I'm saying follow through on the promise you've made. (By making them think they had a trading relationship with your stores, you've led them to expect all this stuff.) Giving it to them is in everyone's interest.

Problem resolution

There are three things a brand representative needs in order to resolve difficulties for customers without damaging the brand relationship. It's worthwhile thinking here not just about store-based sales, but mail order, Internet, franchise and concessions. Stores are usually best equipped to provide all three. New channels, like Internet ordering, can lack all three.

Incidentally, the time I've spent thinking about marketing has taken a terrible toll: I'm left with an urge to give ideas catchy little names. The term I'll give to a proper representative of a brand is an AID.

The name comes from the letters A.I.D. A is for authority. I is for information. D is for delegate. An AID needs to have access to information (I) about the customer and their history. They need to have authority (A) to fix the problem. Finally they need to be a spokesperson or delegate (D) for the brand, which means undertaking the emotional labour we spoke of before. The dictionary definition of a delegate, by the way, is:

A person deputed or authorized to act for or represent another or others; a deputy, a member of a deputation; esp. a person chosen or elected to represent others at a meeting, conference, etc.

The A, I and D are the same three things an ambassador would need to do her job, if you think about it.

Consider the typical Internet order foul-up, where there's no-one at home to receive the delivery and the customer wonders what happened to their package. A third-party courier company will usually handle the delivery. The retailer's help desk won't have information about whether the package is on a van, back at the depot or lost. On the other hand, the courier company won't have any information about the original order and they won't feel any real obligation to the customer. *Their* customer is the retailer.

I won't beat you all up about the Internet. Lots of people thought they'd add a new channel cheaply, and who can blame them. But those who set up a transactional web site and put their store-brand name on it had an obligation to provide the customer with an AID to talk to. And of course many didn't.

When the inevitable snafus occurred, and the customer-brand relationship came under strain, the lack of a satisfactory point of contact would have increased rather than decreased that strain. A customer who was disappointed not to receive their order, would become furious when they discovered that there was no-one suitable to talk to about it.

Representatives are at the heart of the brand. These brand AIDs reinforce and repair the relationship. If you plan to create a brand without proper AIDs for the customer to talk to, you had better make sure your service is zero-defect. With no representatives, the brand has to speak for itself.

I nag because I care

Canny retailers have known for a while that a customer who complains is a customer who cares. With careful handling a customer who is passionately unhappy can often be turned into a customer who is passionately loyal.[1] It all depends on what happens when the customer raises the problem. Does a proper AID present themselves and take responsibility for the relationship? Do they understand and can they help?

---

1   If all your company do with customer complaints is send a gift voucher, you should look into this. For the same money you can often *actually increase* customer numbers, by creating customers who tell everyone about how well you handled their grievance.

Real world example – Capital Estate Services

For a change, this real world example is not a global retail conglomerate. While many household names are investing in state of the art technology, this example was chosen to illustrate what firms with modest means can achieve.

The current chapter talks about a conflict between customers' experiences of service and their subconscious expectations. The continuity that enables a brand to exist is undermined every time a representative treats a loyal customer as a stranger. If the representative doesn't know the customer's name, their purchase history, the background to any complaints they may have, they detract from the impression of a long-established or important relationship.

In some circumstances, technology can help alleviate that problem. It's not possible for staff to know ten thousand customers by name, but with a little help from a computer system they can avoid broadcasting the fact.

Capital Estate Services, based in Galveston, Texas, do most of their customer interaction over the phone; they have invested in some modern technology to help them recognise their customers. They maintain a database of contacts that contains details on all their customers; additionally, managers prepare scripts to guide call-centre staff through both in-bound and out-bound sales calls. They also make use of caller id technology (CLID). Many household phones these days display the number of an incoming call before it's answered; Capital Estate Services have systems that use the caller's number to look up the customer's details in the contacts database. Even before the representative answers the call, their computer screen will tell them who's on the line and what their history with the business is.

Capital Estate Services' annual turnover is $10m, so it's safe to say that any technology that falls within their price range is well within reach for any large retailer. Any retailer running a loyalty card scheme could call up customer details and purchase history from incoming phone numbers. In many firms, loyalty cards are used for direct marketing and not much else. Using them to dramatically improve customer service seems a fitting reward for loyalty.

Though it has a science-fiction feel to it, loyalty cards that can be scanned from a distance are available now. Some high-tech offices issue staff with access cards that unlock doors as the employee approaches – providing the employee is authorised to enter. The same technology in a loyalty card could call up a customer's details on a till by reading the customer's identity from a card in their pocket. Big brother overtones aside, retailers could also make use of existing computer technology that can recognise people's faces. Police use it to spot troublemakers from CCTV footage, but retailers could put it to more hospitable use prompting staff when valued customers enter the store.

In the past, some of this has been technology in search of a use. Understanding the importance of AID points in a business suggests many ways of putting these technologies to work.

Do they behave in an emotionally appropriate way given the role they're playing?

By training staff and setting up processes in support of the brand relationship, retailers have a huge opportunity. Lots of articles and books talk about how much more demanding the customer is these days, and how much more difficult they can be. Well, congratulations! That's what we were trying to do. Retail branding has persuaded the customer to be emotionally involved with our stores. We shouldn't be worrying about it; we should be following through on it.

Our brands and our offers make promises about the treatment customers can expect, about the relationship that is on offer to them. Hopefully, this chapter will have shed some light on the true nature of those promises. Now that we know how to read the contract we have with the customer, we can start to make good on it.

What was that all about?

- Customers have a relationship with your brand.
- That's possible because humans have evolved lots of mental machinery to help them handle relationships.
- Once we acknowledge a relationship we automatically track how it's going – that's why we pay attention to brands.
- Brands use the mental machinery we evolved for dealing with representatives and groups.
- For that to work, retailers have to be consistent and play up the resemblance to a single, unified group.
- The hidden corollary of that is that we must teach our staff to play the role of representatives not free agents.

CHAPTER 4

Employees

This journey

Before I worked in business, I assumed the most difficult thing for business people to pick up would be all the commercial knowledge and skills. It's certainly the impression people get from the outside. In truth, it's much more difficult to acquire all the relevant people skills – the ability to influence, to motivate, to inspire confidence. But at the top of the list of important but difficult things I'd put managing your own temperament.

Think about a good day – one of those days when you're fired up and positive, but calm – everything's very Zen and in tune. What if every day was like that, what would your working life be like? This chapter is about helping your staff get a little bit closer to that ideal.

The chances are that you're not too bad at managing your temperament. You wouldn't be reading books like this if you weren't either on course for senior management or there already. A large part of being 'management material' is about having the right attitude – and that implies having some control over your temperament.

Senior managers are never seen to sulk or be spiteful and they rarely say anything bad about the company. Yet most people feel the urge to behave in those ways. If you're on track for the top, you've probably got those urges under control.

That hard-earned control may make it difficult to accept some of the points made in this chapter. It's all about what makes employees sulky, bitter and demotivated. These are probably not things you have recent personal experience of. But remember most tables of organisation are shaped like a pyramid. There are few people at the top and lots at the bottom. Most of the business is not like you. Most of the business lacks your control, because most of the business is not senior management material.

It's not realistic to expect a large workforce to change. We can't expect them all to master the art of 'the right attitude' and to talk themselves through setbacks and disappointment. And yet the success of the business is bound up with the attitude of its employees. If we can't ask employees to change, what can we do? Can we alter the environment they work in?

This chapter suggests that there *are* ways in which we can make most employees feel less frustrated and more motivated. There are ways to enable them to get more out of their work and to put more into it. And just as with so many other situations involving unhappy people, the key is to understand what's really going on.

Now you know where we're going, a word about how we're going to get there. We're going to develop our ideas about co-operation and personal gain a little more fully. We'll see how personal goals becomes bound up with group goals at work. That leads on to how we think about group goals and how they lead to motivation and job satisfaction. And then we'll bring in some of the ideas from the last chapter to help us put the picture together. But first, it's off to jail.

Synergy and competition

Do you remember the prisoner's dilemma? It asks the important question of when to compete and when to co-operate. Sometimes two people want the same outcome; sometimes they want opposites. Frequently, it's a paradoxical mix of the two.

I might be in competition with a colleague if we're up for the same promotion, but the rest of the time we're working together for the good of the business. But then again, although our business is based on co-operation, it's still in competition with the other firms in our industry. Except that the industry as a whole will co-operate to lobby governments or create professional standards. And although no one wants our economy to be in recession, it's not the end of the world if the economies we compete with are weak. It's a mix of competition and co-operation all the way from the personal to the global.

We can't eliminate competition even if all our goals are the same. In fact that usually makes it worse, because of the way in which goals are personalised. Goals are like those stickers you can buy that say, 'This book belongs to …' You write your name on the dotted line. A room full of people might all share the common goal that: 'I want respect and popularity'. But of course the 'I' refers to a different person in each version.[1]

Straight competition is often zero-sum – my loss is your gain and *vice versa* – but co-operation usually opens up more possibilities. Co-

---

1   It's a bit like the observation that all horse races are the same. A horse usually wins, another horse will come in second and third place is also taken by a horse. It only gets interesting when you start to wonder whether any of them might be the one you bet your savings on.

operation can change the rules, sometimes to the extent that *everyone* gets what they want.

If one of those apocalyptic scenarios that were commonly discussed during the Cold War came to pass, the survivors would undoubtedly do a lot of hoarding and squabbling over food. When there's a functioning economy that sort of behaviour would be ridiculous. You could spend all year growing and guarding your own food or you could work for a fortnight in McDonald's and buy it all from a supermarket.

At the grossest level, there's no question that we're much better off joining a modern society than competing with it.[1] But that's considering society as a single group. As we look more closely, there are lots of other levels at which it's not so clear whether to compete or co-operate.

Scenarios for co-operation

It's clear that a reasonable level of co-operation needs to exist in most business situations. Businesses, after all, are basically about the benefits of co-ordinated groups over solo efforts. Multiple retailing in particular comes from pursuing the idea that two shops make *more* than twice as much money as one does. The *extra* profitability, the synergy, comes from the fact that a co-ordinated team can do more with less.

So, let's think for a moment about how we can set up situations where we aren't all grabbing for the same things. One way would be if our goals were complementary, like that ancestor of the modern deal, the swap – in which both parties would be happier with what the other currently has.

Even without complementary goals, it's possible to co-operate when the outcome involves what economists call 'non-rival goods'. These are things that don't get 'used up' by people acquiring or having access to them.

Information is the best example. If I want to learn Esperanto, that doesn't stop anyone else doing it too. In fact, the more people who learn Esperanto the more useful it becomes to me. In this sense a language can be thought of as just a 'standard' that governs communication. Widespread adoption of a standard adds to, rather than decreases, its value to others.

---

1 'Survivalists' for instance, try to make sure they would survive the collapse of modern society - they make sure that independence is still an option. Of course they totally rely on modern society to assist in their preparations for that independence, by supplying generators, tinned food and plenty of automatic weapons.

Just as frequently, though, people like to have information to use for competitive advantage – for instance, stock market tips. So sometimes non-rival goods get more valuable the more people acquire them and sometimes less. The amount of information available isn't changed as more people acquire it, but the attraction it holds for others might be. (We'll use that idea when we talk about supply chains.)

Another co-operative situation occurs in cases where competition just isn't an option. A lot of goals can only be achieved by a group working together. This is so fundamental to our thinking that many of us never consider undertaking anything big on our own. If we can find a group of people who all want the same outcome,[1] we can put together a group to achieve it. But the group level objectives are secondary goals. We accept them because they lead to personal gains.

That's relevant because it's tempting to think of the group level goals first. We all want our company to succeed, but does that imply that we're always in agreement? There's usually more to it than that. We all want the group to succeed, but we may have diverging views on who should benefit most from that success.

That's not to say we're all completely mercenary, though. Most people view their jobs as a win-win arrangement. In exchange for taking on the good of the company as a goal, the company agree to return the favour by looking out for us. They will pay us, train us and even help out with a pension once we retire. We don't call the arrangement mercenary, we call it mutually beneficial.

Attitudes to work

So how do most of us feel about our employers? How much emotional 'investment' do we make in our job? How many of us consider work only as a means of getting paid? On the other hand, how many of us could say we deeply care about the company we work for? And is it the people we care about or the overall success of the enterprise? How many of us would never consider leaving to work elsewhere – regardless of the pay?

Answers to these questions vary – and some views sound worse than others when you express them aloud.

---

1   I'm playing with semantics a bit here. I've used the word goal to mean a personalised statement about what an individual wants ('I want to win'). The word 'outcome' I've used to mean the facts of the matter ('Jeff wins'). So a group of people might share the goal of winning a race but at the same time they each want a different outcome. Equally one outcome might satisfy several people's goals. 'Jeff wins' might suit Jeff because he's competitive and Angela because she placed a bet that he'd win.

One hint of an answer comes from an observation about dissatisfaction and stress. Whingeing is at epidemic levels in many businesses. A grumbling sense of injustice or disillusionment seems to dominate canteens and coffee lounges.[1] What is everyone so stressed about?

One definition of stress is that it is the tension between the way the world is and the way you think it should be. The less accepting you are of your situation the more it creates extra worries for you. I worked with a guy recently who arrived at work in a foul mood three days out of every four because his journey to work had been so bad. Surely after the first couple of hundred times this would cease to be a remarkable occurrence, but he couldn't let go of the feeling that public transport *shouldn't* be a 'miracle of inconvenience'[2].

Yes, there's a certain amount of complaining that springs solely from a desire to be paid well for doing little. But most of the favoured topics for whingeing are only secondarily to do with making the speaker's life easier. The grumbling is usually about how poorly some department, or the company as a whole, is being run. It's often personalised, admittedly, containing phrases like, 'If they'd listened to me …' or 'How could they treat me like that?' But it's only indirectly about tangible rewards.

People generally either want recognition of their worth, remedy for a slight, or better leadership from above. But if status *were* just a means to personal gain, why not cut out the middleman and whinge about poor pay and too much work? Why do people go on about those other things?

It's difficult to imagine that so many employees would get themselves worked up if they weren't emotionally involved with their jobs. Let's itemise the possible rationale for the complaints.

If employees were only jockeying for status, they'd be unlikely to moan about other people's poor decisions or incompetence; they'd be glad of a few incompetents, because it would make them look good.

Alternately, if they weren't really upset but only talking for effect they'd be ostentatiously reciting the company line, not grumbling.

If they were grumbling merely because they were generally unco-operative they'd complain about the effort they were putting in, not the

---

1 One thing I tell friends who want to get on in the world is 'don't whinge'. Your colleagues and managers will be so delighted and refreshed they will exaggerate all your other qualities. I also believe it dissipates valuable emotional energy that could go into fixing things. If you're not allowed to whinge you either accept things or take action. Even if that action is to leave, it's better than staying and grumbling.

2 A phrase I'm rather fond of which Sir Hubert Wilkins used to describe the bastardised World War I submarine in which he attempted to reach the underside of the North Pole.

results it was yielding – and yet people seem to be very sensitive to their efforts being squandered.

And finally, if we were all just in it for the money would we worry about all the other stuff and let it frazzle our nerves as much as it clearly does?

To me, this pervasive low-level grumbling suggests there's more going on than meets the eye. Many employees are going into work and coming away feeling slightly cheated. There's something they want that many of them aren't getting. What could it be?

Who is on the receiving end of employee loyalty?

Let's think about a situation which might shed a little light on people's relationships to their jobs. Picture the typical retirement ceremony. Somewhere in the speech will be a phrase along the lines of 'Dear old Fred has given this company forty years of loyal service'.

But think. Who has that forty years of service really been given to? To an actual person? Doesn't the very idea of loyalty imply a relationship between two *people*? You can't give loyal service to a building or a letterhead, can you?

But if there is a person at the other end of that long, loyal relationship how *can* it be a real person? In forty years, MDs will have come and gone, and board line-ups will have changed. If the outgoing employee has reached statutory retirement age, it's unlikely that anyone else in the whole company was there for his entire career. There is no single 'real' relationship that has spanned all those years. Why the misleading phraseology?

There's also a suggestion of something going on beneath the surface when a hard-working employee becomes disenchanted. It's almost a cliché for disgruntled workers to moan, 'And after all I've done for this company!' They instinctively appeal their poor treatment on the basis of a relationship that common sense says is just a figure of speech. Are they *really* having a personal relationship with a *business*?

When we talk about employee loyalty, who do we imagine is on the receiving end of it? Who is supposed to keep track of all an employee's contributions to the business over the years? After all, most careers will span more than one role or department. For anyone who's held several positions in a company, it's unlikely that they've had the same manager for the duration.

Even if there is a single manager throughout, a wronged employee

> **The Freudian blurt**
>
> Just as in the customer scenario, I've chosen to use the situation where someone gets upset as illustrative of what's truly going on. People don't rationalise as much in the middle of a tantrum, they let their grievances out in unedited form. That's particularly true if someone's complaint doesn't seem to make much logical sense. A calm person will see that and suppress the thing that's niggling them. But though they may not be able to put it into words when they're calm, once they've got up a good head of emotional steam they might be able to blurt it out. Most people probably don't feel comfortable saying to their boss, 'This company makes me feel unloved'. But if that's the sort of sentiment that appears to be surfacing when people are worked up, then perhaps we should look into it.

doesn't say, 'after all I've done for *you*'. Which is just as well. Managers aren't *personally* benefiting from an employee's dedication (except in a general, makes-me-look-like-a-good-boss sort of way); it's the business that benefits. A manager *might* feel personally obligated if you cleared the leaves out of his guttering, but doing your job well is between you and 'the company'.

We all act as though we have a relationship with the business we belong to. We act as though the business is an entity somehow separate in identity from the roster of employees it contains at any one moment.

The identity of the business is like the philosopher's axe, which has had its handle replaced on a number of occasions and its head. In what sense is it the same axe? Plainly the only sense in which it could be the same is in our minds, if we consider it to be the same. It's not a question of what's real; it's a question of how we think about things.

There was a lot of talk in the chapter on customers about our sub-conscious expectations concerning relationships. As a species we evolved and adapted to life as members of working communities – those ancestral roaming groups that humans formed in the days before permanent settlements. The evolutionary imprint of those times has implications for our behaviour at work. It has left us with an instinctive need to belong, to trade our efforts for rewards, to pursue status[1] within

---

1 If you don't get reassured about your status as part of your job, you tend to look for it elsewhere. But since most companies are rigid hierarchies (whatever the official line), status reinforcement is as ubiquitous as fluorescent lighting. I've known people who can look at ostensibly identical company cars and infer job grade from the absence of power windows or the addition of a CD player.

our group and to build relationships as we go. It's no wonder that when we join a company we tend to become emotionally involved – group membership is a part of us.

The company of strangers

What is strange, though, is that in a very real sense, a company isn't a single group of people. If anything, it is a lot of little overlapping groups.

Although we might feel part of our business, typically we only know a hundred or so people personally. In the retail sector, businesses with many thousands of employees are the norm. In what sense can we say that people we have never met and who don't know of our existence are part of the same group? The only way in which it makes literal sense is in a sort of chain of relationships.

When we join a company, we don't form links to all of it. We wire ourselves into our corner, forming connections with those around us, who in turn are bound to other parts of the extended group. With the exception of the board, most employees have no relationship with the business as a whole, only with their immediate colleagues. Even the board only have a one-way link to most of the company – everyone knows them, but they can't boast the converse.

Yet we don't retain a mental reservation about our membership of the company just because we don't know most of it. We don't think of

---

Linking the extended group

It's important to cross-link the company together in lots of different places otherwise there is a risk of it devolving into something smaller. If you put a divider in a tank of water and add ink to one side, you can later remove the divider and the ink diffuses throughout the whole tank. With people it's almost like you put a divider in and the ink separates out and when you remove the divider it won't mix. Countries that have been partitioned, even if they used to be a single nation, often won't reintegrate.

I used to work for a business that grew too big for its offices and leased a second building. They split the workforce between the two buildings, more or less randomly. Within six months the occupants of one building thought the other bureaucratic and unhelpful, while they in turn were criticised for being reckless and disorganised. Here is yet another drawback to dividing a business rigidly into departments – people will use almost any form of group membership as a basis to discriminate, even an arbitrary one.

ourselves as only being employed by our department. Most of the time the company is the group we identify with. And that's just as it's supposed to be.

If work were an intellectual exercise in making money, then an intellectual definition of the group would be appropriate – a list of employees held by the personnel department. But there's obviously something emotional going on. Does this 'extended group' mainly composed of strangers make sense in an emotional context?

You might think if we were going to form an emotional bond to the group of people we work with, it might be restricted to the people we actually know. But we seem happy to make a conceptual leap and include the whole firm. When we are thinking about the group we belong to, we don't use a personal definition – people we're directly involved with – we use the company's definition. That suggests that the group, the company, is a separate and real thing to us.

Despite the fact that 'the company' is a very artificial concept, made up mostly of people who don't know each other and who'll never meet, it's a concept that seems to slot neatly into our thinking.

The internal brand

The questions we've been asking have all been about uncovering the emotional infrastructure that lies beneath our connection to our jobs. Why do people talk of loyalty to 'the company' and complain about their status within it when it's just a loose coalition of strangers they have a financial arrangement with? The answer is that it clearly represents something more to us. Our attitudes to employment suggest that work is tapping into something more fundamental and more innately human than just salaried employment. But what is it 'the company' represents in our minds?

The answer is tied up with the riddle of retail brands, which we tackled in the customer chapter. The employee thinks of the company as a single entity just as the customer does. In both cases we form a relationship with that entity as though it were a person, even though it's really a group of people.

We overcome the hurdle of having a single relationship with a group of people by treating the members of the group as representatives. That way it doesn't matter that there are lots of them, the relationship they represent is the same. In the case of the company, the representatives are our managers. That's how someone can imagine they've given forty years of loyal service to 'a company'.

Just as the customer is comfortable treating the myriad interactions and experiences they have in your stores as though they were all somehow part of a single relationship with the brand, employees do something similar on the inside of the business. They act as though there is an internal version of the company brand with which they have a bond.

Maybe you're thinking about the phrasing of the statement 'internal version of the company brand'. It's a strange sounding thing. You feel you have to ask the question, 'Why would our brains have evolved to handle "internal brands"'? But we'll see in a moment that they evolved to handle something else, something just similar enough that the same mechanism can be reused to think about modern employment.

But isn't loyalty dead?

Before we say any more let's check we're not wasting our time. Even if we uncover the mechanism behind employee loyalty is it relevant to anything? After all, isn't loyalty to the company dead?

Increasingly, people flit from employer to employer. First businesses realised they could no longer offer employees jobs for life, and then many employees decided to withdraw their lifelong commitment too. Perhaps these days employment is just a temporary convenience for employer and employee. Perhaps the relationship with the modern employee has no more emotional depth than you'd experience with a vending machine.

That may be the reality for more and more people, but that's not because it's what we want or what we find satisfying. Everyone these days is transforming themselves into consultants, contractors and freelancers, but not because it's an ideal we've always aspired to; it's because for some people the benefits of a 'permanent' job no longer outweigh the hassle.

We all want camaraderie, team spirit and the good feeling you have when the whole group achieves something. We all want that shared feeling of triumph. But some people have given up chasing it. They either haven't experienced it, or if they have they don't consider it makes up for feeling unsatisfied or exploited the rest of the time.

These people reason that if they're going to feel isolated or unfulfilled, they would be much better off doing it on their own terms and for better pay. Traditional employment, for those who opt out, has started to seem like a relationship gone sour. Rather than expend any more effort on it, they've decided to get out.

That's not to say freelancers are all happy 'being single', I think most of them are *happier*.

As a generalisation, I'm saying that the move to freelance work is not a positive thing. It may evolve into something positive as affiliations of freelancers learn to build themselves communities, but I believe it's primarily a rejection of the failings of the workplace and not the joyous blossoming of the self it is often made out to be.

"Over the last ten years or so, large companies have adopted a number of approaches to make themselves more competitive, usually (although not exclusively) through cost-cutting measures. The great attraction of process re-engineering was the likely reductions in headcount through the automation of standardised processes using technology. Although this is rarely feted as the main goal of business change programs, the growing popularity of 'downsizing' took hold during the 1990s and people who worked in large businesses generally knew what was coming when the consultants arrived. Leaving aside the issue of whether or not these change programs, and the reductions in costs and headcount actually delivered any long lasting benefits, we can safely say that the feelings of loyalty between the employee and the company were greatly eroded as a result. Employees have always known that 'indispensable' is not a word generally valid when describing their role in a company, but as company after company took the axe to accounting departments and out-sourced everything from distribution to HR, they became aware that they were in fact all too dispensable. A recent study in the retail sector showed that staff turnover is 26 per cent (the highest of any sector), and that at any one time more than half the employees in a retailer are actively thinking about leaving for another job. Whatever the rights and wrongs of employee transience one has to admit that staff loyalty is not what it used to be." – Dan

Where does contentment come from?

When we talked about customers there was a section entitled 'I complain because I care'. You could say of employees, 'I whinge because I'm emotionally involved'. It's perhaps the least productive response open to people, but whingeing clearly indicates that an employee's happiness, or unhappiness in this case, depends on more than being paid well and given interesting work.

Many of the things in life that bring us contentment are unconscious, even instinctive things. People don't calculate their level of fulfilment, they just experience it; it's emotional and innate, not intellectual. Lack of contentment, at the subconscious level, has a tendency to make people fret, pine or grumble. But what is the basis for contentment in the workplace and what undermines it?

Lack of money, for instance, is not especially insidious. In a buoyant job market, there's often something to be done about it. If someone thinks they could get more money somewhere else, they look for another job. They don't feel directionless, irritable, let down or bitter; they just find an opportunity elsewhere and leave. And yet there are employees feeling resentment or bitterness. Those emotions are symptoms of a more intangible and old-fashioned complaint than low pay – they're indicative of relationship troubles.

It doesn't seem like much of a revelation: people care about their jobs. But most people are very good at rationalising away any emotional reaction they have to the workplace. They are aware that they should be calm but positive at all times – perhaps permitting themselves the occasional moment of jubilation.

People find any other emotional reaction to work unsettling. They look for ways to ignore, dissipate or suppress those unwanted feelings. If they feel angry or despondent, they try to overcome it. They rarely spend time trying to understand the basis of those feelings. Perhaps people think that dwelling on inappropriate emotions will strengthen or encourage them.

The truth is that there is a powerful emotional bond tying many people to their jobs. When that relationship comes under pressure or is out of balance it *can* provoke strong emotions in even the most dispassionate and level-headed employee. And there are lessons to be learned from those reactions.

In a way, many people feel something analogous to love for their jobs. Unfortunately, it's too often in the doomed or unrequited sense of the word. What's exciting is that there are things that we can do to improve that situation.

It's just implicit in the relationship

Let's think a little about the baggage that goes along with relationships. A romantic relationship, for instance, might start with a first date. First dates are about things like attraction, compatibility and maybe humour. If the relationship continues, other factors come into play. Somewhere down the line we start expecting a partner to be supportive or understanding, or to ask what was wrong with our day. These expectations are just implicit, we don't agree them up front and we don't really discuss them unless we notice they're not there. It's just part of the deal.

It's too legalistic a word, but relationships are contracts. That's not to dehumanise them, or try to make them sound selfish. For a relationship to matter to us we need to know we can rely on the other person, that they will be there for us. To trust someone is just another way of saying that you have an unspoken arrangement, an implicit contract with them.

Many of the implicit rules and regulations concerning relationships come from our culture. Each culture maintains a list of standard relationship types and some of the things you might expect from them. Some societies have entries that aren't on the American/European list. In Japan, the older-brother/younger-brother[1] relationship is a strong one. And not just among real brothers:[2] it is a common form of friendship between two men of slightly different age and seniority. Brits find the idea a bit strange although we are more comfortable if there is a larger difference in age – then we recognise the mentor/*protégé* relationship.

While the templates and some of the byelaws of relationships are dependent on culture, there are many universal and invariant features. The expectations we take with us into the workplace include a lot of unformed, instinctive attitudes and reactions. People don't work this stuff out; they just feel it.

Employees tell themselves they are there for the money and the various challenges, but pretty soon most of them start to expect more. They begin to want a sense of community. And they start to expect an appropriate position in that community. They want a bit of appreciation. For many people, the challenges and the money are important, but it's often their standing in the firm, or lack of it, that has the biggest influence on their happiness.

Auto-tracking the internal brand

When we talked about customers, and how they relate to the (external) brand, we said they have a sort of auto-tracking mechanism that works out whether the relationship is in debt or credit. They are always monitoring how well the company is treating them. In the case of an external brand, it's often fairly easy for the customer to shop elsewhere if they feel let down. It's a relationship that can arouse powerful sentiments, but it's still just a trading relationship. Not so for employees.

---

1   It's also one of Confucius's five cardinal human relationships: father-son, emperor-subject, husband-wife, elder brother-younger brother, and friend-friend.

2   Here's a little snippet from an old news report that Dan noticed, '*Bookseller denies nepotism charges.* Barnes & Noble, the largest US retail bookseller, on Wednesday defended itself against charges of nepotism after Leonard Riggio appointed his brother Stephen Riggio to replace him as chief executive.'

We suggested that employees build a picture of the company too – an amalgam of all the individual interactions and relationships. In effect they create an internal brand. And things are different when people think about a business from the inside. How they feel about the company they work for goes beyond the idea of a trading relationship, it becomes personal.

For the customer, the brand represents a community they sometimes do business with. For the employee, the brand is *their* community, the one they are a part of.

You know when you buy something over the Internet? You usually have to fill in a shipping address for where you want the goods sent, and an invoice address (if it's different), as well as work, home and fax numbers and an e-mail address. I rarely fill all of them in – I don't bother with a fax number for example – but the empty fields are there nonetheless.

Brains are like that. Evolution has prepared us for certain types of relationships. We've got mental space reserved for thinking about family and friends, community and trading relationships, and potential mates and rivals. We have special-purpose mental modules, which we talked about in the last chapter, all ready to go to work on each type of relationship once the details are filled in. We can leave some of the spaces blank, but the mental machinery for processing that data is whirring away, ready for action nonetheless.

What if we're missing an important type of relationship? Our minds expect it but it's absent from our environments. What if some important details aren't being filled in by twenty-first century living?

Some businesses talk about themselves as a metaphorical family. I tend to associate that practice with American management, which is often more overtly enthusiastic about itself (heaven forbid anyone in the UK should get over-excited about anything). They choose to compare the business with a family because they are looking for an analogy that captures something more fulfilling and more personal than just a financial arrangement.

Family is a natural choice as a metaphor, but only because most of us don't recognise that there used to be a really important kind of relationship that involved more people than a family, one that's even more appropriate as a metaphor for business: the community.

Real world example – John Lewis Partnership

The unusual ownership of the John Lewis group sounds almost Marxist, bringing to mind rhetoric about the means of production being placed in the hands of the workers. The employees of UK retail group John Lewis are co-owners of the business – it is structured as a partnership and has had no shareholders since 1929. And yet there is no suggestion that it is any less commercially viable than companies with ownership along more traditional capitalistic lines. They currently employ nearly 60,000 'partners' and have sales of around £4 bn.

To quote the company's brochure, the partnership is 'the embodiment of an ideal, the outcome of nearly a century of endeavour to create a different sort of company – one that would be absolutely honest with its customers, fair to its suppliers and ensure for its workers the maximum benefit from their work.

Their unusual system of ownership may be responsible for the high level of empowerment among store staff. Department managers in Cole Brothers (part of the group) are encouraged to contribute to merchandising and layout schemes. While such involvement is not unusual in the industry, in my experience it is more usually in spite of company policy rather than encouraged by it. On the face of it, such empowerment might be a bad thing as it runs counter to the principle of standardisation on which profitability in multiple retailing is based. It would be interesting to know whether the dividend in staff morale and motivation outweighs the risk of an expanded cost base.

Another unusual feature, popular with many partners, is freeing department store sales-staff from chasing commission. The group often break with retail dogma to ensure that store staff will sell products on their merits not their margins. Conventional thinking would say that profits won't be as high if sales staff aren't incentivised on their sales. But this retailer has built up quite a reputation with customers, based on the trustworthiness and impartiality of their staff. Perhaps repeat sales from customers happy with the pressure-free advice they received offsets some initial sales lost.

Other innovations include a group 'Council', mainly elected by staff, who call in the Chairman and senior directors once a year and quiz them on their running of the business. The group also make management information available to staff below management grades who wish to see it. Staff have access to various, fairly lavish, leisure facilities including country clubs owned by the group; they are also encouraged, and often financially assisted, in pursuing various educational goals. Support is also available to staff suffering from ill health or other hardships.

Recent history notwithstanding, in the last seventy-five years the group has built itself up to be a major force in UK retailing while subscribing to various policies considered by many outsiders to be neither stringent enough nor commercial enough to bring financial success. John Lewis Partnership are an excellent case study to ponder for any retailers considering the costs and benefits of more nurturing or indulgent management styles.

We're a species of team players

Remember our ancestors travelling in groups of thirty or forty adults across the African savannah? Our brains evolved to help us get the hang of living in a community, because being a loner wasn't really an option. Those who didn't figure out how to work together ended up inside something big and stripy. The mental machinery that helped us form those groups is still up there, trying to make sense of the modern age, trying to process our community relationships for us. There's just one problem: we're not part of communities any more.

Modern day communities, small villages for instance, aren't actually that much like the groups our species evolved with. We're all too separate, disconnected and independent. The communities of yore were tight-knit with lots of mutual dependence and teamwork. They had a definite hierarchy and they focused on getting things done – in other words they were more like the modern workplace. If our mental 'community module' is able to work with any set of twenty-first century relationships, it's most likely to be the ones at work.

On the other hand, the workplace doesn't fit exactly into the mental compartment we have available for community. Companies are too big and too impersonal. Emotion would have played a big part in ancestral groups, whereas most companies discourage that sort of thing.

In fact, when we discussed emotions in the workplace, we said that companies tend only to allow a few negative emotions – aggression for instance. You won't hear a company briefing that extols patience, or generosity or tolerance – only toughness and beating the competition. The only 'company approved' positive emotion you might hear a speech about is a rather sanitised sentiment known as team spirit. It's not something most people would instantly think of if you ask them to list emotions, but it's very real and very relevant to our discussion here. And in its undiluted form it's very powerful.

I said that the original hunter-gatherer communities were much closer and more action-oriented than modern communities. There's a word for a mini-community like that, it's called a team.

Actually, the modern emphasis placed on 'the team' suggests that many people are vaguely aware that teams have some natural resonance for us, that they are capable of stirring up strong, motivating emotions. But we don't usually stop to question *why* we would bond emotionally as teams. Nevertheless, the popularity of outward-bound-style team-building courses suggests that some people recognise the potential of that bond.

These outdoor-based team-building exercises come very close to simulating ancestral groups. There's plenty of action, group goals, competition and co-operation, as well as a dash of physical hardship.[1]

We possess a partially dormant repertoire of group-level instincts and sentiments that these days often lack a focus. There is a whole layer of relationships we are capable of for which most of us have no outlet. Our group-level mental machinery is only partly successful in substituting the workplace for the ancestral community, because it's only a partial match to the original structure.

We dimly sense that team spirit taps into something that, in its own way, is as primal and powerful as family. We just haven't been very good at uncovering the rest of the mental machinery that goes with it.

Caring and sharing

There's a joke that has been doing the rounds about working in retailers. A central buyer has died and gone to heaven. St. Peter says that the buyer's life score is borderline, and he can choose whether he wants to spend eternity in heaven or hell. A day trip is arranged to each for research purposes. Arriving at hell's door, the devil greets the buyer cheerily and says "come on in, all your old pals are here". The buyer meets up with all those sales and marketing directors and distribution managers he worked with during his life, and a day of partying and drinking ensues. At the end of the day the buyer returns to heaven where St Peter shows them around. Loads of people are sitting on clouds playing harps and there's not a drink in sight. Slightly unsure, the buyer makes his choice: "I'd actually like to return to hell, if it's all the same to you". On his arrival the next morning with all his luggage he is dragged through the door by a hideous demon, stripped naked and set to work picking up heavy rocks in a muddy field, amid the wailing of all his erstwhile drinking buddies. "Good grief!" he cries, "What happened to the party, the drinking, the fun, the laughter of yesterday?" "That was an interview", says the devil. "Now you're part of the team". – Dan

---

The perils of imaginary relationships

Do you find you go through a honeymoon phase when you start working for a new business? Maybe you did when you were younger. You

---

1 I asked my brother about these courses because a former employer sent him on one. He said he'd been extremely sceptical beforehand, but at the end of the course he felt a strong bond to the rest of the team. Unfortunately, as they were all from separate parts of the company, he never saw any of them again.

imagined that if you worked hard, you'd be appreciated for your innate worth and unique skills and all would be well. Sometime soon after, reality intruded, and the honeymoon was over. Depending on how much of a bump you came down with, you might even have started to feel you'd made a mistake taking that new job.

I'll illustrate the onset of disillusionment that I'm talking about by reference to something that happened to me a long time ago. If you were ever idealistic or eager to please, you've probably had a similar experience.

Sometime in the Eighties I was working for Philips Electronics as part of the team that kept the British part of their global computer network operating.[1] I had come in on a Sunday to make some changes and I discovered a serious problem. It ended up taking all night to get the network repaired and I was due to start work at seven that morning. When my boss got in I called him and told him I'd been working since yesterday lunchtime and could he get someone to cover for me because I was exhausted and needed some sleep. He said he'd do what he could, but eight hours later, when my shift ended, it was clear he hadn't considered it a priority. After a twenty-eight hour day at work I was feeling hard done by.

I felt I'd put myself out for the company and it hadn't been reciprocated, even though a day off was company policy in the circumstances. I felt foolish for working so hard. I said to myself, "What sort of ungrateful company would treat their staff like that?"

Before you think the moral of this story is 'don't work for Philips' I should probably say that I met many people with very different experiences. One guy had been sponsored through his M.Sc. by Philips and couldn't say enough good things about them.

I remember thinking that it was almost like we were talking about two different companies. Having read the previous part of this chapter, you can no doubt see what nonsense it is talking about Philips like that. We might as well have compared notes on whether Philips employees have a sense of humour or not, or whether they like the colour blue.

When I worked for them they had a third of a million employees worldwide – that's the population of a fair sized town. Tens of thousands of them would be fabulous people and probably there were a few hundred

---

1 Genius that I am, I'd worked out that giant global networks of computers would be 'the next big thing'. I'd also worked out that the whole thing would be built using big old IBM mainframes, so I became an expert on linking them together. It turns out they were just about the only type of computer *not* used to build the Internet. How I avoided buying a Betamax video recorder at about the same time I don't know.

who were swines. What else can you expect from a group of over three hundred thousand people?

I had been bundling up my day-to-day dealings with my boss, his boss, my colleagues, plus a few people in other departments and labelling those experiences 'Philips'. The M.Sc. guy had done the same and arrived at a different conclusion.

The company talks with the manager's voice

Looking back on it, if I was going to be cross with anyone over that incident, it should have been my boss, not the company. And in his defence, it wasn't as though he had spare staff he could have sent to my rescue. He could have given up a day of his own time and covered for me himself, or he could have made himself unpopular and got his deputy to do it – a deputy who would have been very unhappy about it. From his point of view, I was an employee asking that he wreck his day for me. I hadn't fixed *his* network, I'd fixed Philips' network, but nonetheless I expected him to make the sacrifice.

The heart of the matter is that as my boss he was acting as an intermediary between me and 'the company'. To my naïve perception, anything he said to me was always as a sort of company spokesman. Remember when we mentioned the military phrase 'You're not saluting me, you're saluting the uniform'? When my boss declined to help me I felt sure it was Philips who were letting me down.

The relationship auto-tracking bit of my brain said they owed me, but their representative (my boss) certainly didn't act like it. It was only natural to feel a little betrayed. I mention it because this sort of thing is going on in every office every day.

If you don't recognise the relationship with the brand, you won't understand that you're seeing cause and effect. My boss wouldn't see why *me* staying late meant *he* had to give up his day. No one had explained that part of being a manager to him.

In stores, few staff fully appreciate that when they speak it's the company the customer hears. Inside the business, managers too will frequently fail to make the distinction between their role as local spokesperson for the business and their role as individuals.

If managers want to keep staff happy, they will have to learn to perform 'emotional labour' in the same way store staff do. Whether they like it or not, it falls to them to keep the employee's relationship with the brand running smoothly.

My manager could have asked himself how the company should behave towards me and then taken it upon himself to make it happen. If he felt a representative of the company should have thanked me, he could have done it himself, been that representative. But you can't blame the guy, because very few people understand the duality of the role.

A manager might be forgiven for thinking that there are two people in an employee relationship: him and the employee. A manager may often miss the invisible third person – the company – because its representative looks and sounds just like him. As long as he's a manager, he will regularly be speaking on behalf of that third person.

Are you saying that as my manager?

Things would be clearer if we used an idea you could imagine that pioneering milliner, Edward De Bono, coming up with. We could give managers a hat with the words 'I am speaking on behalf of the company' written on it. If they upset you when they were wearing the hat, you'd direct your sense of injustice towards the company; if a bareheaded individual ruins your day, you take it up with them personally.

You can see why people sit in the canteen whingeing. Employees are making all sorts of connections between their own actions and the actions of their managers, and much of it is being amalgamated in their minds into one big relationship with the brand. Most of the time, no one is managing that relationship from the brand's side.

Have you ever seen a TV farce based around the idea of identical twins?[1] Imagine if no one realises they're twins, everyone thinks they're the same person. You could do a favour for one twin and get no sense of gratitude from the other. One twin could insult you and the other would show no remorse. If you thought it was just one person, you'd fall out with them pretty quickly (and much comic hilarity would ensue, at least in the TV version).

Representatives of the brand are like that. *They* know they're individuals, but to employees they're somewhat interchangeable.

By nature, humans like to join groups – we join clubs, societies, communities, organisations and companies. But obviously a group is a disembodied concept; we can't hold a conversation with it, even though we have a relationship with it. So we manage our relationship with the

---

1   For some reason, on TV one of the twins is usually evil.

group *via* the people in charge. The role of leader is synonymous with chief spokesman in our minds. That's really what authority means: empowered to speak for the group. When the chief spokesman says 'we' are going to do something, who is in a position to dispute it? It would still be the same group if the leader were replaced, but for most day-to-day purposes the leader *is* the voice of the group.

Let's take these concepts and put them together. We have:

- Companies trigger feelings of community.
- Sense of community or team spirit is something that we are programmed by evolution to have strong feelings about.
- Communities have leaders who speak for the group.
- We automatically keep track of our relationship with our community.
- We manage that relationship *via* the community's leaders.
- Much of our sense of contentment and our motivation comes from our relationship with the community.

If you combine all of these things you come up with an exciting possibility. Companies have the potential to fire up one of the strongest motivating emotions humans are capable of: team spirit. And all they have to do is manage the relationship properly.

Primal teams

Some studies have been done into why soldiers are sometimes prepared to lay down their lives. Is it patriotism? Is it to save little Jenny back home? The consensus is that it's because of team spirit. It's because some people would do anything for the 'guys in their unit' – including die.

It'd be nice to get a little of that sentiment going in the workplace, wouldn't it? Maybe not the dying bit. People are never going to 'make the ultimate sacrifice' to save a few shops, but you could still get them pretty fired up.

The great thing is that a lot of team spirit happens naturally; you just have to get out of the way. I mentioned the honeymoon period when you join a new business. It's a feeling of optimism and enthusiasm. It's based on starting a new relationship with a new community.

I also pointed out that no one is managing the relationship from the company's end, because nobody really understands it's there. How long is a new relationship likely to remain upbeat and full of energy when it's neglected? The modern business is consistently wrecking most people's team spirit by ignoring the relationship it's based on. They don't see what's going on, so naturally they keep walking all over it.

If we find a way to stop the slaps in the face we unwittingly give our employees, we might allow that team spirit to grow. We might generate powerful feelings of loyalty and we might help people feel content with their jobs.

How might something like that work?

Just stop screwing up

One important point is for managers to recognise their role as local spokesperson for the brand. A manager needs to set aside his own point of view, when donning the management hat, and say 'What should the brand representative do?'

It's like the situation with customers in a store which we discussed in the last chapter. A manager is like a new actor playing a long-running role. It's like the way they keep getting new actors to play James Bond.[1] When Pierce Brosnan took over, Bond didn't get amnesia, he still knew how he liked his Martinis, he still got into a fight every time he put on evening dress. There's just a new voice saying the lines.

From the point of view of the employee, the role of 'My Manager' starts with their first boss, but inevitably there will be substitutions over the years. As individuals, we start from scratch with each new boss. But when our manager talks about our performance, our future with the company, our status, we expect continuity. The goodwill we've built up in the past isn't supposed to be between you and your boss, it was supposed to reside with the business.

If status and standing in the business were like the balance in your bank account, you wouldn't be too pleased if you found yourself broke every time a new branch manager was appointed. None of the money you paid in previously counted because the new manager said, "that was all before my time".

The employee keeps track of all the debits and credits in their relationship with the brand. We need to find some way of keeping track from the brand's side of things. And the two sets of records need to be compared. The brand and the employee need to agree on how the relationship stands. We need to find a way to maintain continuity even when the manager/representative changes.

---

1   I shouldn't have to spell out the more obvious ways in which being a manager is *not* like being James Bond.

If we are going to start keeping records we will need to be a lot clearer on what constitutes obligation and what kind of behaviour will be rewarded. And once we decide which kinds of behaviour to reward, we have to make sure we are aware of who is displaying it.

Consistency is the key

It will also require a lot more consistency in management. It's a big enough problem handing the employee relationship over from an old manager to a new one, but it gets a lot worse if the new manager has a different set of values. Maybe your old boss thought you were great because you showed a lot of initiative. How does that leave things with a new boss who values obedience instead? How does your high standing in the team transfer over when the behaviour that got you there is now out of favour?[1]

In ancestral communities, lack of consistency would have been less of an issue. For a start, the leader would probably be aware of what most of his lieutenants were doing because the group size was much smaller. It would also have been easier and more acceptable to go directly to the leader with a grievance. When we talked about customers we saw how they have a natural instinct to work their way up the management hierarchy with a complaint. Someone who does that sort of thing from within, as an employee, may get a reputation for being a troublemaker.

Here's a question. Why do employees do what their boss tells them to? It's because he speaks for the company. If they don't do as their boss asks, they risk damaging their relationship with the business. So surely doing what their boss says should enhance their standing with the business. Anything that breaks that link is going to leave employees feeling cheated.

The don'ts of managing employee recognition

We'll use the analogy of the bank to recap and extend the list of management behaviour likely to demotivate people. Just to be clear, the bank account represents the employee's standing or goodwill with the business which they've been paying into with their diligence and hard

---

1 I think it's different if the employee changes role, they expect to behave differently. But when the representative (the manager) changes, the ground rules shouldn't change – just as with a change of bank manager.

work. If you're going to manage people's accounts satisfactorily you need to bear in mind the following:

1. *Let everyone know what your bank charges and your terms are.*

   Employees need to know what will be rewarded and what will get them into trouble.

2. *The charges shouldn't vary by branch.*

   Your progress in the company mustn't depend on who your manager is; the same behaviour should be rewarded throughout the business.

3. *Lost transactions are not acceptable. A large cheque shouldn't just go missing.*

   Managers have to be perceptive towards the behaviour the company has decided to reward (or punish). Otherwise why should employees bother?

4. *A change of branch manager shouldn't affect your bank balance.*

   We've covered this one. Who wants to keep starting from scratch?

5. *Supply regular itemised statements and overdrawn notices.*

   Employees must see that the company is paying attention. Regardless of their personal views, managers must give feedback to employees about their behaviour. That feedback must be based on the company's values not the manager's.

To pick up a couple of those points. Often, good behaviour only needs to be recognised verbally. If an employee does something exceptional, all they need is a pat on the back. But please let me make this plain, the reason those words matter is that *they acknowledge the debt from the company's side*. Hollow speeches aren't the key to motivation. The words are symbolic; they say, 'We noticed, we will remember'. If the business hasn't noticed, if it won't remember, a manager who gives one of those little speeches of recognition is storing up trouble for the future.

It is distressing to read management books that imply staff only need a kind word and a pat on the back and don't mention the follow-up. That's like advising banks that all you need to do to run a bank is send out statements. You send out statements to reassure customers that you're keeping accurate records. It's all pointless unless you also honour those statements.

A challenge

I think we'll leave it there, although there's plenty more that could be said. Hopefully this chapter will have given you a new and illuminating way of looking at employee relationships. It should also have given you the basis for fixing problems you probably didn't realise you had.

Many of the best managers seem to have found their way to roughly this point, but they've done it almost subconsciously, without an underlying theory of why it works.

Personally, I find the possibilities inherent in these ideas very exciting. Team spirit is an innate part of us and something that will develop automatically, under the right conditions. You don't need to invent new ways of firing up your staff; you need to understand how to encourage the process to occur naturally.

Many aspects of modern management interfere with and upset this process. Without meaning to, we routinely violate the basics of good team leadership. Modern management, without realising it, continually triggers our mental 'bad leadership' alarm. If we can just stop shooting ourselves in the foot, we might be able to reverse the move to freelancing. We might be able to eliminate the whingeing. We might be able to guarantee our employees job satisfaction. There's a challenge for the new century if ever I saw one.

What was that all about?

- Employees have a relationship with the company that echoes the relationship with our ancestral communities.
- Managers are the intermediaries who manage that relationship.
- Because managers don't realise they are spokesmen, they continually say or do the wrong thing.
- If our relationship with our companies was managed in harmony with our subconscious expectations we might all experience job satisfaction and high motivation.

CHAPTER 5

Suppliers

This journey

So after chapters of strange science and exotic explanations of the mundane what do you need to prepare yourself for here? This chapter is both less speculative and more controversial.

Just like previous chapters I'm going to show you scenarios you'll recognise but tell you there's more going on than meets the eye. The difference is that I'm not going to be uncovering any new forms of behaviour here; I'm going to be talking about the old familiar kind. I'm going to show you a situation that's considered by many to be simply 'good business' and ask you to believe that it's an unhealthy state of affairs that's undermining your business.

It may be a struggle to accept that what I'm describing here happens in your business. I'll show you the worst-case scenario and you can judge how much of it applies to your company. Even so, it might be an uncomfortable experience from time to time, so I'll need to ask for your patience and open-mindedness.

This chapter promotes the ideas of collaborative commerce and supply-chain integration. It would be difficult to persuade you that the many obstacles to such a scheme are worth overcoming if I didn't first show you what's wrong with the *status quo*. And unfortunately there's a lot wrong with it.

I've mentioned elsewhere that one theme of the work that Dan and I have done together is that we tend to ask the awkward questions. We try to pick our moments, but if there's some glaring problem that no one's talking about, we talk about it.

On his more cynical days, Dan has suggested that businesses use the word 'strategic'[1] the same way religious folk talk about 'faith'. Saying something's 'strategic' seems to mean 'no explanation required'. Well, retail isn't a religion; there are no questions that must not be asked. The

---

1 I attended a talk on finance at the London Business School last year. I learned that, at the highest levels, finance is pronounced "f'nance", with no 'i' and strategy is pronounced "straadegy" with a long 'a' followed by a 'd'. Useful stuff.

problem we'll talk about here is one that potentially afflicts a large part of retail and yet it's not discussed openly.

I should warn you that as part of the discussion I'm going to take some pretty big swipes at buyers and commercial directors, though I suppose I'm not exactly the first to do so. If you work in a non-buying discipline, you may even consider that sort of thing good clean fun. Just don't get too comfortable, commercial teams may have painted themselves into a corner, but they didn't do it without some help.

We'll be talking about a supplier relations dilemma, faced by many retailers, in which there are two options. Option one is the essence of tough-guy management and provides the all-important 'quick win' that everyone loves. The second is uncomfortably touchy-feely and has a bigger payback in the longer term, but unfortunately nobody gets to kick any ass. You've guessed it; I'm going to try to spoil all your fun by recommending the peace-and-love scenario of option two.

It's a tough sell, though, as long as the bare-knuckle alternative continues to bring results. And, until someone takes the plunge and really gets collaborative commerce up and running, a precarious sort of complacency reigns, at least in the UK.

Even if you don't like the looks of the collaborative alternative, I hope you'll come away with a new and unsettling picture of your supplier relationships. I'm going to try to do for supplier rebates what the movie 'Babe' did for bacon sandwiches.

The benefits of vertical integration

We'll get to all the dark deeds soon enough, but we're going to begin with some very top level thoughts about the structure of businesses.

Let's start by thinking about a single product being made, shipped, displayed in a store and then purchased by a customer. The various organisations involved in the process, up to the point where the product is dropped into a shopping bag, run the length of the supply chain.

Actually defining the supply chain can be a bit tricky. A retailer buys from many suppliers and a supplier usually sells to more than one retailer. It's difficult to say where one 'chain' ends and the next begins. So instead, let's think about that single product again and call its passage from manufacture to consumption a supply 'thread'.

It's unfortunate, in a way, that the world has settled on the word 'chain', because a chain is made from hundreds of short links – it's not a good

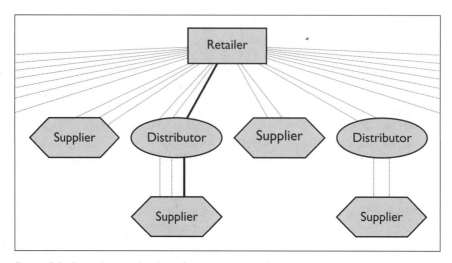

Figure 5.1 A single supply chain for a single product

analogy. A better metaphor is threads making up a rope or wires making up a cable – one strand for each product.

Let's look at the next product into the customer's shopping bag. The manufacturer and supplier may be different from the previous product, but the two threads meet at the retailer. A retailer's position in the economy drawn in this way is a myriad of threads starting out in lots of different places but converging down to a single bundle in the store.

When you consider any individual thread, it's not clear why there is more than one organisation involved. Why couldn't the same business both manufacture a product and sell it to a consumer? Why consider them separate when they are two halves of a single process? Neither is much use without the other. Yet manufacturing and retail are separate enough to be considered different industry sectors.

It seems clear that the designers of a product, right at the beginning of a thread, would be experts on its virtues. Who better to proclaim its benefits directly to the customer? In fact, doesn't it seem that the inventors of the product would also need to listen to, as well as talk to, the end customer in order to design products for them? The parties at both ends of the thread have good reason to talk to each other, yet the interface with the customer is in a different business from the product designer – in fact it's in a different business sector.

It also makes sense that day to day information about rates of sale and stock levels in shops should be communicated swiftly back up the thread where it can be used to adjust the rate of production. As soon as stores are aware that a product is selling unexpectedly slowly/quickly, factories need to reduce/increase production. That information should be communicated without delay.

The metaphor of wires in a cable becomes particularly apt if you picture an old-fashioned telephone cable with each individual strand carrying a conversation about a different product. Anything that interrupts that conversation will leave the factory guessing what's going on with the customer.

By convention, we think of the supply chain running vertically down from source to outlet. If we were to follow one thread back to its origin 'upstream', buying up all the businesses it passes through, we would be building ourselves a vertically integrated business.

Once that vertical integration is complete we would be in a position to efficiently synchronise production of the product with demand from the end customer. The flow of information would now be taking place entirely within our corporate boundaries.

We could also use the information we gather at the customer interface to guide our manufacturing R&D – matching our new products to our target customers. Vital information need only flow from department to department not company to company.

Before we get on to the drawbacks of vertical integration, let's just pause and say, "Doesn't it sound so far like it would be a good thing?"

Of course if we were to vertically integrate, then following one product thread back to its source wouldn't be much good. We'd need to buy up the businesses along *all* the product threads that ran into our business. *Now* all the relevant flows of information take place within one organisation.

Clearly, information won't flow as freely if the lines of communication need to jump the gap between separate businesses – which is the situation in an unintegrated supply chain. Like with neighbouring countries, a lot will depend on relations between the two firms, but in many businesses passing information to suppliers is as problematic as crossing the Iron Curtain used to be during the Cold War.[1] So why doesn't everyone get the information flowing by vertically integrating and putting the pieces of the supply chain back together?

---

1 This piece of imagery comes to mind because some people have said that the economic problem with communism is that at worst it severs the link between supply and demand and at best it forces the link to take a roundabout route. Senator McCarthy would be proud; I can now denounce opponents of collaborative commerce as communists.

The goals of manufacturing

To understand why, far from being integrated, most supply chains are growing more fragmented we need to look at the goals of the individual players. We'll start with manufacturing.

Business expansion should be the search for economies of scale. A combined manufacturing facility that made all the different products a retail outlet requires would be a very strange place; it would be short on economies of scale.

Factories set up to run efficiently may produce lots of different products, but they generally don't offer variety as a High Street shopper would see it. A factory might make 130 types of light bulb. That's plenty of choice for the trade customer, but something of a bore for the novelty-seeking shopper.

The most attractive manufacturing synergies (by which I mean economies of scale) come from assembling a portfolio of products with similar production requirements. A factory with its massive machinery constitutes a huge chunk of capital investment. Efficiently utilising those fixed assets is a prime consideration for a manufacturer. Being able to make a range of popular products with a single production line makes a lot of sense.

Efficient factories also need to get the most from their permanent workforce. If possible, workers should neither be idle during their normal shifts nor required to work lots of extra hours at overtime rates. The ideal situation, in terms of most 'bang for your buck', is when each employee's workload exactly matches their contractual hours.

Of course, permanent staffing levels can be adjusted, but not on the same timescale as the rise and fall of orders. Laying off skilled staff and then wishing you had them back six months later is a terrible approach – for all concerned.

That Goldilocks and the Three Bears situation (where demand is not too hot, not too cold, but just right) forms an 'efficiency zone' centred around the most efficient level of production. Keeping the business in that zone is the goal.

Imagine that the light-bulb factory I mentioned makes domestic bulbs, flashlight bulbs and auto bulbs using roughly the same equipment and skills.[1] That's three different sectors with different economic and seasonal cycles. When one sector is quiet, there's a fair chance that

---

1   I suspect no such factory exists in these days of sealed metal-halide headlamps and krypton flashlights. But thirty years ago they were all glowing wires in a little glass bulb.

another will be brisk. Production facilities can be switched to whichever sector or customer is placing the orders and the fixed assets need never sit idle. Design and operational expertise is similar across all three product types so efficient use is also made of the workforce.

And yet, no matter how diverse the manufacturing product range might seem from within the industry, it is unlikely to constitute a credible retail offer. It will generally be too samey and too small. There is no high-street bulb shop, but several big retail outlets stock a small range of bulbs. You're not going to be able to use the bulb manufacturing facilities to make the plugs, extension leads and fuses your customer will expect to find adjacent to the bulbs in your household electrical display.

So we have a manufacturing product range that's relatively small, based around use of the same machinery and skills. This contrasts with a retail range that's much broader and based around customer expectations. Unless you can arrange for the two to coincide, there's a limited advantage to owning both businesses.

What about a better example, say clothing, where lots of variety is possible from a limited range of manufacturing technologies? Might the manufacturing and retail ranges be more compatible in that industry? In theory, the same company that owns the retail outlets could also own the garment factories.

Even here there are problems. Most clothing stores sell belts and shoes, which are very different from dresses and shirts. Think of all the other products it's difficult to make with a sewing machine: bags, jewellery and cufflinks, knitwear, hosiery and sunglasses.

Imagining owning production facilities for all of those products. That's a lot of different types of manufacturing. Would a single retail chain be able to keep each factory working efficiently? Once you've made the fifteen types of men's and women's belts you need for your stores, wouldn't you be tempted to keep the machines running and make a few more for other retailers? And if your factory were busy all year, wouldn't it be over-stretched preparing for Christmas? A factory tied to a single retail customer will struggle to keep its production capacity in the 'efficiency zone'.

If the manufacturer is a 'free agent' they can have a selection of customers. That gives a factory a better chance to keep production (supply) at a constant, optimum level and then arrange for appropriate order levels (demand) to match. A factory can turn away orders if they're swamped, or if demand is declining they can go out and look for new accounts.

Real world example – Zara & Inditex

If you've been committing every priceless word of this book to memory, you may have spotted something of a contradiction. Dan's introduction mentions the great success the clothing store Zara have had, much of which it owes to vertical integration. Yet, in this chapter I lay out the reasons why vertical integration is impractical. Who's right?

Well, you'll be relieved to hear that there's no contradiction – providing it's clear that I'm talking about *exclusive* vertical integration. The failings I'm pointing out occur when in-house manufacturing have as their sole customer in-house stores and the in-house stores source only from the in-house manufacturing. In other words, I'm talking about a closed system. As noted, the only way to make this system as efficient as a free market economy is to make it as large as one.

There are two scenarios for maintaining peak efficiency when vertically integrating and both of them break that exclusivity. First is to run the factories at optimum levels, ensuring that their output is always less than the requirements of the stores, and then allow the stores to source the remainder of their stock externally. The external links handle the fluctuating store demand. The second way is to make sure that production capacity is always greater than the stores require and allow the factories to sell their excess production externally. The external links handle the excess supply.

These scenarios can be blended by allowing most of the in-house production to form most of the stores' range, while allowing both to have links outside the group.

The second scenario (with the external retail customers) in its pure form means making everything in-house, which even for a homogenous product group like clothing is a challenge. Zara & Inditex use the first scenario, allowing the stores to source outside the group. Inditex also run five other store brands which helps keep the factories fully utilised. Though I couldn't find a specific example, I would imagine they also supply stores they don't own from their factories.

In fact, from the Zara stores' point of view, the business is only about 50 per cent vertically integrated, but since this is in the product categories with the shortest lifecycles and most volatile demand, it has a profound effect.

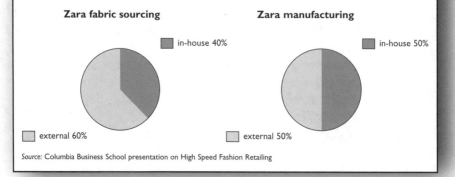

Zara fabric sourcing   **Zara manufacturing**

in-house 40%   in-house 50%

external 60%   external 50%

Source: Columbia Business School presentation on High Speed Fashion Retailing

The unpleasant drawbacks of vertical integration

With vertical integration, matching supply and demand will be a constant thorn in your side. It's not a piece of cake in a free market but it's much easier. Picture all retail businesses being little pockets of demand on one side of a divide and factories being pockets of supply on the other. It's clearly easier to balance supply and demand when you're free to make whichever connections across the divide you want. If instead you package up each retail outlet with a couple of factories the chances are they will spend a lot of time out of step with each other.

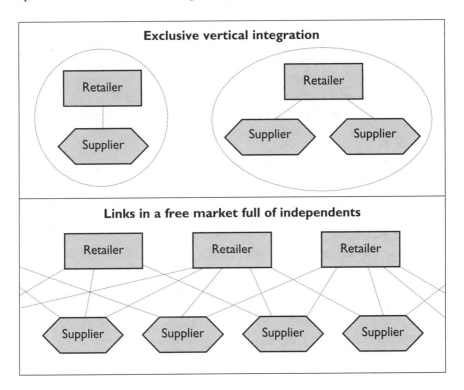

Stochastics[1] start to lend a hand if the retail + factory parcels are big enough. If you buy enough retail brands and factories, the fluctuations start to average out. You begin to have something similar to the free market

---

1   If you flick back through this book, you'll see I've done a pretty good job of not throwing around lots of 'ten dollar words' like 'stochastic'. I haven't used 'substantive' because it sounds better than 'substantial' and most of the time I've said 'use' rather than 'utilise'. I'm allowing myself this one as a reward for restraint elsewhere.

situation, except that it's all one company. If your retail and manufacturing consortium gets big enough, it might approach the efficiency of a network of independents. But all you've done is to approximate the efficiency of a free market by *buying* a free market. It's not a workable solution.

Short of taking over the whole high street, the problem remains. Either fluctuating retail demand keeps throwing the factory production levels out of whack, or constant levels of production leave the stores alternately under- and over-supplied. And woe betide the retail outlets that want to replan their range. That requires a major retooling exercise in the factories and possibly the construction of new facilities. You'd really have to think twice before your store listed a couple of dress watches in its accessories range if it meant building a watch factory.

Just as the manufacturing portfolio is put together to make good use of a factory, the retail product portfolio is designed to 'make good use of' the customer. Though they sound similar they require different approaches. The manufacturing product portfolio is designed around efficiency. The retail product portfolio, on the other hand, is about effectiveness. Which is another way of saying it's about the offer; it's outward facing.

A retailer has to accomplish a lot more with its range assortment than just including a few great products. The range must capture the customer's imagination, it must make shopping easy, it must be coherent and simple but offer novelty and excitement in the right places, it must build the brand, suit the customer's purse and fit with the overall offer.

So, manufacturing and retail ranges have very different compositions. The two industries also have very different concerns about volume. Manufacturers are trying to hit their cruising speed and stay there. Retailers have their foot hard on the gas trying to get out of second gear. Essentially the reason for this difference is that economies of scale kick in much sooner for a factory than a multiple retailer.

The goals of retail

What are economies of scale? They're nothing more than an expansion in which income tends to rise faster than costs. When you go from two hundred to four hundred stores, you don't need twice the head office staff. There isn't twice as much marketing to be done. The payroll or replenishment runs on the mainframe don't require twice the staff to administer them (although they may run for twice as long). For a multiple retailer, bigger should be more efficient.

There's also the fact that there's a larger product portfolio to support in retail than in manufacturing. Retail product ranges are, or at least should be, targeted to provide customer solutions, something we mentioned several chapters ago. A complete customer solution will require a certain amount of choice at each level – choice between product categories, product types and styles, brands, pack sizes and prices.

It's an open question whether you let your product area suggest the customer solutions you tackle, whether you let your customer solutions define your target customer or whether your target customer shapes your choice of product area. Wherever you start, you should end up with one or more solutions fully catered to. The goal is to target as many customers with as many solutions as possible using the minimum number of products (and other resources). The costs go up with the products and resources, the revenue with the solutions. With one or two exceptions,[1] the number and variety of products required for a compelling offer is beyond the scope of an efficient manufacturing product portfolio.

Once a retail offer is created, economies of scale come from replicating it in as many outlets as possible. By standardising every aspect of the stores, the central administrative burden of running an extra store is kept to a minimum. The hundredth store will contribute just as much revenue as the first did, but its contribution to central costs will be tiny. So every new store a multiple can open increases the company's net margin percentage.

Some thoughts on replicating the offer

We're going to carry on thinking through the logic of retail expansion even though it takes us away from suppliers for a while. The dilemmas and the goals we uncover will shed considerable light further down the line.

The 'replicate the offer' formula for profit growth works for any expansion where the stores are pretty similar to each other.[2] The easiest way to achieve that sort of expansion is just to spread geographically. The natural limit on that sort of expansion is the point at which the offer needs

---

1 Car showrooms are one example where a store can get away with only ten products all of the same brand and (at least in principle) made in the same factory. Even so, most customers would probably like it if they could compare the BMW to the Mercedes under the same roof. Showrooms featuring directly competing brands aren't all that common because cars are one of the few examples of manufacturers owning their own retail outlets. So cars are a rare example of vertical integration.

2 We've gone into considerable detail about why standardisation is important externally in building a brand and here we see that it's important internally in making a business efficient. I don't want to turn store staff into mindless zombies, but there are a lot of reasons to be cautious when 'empowering stores'.

to be altered for further expansion – when there are no more locations suitable for a 'cloned' offer. Then you have to adapt the offer to suit a new set of locations.

The cheapest alteration to the offer is to use a subset of the standard one. For many retailers approaching geographic 'saturation', a smaller format store, kiosk or a concession allows the expansion to continue a little further, populating nooks and crannies of the retail landscape unsuitable for the standard offer.

This logic can also be applied to expanding (rather than reducing) the offer, maybe moving to a larger, out-of-town format. Unfortunately, many of those attempts are sorry affairs in my experience. The extra product range required to fill the new extra-large store tends to be provided by some sort of behind-the-scenes bodge. The extra range also tends to contribute a lot of indirect costs as well as a lower margin than the core range.

The retailers who handle the outsize format best are those whose customers are always clamouring for a larger and larger product range anyway. So in a sense, the outsize format is the 'natural' size for their outlets and the original formats are the cut-down version.

Another way to geographically expand is to 'go international'. Again, in my personal experience, this is often done very badly. The principle of multiple retailing can be summed up in the following checklist:

- Assemble an attractive offer
- Standardise the store
- Push as many costs to the centre as possible
- Make the centre efficient
- Open lots of stores

Once the store estate crosses an international boundary it frequently needs to modify its offer. Language, legal or taste differences often result in alterations that require considerable extra work at the centre. Imagine for a moment the work involved in modifying an English-speaking business to use two languages for all store signage and marketing, all store instructions and employment contracts, all help desks and hotlines.

Relying on central services located the far side of a national border can be difficult in other ways too. Logistics efficiency may drop as stores are being supplied from warehouses in another country. Running stores effectively in a second country can often be done only by providing a second set of central services in the new country. This is hardly efficient, particularly if the second estate is small. The cost of the second centre needs to be spread over as many stores as possible.

Never do what one consultancy client of ours did (we weren't involved in this decision by the way) and open fifty stores abroad, but spread them over six different countries. None of these national operations were anywhere near 'critical mass' for an efficient operation. The overseas stores had very little support and consequently had an amateurish feel to them.[1] Unsurprisingly, this expansion proved a lot less profitable than their home market where the centre had over a thousand stores sharing its costs.

Global economies of scale

An efficient global business would separate sourcing from store ranging so that a product could be bought anywhere and sold anywhere. Sourcing includes finding new products and arranging buying terms. Ranging is deciding which stores to sell which products in. If you link the two, giving both tasks to the same person, large companies will start to encounter problems.

With a combined sourcing/ranging role, sourcing gets inefficient as the number of ranges grow. Ranges need to vary by brand, perhaps by store type and by country. Sourcing doesn't necessarily have to vary at all. But with a combined role, each range planner is doing their own sourcing. Sourcing complexity grows because range complexity grows. For reasons we will soon explore, one range planner will be reluctant to use another's sourcing, and so unnecessary duplication and inefficiency arises.

That combining of roles also means the net isn't cast as wide in the search for new products. That's a concern for any multi-brand retailer and a disaster for an international one. We'll have more to say about splitting ranging from sourcing when we think about barriers to collaboration.

At any rate, as far as stores are concerned, national boundaries often provide a barrier to expansion, or at least a hump the business has to get over. There is a whole level of economies of scale above the national level, but they require such size, capital investment and above all organisation to reach, that very few businesses operate in that league (see display panel).

---

1   You may or may not know it, but rules about which promotions or sales a store can run, and what signage it must have, vary considerably from country to country. Unbeknown to bosses, by following head-office instructions these stores were routinely running illegal promotions (that were perfectly proper in the country they were devised in).

An aside about post-merger integration

In fact a much more attainable synergy eludes many 'group' retail businesses. Dan and I both had experience of multi-brand retail groups that couldn't make the leap to full integration in the days before we became consultants.

My experience was with a group that comprised DIY, general merchandise, health & beauty and electrical brands, as well as a property company and a music wholesaler. Sadly, the obvious synergies were never pursued and the group is now coming apart into more homogeneous, product-centric chunks.

Each operating company (op-co) retained its own warehouses and trucks, its own head-office and its own IT systems. Properties were owned at the group level, but everything else was an exercise in duplication and needless variety among the operating companies. It's also true of the other multi-brand retail groups I've seen since.

The logic of acquisition was never carried through to internal integration. If you picture the supply chains of the individual businesses, they barely touched each other. Perhaps some supplier deals were negotiated at the group level, and a little bit of new product sourcing too. (Imagine a few of the threads of the supply chains twisted together right at their source.)

But the possibility exists to use the same logistics infrastructure right across a group. The supply chains of all the op-cos could be plaited together all the way from suppliers to stores. Next-day replenishment would become a practical possibility, because multiple nationwide brands usually means multiple stores in the same town. A truck may well be going to one store in the town every day – a quick top-up delivery to one of the others is easy to arrange.

You can work through the other possible synergies yourself. Each brand would have different requirements for head-office support, but that doesn't necessarily imply separate head-offices. Why couldn't that support come from a single pool of personnel sharing resources and office space?

In some companies integration was just never attempted, in others an alternate philosophy was pursued. There were two reasons for taking the alternate route, one regrettable the other rather ingenious. The regrettable reason has to do with commercial team structures, which we're coming on to. We'll deal with the ingenious reason first.

Investing in efficiency

One of the goals of profitable multiple retailing is to drive down the costs at the centre, but there is more than one way to do that.

In an internally-integrated multi-brand group, efficiency comes from building the enormous shared facilities required for the whole group and then meticulously devising the processes needed to support each of the multiple brands. Many of these innovations would require the dismantling of the traditional commercial team structure. Sourcing and supplier negotiation would be handled once at the group level, but store ranging would be kept separate so that it could vary brand by brand.

Creating this kind of integrated group requires investment and a completely new set of head-office processes. It also requires some uncomfortable organisational changes.

The ingenious direction that many retailers took also relied on investment and slick processes, but they found a less painful approach; they got someone else to do it.

Getting out of non-core areas

It seems obvious that integrating functions such as logistics across a number of retail brands can bring considerable gains in efficiency. The rationale makes most sense *within* a multi-brand group, but there is no rule that says all of those brands must belong to the same business. Of course few retailers will want to share their in-house capabilities with a competitor. And few competitors would want to risk their stock travelling second-class, while the owner's stores received priority.

The easiest solution is separate service providers with no retail brands of their own. A pure-play logistics company is free to offer services to several retailers on an equal basis and many of the same economies of scale still apply.

The offer of efficient, and therefore cheap, logistics provides the 'pull' to lure retailers away from maintaining capabilities in-house. There is also a 'push' that comes from retailers wanting to rid themselves of 'non-core' investments.

I mentioned that investment and process design work are required in order to achieve any sort of efficient operation. Increased efficiency comes from getting the same level of effectiveness at a lower cost. Businesses will have their highest efficiencies in core areas, the areas where they have the greatest expertise. Otherwise, they need to reevaluate the business they're in. It naturally follows that a business will want to deploy the bulk of its capital in those core areas, where it is confident it can generate the highest return. That means trying to avoid investment in non-core areas. Out-sourcing functions like logistics is a way of achieving that.

Specialist service providers

For a specialist logistics provider, buying warehouses makes more sense than renting them, and purpose-building them is even better. Capital requirements go up when you own your own fixed assets, but running costs go down as you cease to pay rents and leases.

The question of whether, overall, you come out ahead will depend on how skilfully you deploy those assets. If you lease, you pay someone else's operating margins, if you buy, you pay your own. If you're expert in what you're doing, your margins will be narrower, so you're better off investing.

A company with specialist logistics knowledge should be able to get more logistics capability out of cash invested in fixed assets than cash spent on paying someone else to do the work.

As pure-play logistics providers continually improve the state of the art, many retailers find their in-house capabilities falling behind. The wider the gap gets, the more it makes sense for retailers to abandon the struggle and out-source. Not all retailers give up the fight, but for many there doesn't seem to be a compelling reason to compete. The same logic applies to various other support roles, like payroll, advertising, security, maintenance and so on.

So, many large retailers have tended to look for efficiency externally, rather than creating it themselves. Granted, that only applies to non-core areas, but there can be as many of those as you want there to be.

I'm not a big fan of out-sourcing as it's generally approached now. It's my feeling that service levels nearly always suffer, but in terms of return-on-investment it does offer some benefits. Out-sourcing allows retailers to reclaim capital from non-core functions and put it to work in areas where they could get a better return on it – say by opening new stores.

We asked some time back why retailers hardly ever vertically integrate. We can see that the answer to that question is in the two ways in which retailers have chased economies of scale. Firstly, they have been looking to replicate their offer in as many markets as possible, trying to achieve saturation in each. Secondly, they have been narrowing the scope of their in-house operations in order to focus on core activities.

The second one of those, eliminating non-core activities, is clearly at odds with expanding into manufacturing. The first, replicating the offer, is about having a lot of shops sharing an efficient centre. If it implies any sort of integration, it's horizontal across regions and brands, not vertical.

Hopefully we can now see how the pursuit of their respective synergies has pulled the retail and manufacturing sectors farther apart. Many retailers have withdrawn from the activities that lie closest to the supplier, such as logistics. Manufacturing, in turn has clustered tightly round its own set of production-based synergies.

Vertical competitors

How has this left relations between the two sectors? Let's think of the profitability of an individual thread in the supply chain. Under normal circumstances, selling the product to an end customer generates the revenue for the whole thread. Thereafter, it is just a question of how that revenue is distributed along the thread to each of the parties involved. What fraction does the retailer keep, how much gets paid to the supplier?

We've already encountered zero-sum scenarios and here's a good example of one. The selling price of a product can be shared out between retailer, distributor, shipping agent and manufacturer in any number of ways, but if someone wants more, someone else has to have less. For a given selling price, total income per unit is fixed and the impact of any redistribution among the parties sums to zero – hence the name.

With this in mind, supplier and retailer become 'vertical competitors', jostling for a share of the product's profit margin. After all, no shift in the *status quo* can benefit everyone; someone always loses out. It seems obvious that the relationship will become adversarial.

In many ways, the relationship between supplier and retailer is like a tug of war. Both parties are trying to drag as much margin over to their side as possible. Unfortunately for the manufacturing sector the retailers are often bigger. We've already seen how multiple retailers are intent on expanding their business in the search for profitability. Leaving aside the giants like Procter & Gamble, the High Street is dominated by retailers who have achieved nationwide expansion. They will be much larger than the majority of their suppliers. This leads to rather an uneven tug of war, in a lot of cases, with margin gradually being dragged out of the supplier's hands.

Our initial observation was that manufacture and retail are two parts of a single process and harmony between the two is an obvious goal of a healthy supply chain. We've also seen why achieving that harmony with a single integrated business is not practical. Now we see that with a fragmented supply chain the various parties are locked in competition with each other. Far from a state of harmony, the retailer and supplier are naturally at odds.

The rise of the retro

When we introduced the ideas of co-operation and competition, we stressed that it was a good thing if competing parties had different goals because it meant there might be room for compromise. Are suppliers and retailers after exactly the same thing? Are they both solely focused on a larger share of the selling price?

> ### A young person's guide to buying terms
> On the off-chance a non-retailer is reading this (having fun?) here's what those financial terms mean. What you pay for a unit of a product is your cost price and what you sell it for is your selling or retail price. Cost of goods sold is the total cost of acquiring the goods in a condition ready for sale. Usually that's pretty much the same thing as the cost price. You take the sales (minus VAT) and knock off the cost of goods sold (COGS) and you're left with your unit gross margin. You multiply that by the number of units sold at that price to get what is normally just termed gross margin, or cash margin. The ratio of the gross margin to the sales (minus VAT) is the gross margin per cent.

Well, there is a little room for manoeuvre. We said that manufacturers need to make optimum use of their assets and workforce and that means matching supply to demand. One way to do that is to artificially adjust demand so that the factory can keep operating at its most efficient level.

Suppliers adjust demand by offering the retailer incentives to change their ordering patterns. Effectively they run promotions aimed at the retailer – although they don't present them in those terms.

A retailer-targeted promotion might work like this. By prior agreement, the retailer might lower the selling price of a product by 10 per cent. At the end of the promotion, the retailer totals up how many products were sold and asks the supplier to pay the missing 10 per cent of the revenue. The supplier reimburses the retailer retrospectively[1] (hence the name retro) for the cost of running the promotion.

Ostensibly it's a customer promotion, but from the supplier's point of view it's a retailer promotion. The retailer orders more at a time that's convenient to the supplier.

Another incentive involves offering the retailer a volume discount if they order more than a certain quantity of product in a year. The point at which the discount is triggered is set a little above what the retailer is expected to buy. If the supplier thinks the retailer will buy a million units in a year, they might offer a discount for buying 1.1 million.

To understand the appeal of an offer like that you need to appreciate the panic that occurs in some retail businesses close to year-end. The board may be desperate to reach, and ideally exceed their profit targets, and a lot of short-term decisions might be made to help that happen. Travel budgets could be frozen, ordering delayed, inventory run down, in an effort to buff the figures for the annual report.

Amidst all this panic and pressure, a buyer might notice that they are within striking distance of a volume discount. They just need one more large order to trigger a lower cost price for the year. Because most of the orders have been paid for, the supplier will give the discount as a rebate. The buyer will receive a sizeable cheque that doesn't appear in any existing financial projection, which means that cheque represents pure profit. Imagine being able to tell your director that you've single-handedly added an unexpected million to the bottom line in the last couple of weeks of the year.

The fact that our hypothetical buyer might go badly overstocked to get the cheque is something for him to worry about next quarter. After all, he can always run a promotion to help clear the stock down to normal levels; it just means a little margin erosion.[2] Alternatively, he can let the stock levels sell through on their own by holding off on placing orders for a while. But if he does that, there's no way he can reach the volume required to trigger a rebate next year. And the bad news is that his boss will probably be expecting that cheque next time around.

---

1   If any of this is unknown to you, you may wonder why the supplier doesn't just drop the cost price if he wants the retailer to buy more. The answer is that the retailer might then place an order for three years' worth of product. The supplier wants the retailer to return to paying full price once the promotion is over.

2   Congratulations if you spotted straightaway that the buyer has just shunted some of next year's profit into this year.

This all makes the supplier sound like a Machiavellian genius. It's almost as though they've manipulated the retailer without them knowing it. But retailers pretty quickly get addicted to retros and triggers and they start demanding more.[1] And if they don't get it, they are usually in a position to get tough.

Pressure on margin

Let's look a little more at the position the buyer is in. In most retail businesses there's enormous pressure on margin, and the buyer is responsible for it. One glance at a Profit & Loss account and you can see where the problem comes from. You start out at the top of the report with all that sales revenue and then work your way down until you get to the profit line. Hopefully there's at least a little loose change left by that point.

> ### I've seen some ugly P&Ls in my time
>
> Dan and I spent a lot of time talking to a retail business with sales of nearly €2 billion per year, but which was making less than €10 million pre-tax profit. For every euro they received, more than 99.5 cents went on paying bills. You have to wonder why the owners didn't put their capital in a building society. The business had been growing by acquisition, not organic growth, for years and they'd neglected to uncover any economies of scale in their expansion. They didn't standardise the offer; instead each business they bought added to the capabilities they felt they had to support. At the same time, they devolved as much work as possible to the stores, which further undermined the principle of an efficient centralised business.
>
> It's now under new management.
>
> It was my experiences with that business that made the following cynical statement of the principal/agent problem catch my eye: 'Owners are happiest with a profitable business whereas directors just want a big business.'

It goes without saying that everyone is either trying to make that revenue line bigger, or one of those cost lines smaller. Unlike everyone else, commercial teams have most of the responsibility for the revenue line as well as sole control of the largest cost deducted from it: the cost of goods sold. They're always in the spotlight.

---

1   From time to time Dan and I try to persuade retailers to cut down on the amount of supplier-funding they rely on. The response is very like what happens when you try to pry a juicy bone away from an Alsatian. I'm hoping it's less dangerous in print than in person.

Just consider the impact of gross margin per centage for a moment. Imagine a business with an average of 35 per cent gross margin, which is taking €1 bn per year. Let's imagine their net-margin is 3 per cent, which means €25 m profit (using UK VAT levels).

If there's some way that a retailer could improve their gross margin percentage from 35 per cent to 35.5 per cent their pre-tax profit will jump to €30 m – an increase of 17 per cent. (I've assumed they hold the sales price constant, so volumes are unaffected).

If you're anything like me, you'll have forgotten all of those numbers already. The point is, half a per cent on the gross margin percentage would supply all the operating profit growth the shareholders could want.

Consider too what's involved in achieving 17 per cent net profit growth by any other means. If you get it from reduced internal costs or boosted sales it's likely to involve masses of hard work, significant investment and a lot of planning – perhaps a major store opening programme or a company-wide efficiency drive. Whereas, it's just possible a company could achieve the same thing by getting all of its suppliers in a room and telling them that anyone who couldn't give them 0.75 per cent[1] off the cost price will never get another order from them. It's an afternoon's work and it costs nothing.

Remember how we said that there are plenty of national retailers who are much larger than the majority of their suppliers? That means many retailers may have suppliers who have no other customers; a retailer might buy their whole annual output and then go shopping for more. It's certainly not uncommon for a single national retailer to account for 50 per cent of a supplier's sales. Frequently, a supplier needs a major retailer a great deal more than a major retailer needs a particular supplier.

Depending on the departments and the companies you've worked in, you may wonder whether a retailer would threaten their suppliers like that. But I can tell you, that sort of thing happens.

The retailer doesn't need to think of it as coercion, 'do this or you're out'. They might imagine themselves giving the following speech, "We are under pressure to hit a very tough profit figure. We can only achieve it if we find some very attractive buying deals. We would rather not look elsewhere; we would rather leave the business with you. Can you help us?" But once the suppliers have worked it through in their minds they know it means, 'Do this or you're out'.

---

1 Just in case the numbers aren't obvious – if the cost price makes up two-thirds of the selling price (minus VAT), a cost price reduction of x per cent only gives you $2/3x$ per cent margin improvement. So to get 0.5 per cent margin improvement you need 0.75 per cent cost reduction. Yawn.

When this occurs, it's clearly a pretty adversarial situation. Would you be comfortable with it[1] as a negotiating tactic? Maybe there's nothing wrong with it because it's business, not personal, and there are no laws or professional guidelines to suggest you shouldn't exploit an advantage when you see one. Personally, I think it's a bit aggressive, but then no-one in their right mind would put a pushover like me in charge of a tough negotiation. So we'll leave aside whether it constitutes 'playing nice with the other kids' or not and simply enquire into its business merits.

However, before we condemn the aggressive approach, we should check we've got some practical alternatives. Why would commercial teams opt to use a 'gun to the head' negotiating tactic? One important reason is that there might be a gun to their head too.

We're going to get into some detail now about commercial teams. In particular we're going to have a great deal to say about the role of the buyer, as it stands in FMCG retailing, as well as the implications of that role.

If you're not a retailer or are only interested in the big picture, you may want to skip the next major section. Make your way to the next big heading, which is called 'Collaborative commerce assembly point'. Immediately before it starts you'll find the bullet point summary of what you've skipped.

On the other hand, if you're a career retailer, I'm fairly confident you'll find the next section fascinating.

It will be uncomfortable reading if you think I'm referring to your business, so it might be wise just to take it in before you consider whether it describes your organisation or not.

All I'll say on that score is that Dan and I consider the problems described here to be very widespread.

---

1   As Barry Gibbons says, don't do anything in business that you wouldn't be comfortable telling your Mother about. If you haven't read, *If You Want to Make God Really Laugh Show Him Your Business Plan* you should. It sets the standard for management books you laugh out loud while reading.

The flawed buying role

Buyers under pressure

Now, unless your experience has been very different from mine, you'll agree that for many buyers their annual sales targets must seem like cruel and unusual punishment. Their reward for having a good year is an even higher target next year. The buyer who brought in that big cheque two weeks from year-end was a hero, but if he couldn't do it again next year he wouldn't be quite so popular.

Sales planning is one of those processes that doesn't sound right when you explain it. You start with a top-level figure for how much you want to make next year and then you begin sharing that target out between the various product categories. At the same time you start at the bottom working out which products you're going to sell and how much you can grow sales and margin for each of them. Then you begin totalling up. The top-down allocation of targets meets the bottom-up[1] aggregation (somehow) and a sales plan is born.

Top-down targets come from the board, bottom-up projections from the commercial teams. What happens if the guys at the top want more than the guys at the bottom think they can deliver? Put another way, if employee and director disagree, who wins? I tend to put my money on the guy with the parking space nearest the front door.

And we mustn't forget that these are people we're talking about, so there's a psychological element to consider when handing out targets. Setting 'motivational targets' or 'stretch budgets' can encourage employees to achieve more than they thought they could. This sort of thing is standard practice amongst sales forces[2]. But to many of us, being told to achieve 10 per cent more than we consider humanly possible

---

1 A famous industry analysis company recently undermined one of their rather expensive reports on retail by using the term 'bottoms-up', rather than 'bottom-up', planning. Although I could be wrong and there really is an approach known as 'bottoms-up planning'; perhaps it's where you submit the sales figure you think you can achieve and then pour yourself a stiff whisky.

2 Dan knows of a sales manager who finds an excuse to fire someone in the first week whenever he takes over a new team. Apparently, it saves a lot of time later when people wonder if he's serious about the targets he's set.

doesn't sound motivational at all.[1] Still, that's the way these things are often done and buyers are rarely of a retiring disposition. In fact, in certain business the enormous pressure has forced buyers to behave in ways that don't necessarily benefit the company as a whole.

Before we say any more, I want to remind you that I'm describing the worst case here. I've had personal experience of each one of these questionable practices, but I've also encountered businesses guilty of none of them. I'm criticising the behaviour I'm describing here, not the people or the companies.

The buying role itself

In many garment retailers, there is a two-person team I'll refer to as buyer and merchandiser (although the names sometimes vary). The former talks to suppliers and dreams up products, the latter thinks about stores and stock, and tries to make sure the numbers add up. I'm sure it has its disadvantages, but it is a far more sensible arrangement compared with the flawed approach adopted by many FMCG retailers.

As central stock replenishment software has automated many of the traditional stock management tasks, some retailers have allowed the merchandiser role to wither away and have piled responsibility for everything on to the buyers. This is true of many general merchandise retailers and can occur in any product area with short lead times and reasonably predictable demand – because those are the areas most amenable to automated replenishment.

Unfortunately, category management has frequently made things worse – although its heart is in the right place. In principle it involves breaking down the old departmental structure and creating teams based around product categories. A category team has its own buyer(s), logistics people, merchandisers and so on. What actually happens in a lot of businesses is that the buyers control the teams and everyone else becomes their support staff.

I'm pleased if you think I've got this dead wrong because it suggest that your experience of category teams is more egalitarian than mine. The majority of my personal experience suggests that category management means 'buyer in charge'.

---

1   In the world of sports 'stretch budgets' are a way of life. I believe I've mentioned that the phrase "Get out there and give me a hundred and ten per cent" is not considered to be a humorous remark or even a cue to discuss the meaning of the expression 'contradiction in terms'.

Why does that matter? Should we be worried? Well, let's list the tasks an FMCG buyer might be expected to perform. Many will find new products, negotiate deals, plan promotions and set prices, they'll usually have the last word on visual merchandising, they'll plan store product-ranges and they usually have a lot of influence over which stores those ranges go into.

With that sort of workload they share the typical retail operator's need to chase a hundred little details every day. What with all the range and sales planning they do, they have to be strongly analytical and numerate. In order to drive new product development and visual merchandising they need to be creative and have some design flair. Because a large part of the company's profits depend on negotiating good buying deals they need to be expert negotiators. They must also co-ordinate the activities of a lot of other people, so they have to be good people managers. They also have to be highly commercial in their thinking, but also in touch with what the average customer wants. Add all that up and you've got a hell of a job description.

All in all, I believe that in many businesses it's an unreasonable list of skills and an impossible role. It's almost not realistic to expect anyone to do it all well, and there are even some aspects of the job that conflict with others.

For instance, it doesn't seem right to expect a professional negotiator to be a self-effacing team player. Some buyers manage it, but it's a tightrope walk. If you hire someone because they're a genius at getting their own way with suppliers, can you blame them when they tend to dominate the staff around them? It's no wonder buyers often take over category teams – they're handpicked to have that sort of personality.

In theory, buyers are all on the same side, but the role, the personality type and the system of rewards and incentives all encourage competition. The structure of management reports pits the buyers against one another and the traditional Monday trading meeting is where some companies allow the losers to be mauled in front of their colleagues.

Many companies also have a serious problem with badly chosen KPIs[1] for their buyers. Buyers are often incentivised on revenue and direct selling costs, for example gross margin, sales, GM percentage or something similar. But buyers always have influence over a lot of other costs that aren't factored into their KPIs.

---

1   Key Performance Indicators (KPIs). They are whatever you measure to tell you how things are going. Your KPI could be as simple as sales or could be some complex calculation. KPIs are often used as the basis for employee bonuses.

Naturally, the more pressure buyers are put under to perform, the more they draw on the resources around them to achieve better results. In some companies that means driving up logistics, inventory, store and finance costs – which buyers are not usually measured on – in order to improve the things they are measured on.

Again, let me be clear. I'm not saying that buyers maliciously undermine the profitability of the business. I'm saying that the harder they are pushed, the more resources they marshal in pursuit of top line sales. It is not part of the buyer's job to work out the budgetary impact on other departments. But the effect is always to improve the buyers measured profitability while driving up costs for other departments.

In certain companies, buyers will push up the number of products in their range beyond a level that is profitable for the business as a whole.

These extra products don't have to be highly profitable, because it doesn't cost the buyers anything to stock them. Obviously it costs the business money to keep them on the shelf and in the warehouse, but the buyer is not penalised if a product costs more than it makes. Whatever money a product generates is added to the buyer's total. The more products a buyer lists, the higher the buyer's total margin, but meanwhile the net margin might actually be falling.

Buyers in some companies may also fail to clear leftover stock when they replace old products with new. A constant trickle of new products is much more costly in terms of hours store staff spend remerchandising, but it gets the new products earning revenue as quickly as possible. Some companies leave stores to figure out what to do with the old lines.

Other companies may place no restriction on buyers buying early and in bulk to get a good price. Storage and capital[1] costs might negate the benefit to the business, but they are not factored into the buyer's margin.

There are many more examples. Many buyers get no reward if they keep these knock-on costs low, but they are penalised if they don't do everything in their power to drive their own KPIs up.

It's like being given someone else's credit card at the same time you find out you're overdrawn at the bank.

And even if knock-on costs were monitored there would still be one source of revenue buyers wouldn't be penalised for using: suppliers. Surely no one would criticise a buyer for boosting his margin by pushing

---

1   In theory an Open To Buy discipline would limit this sort of thing, but firstly it only manages working capital requirements not return on capital employed and secondly a lot of FMCG businesses have let OTB fall by the wayside. For replenished products with stable demand OTB isn't necessarily a good idea, but that means it should be replaced with something better not just abandoned.

costs out of the business and onto the supplier. Alas, that's just what I'm about to complain about.

The tyranny of artificial targets

Let's consider how a hypothetical buyer might use suppliers to get him out of a fix. It's not that uncommon for companies to get to the half-year mark and realise they're in danger of missing their profit target. One 'operational lever' they can pull to get back on course is to 're-visit' some of their sales targets. On many occasions I have talked to buyers who have had their sales or profit targets unexpectedly revised upwards halfway through the year. In order to respond to these new targets, buyers often have to reopen negotiations with suppliers which all concerned thought were concluded.

At the beginning of the year, buyers will push their suppliers hard for concessions. Once they are satisfied that they have got the best deals possible they can let the suppliers off the hook, patch up relations with them and get the year underway. Coming back six months later and demanding more looks a lot like negotiating in bad faith. In order to give these late demands teeth, the buyer has to threaten all the things they threatened at the beginning of the year. Whenever I've seen this situation occur, it has the effect of educating everyone involved about what to expect in future.

The first effect is that suppliers realise however much pressure a retailer puts them under, they will probably need to hold something back for later. A supplier who truly did offer their best price at the beginning of the year would be in big trouble if the pressure were reapplied two quarters later – they would have nothing to offer.

The second thing that will happen is that the buyers involved realise they need to hold something back as well. If they pass along every concession as they negotiate it then they might come unstuck mid-year if the bar were raised. They start to think of ways to keep a little something in reserve.

Again, it's important to be clear. I'm not accusing buyers of anything illegal (there are plenty of ways to achieve these things without going that far). I'm just saying that if a business makes impossible demands on their buyers then a smart buyer will find a way to survive.

In the businesses I'm talking about, the finance department frequently grumbled that they were not being fully briefed on some of the big money deals the buyers were doing. They commonly attributed this to a cavalier attitude on the parts of the buyers. In fact, the buyers were often being disingenuous. They knew if they documented everything they had planned it would get added into their targets and then three months down the line the targets might go up.

These companies' IT departments also tended to be bemused by the buyers' failure to fully use the systems provided. They imagined the buyers doing all their deals on napkins and the backs of cigarette packets. The IT people assumed that more flexible or intuitive software was required to encourage reluctant buyers to rely more on systems. They were unaware that it was sometimes in the interests of buyers to circumvent the systems, so the functionality of the systems was largely irrelevant.

Punishing compliance

Have you come across businesses like this and practices like these? They tend not to be discussed openly. There's a lot of money at stake. Even if companies acknowledge that they have taken a wrong turn with their supplier relations, they need to have an alternative in place. Merely blowing the whistle on short-sighted behaviour is only half a solution. Taking the pressure off suppliers once it has been applied will only lower the retailer's margins. They need an alternative method of achieving profit growth.

Before we look at the remedy, let's understand the problem a little better. Let's look at the extremes some commercial teams are going to.

How does a buyer go about keeping some margin in reserve? What are the *sotto voce* buying deals I'm talking about? Well, there are two requirements for concealing the true picture from prying eyes. First is to get as much money flowing in both directions as possible between retailer and supplier. That's so that no-one outside the commercial team can make sense of the situation. Second is to make as many deals as possible contingent upon something that few people, except the buyer, have control over or understanding of. For instance, a volume rebate can appear a very remote possibility to everyone else in the business until the buyer places an unexpectedly large order.

Wherever you find this situation, you tend to find that the suppliers have played their part in creating it by agreeing to or even suggesting all these roundabout payments. Suppliers are forced to take part in some very uncomfortable negotiating, so understandably they make use of the props and ploys of hard bargaining to help them protect their position.

Real world example – short-term margin madness

In the olden days, some dishonest managers misreported company accounts in order to hide their own embezzling. Today it seems that the management of more and more firms are bending or outright breaking the rules of accounting to hide nothing more sinister than lacklustre trading performance.

For any who doubt that professional managers from respected firms would indulge in any of the activities described in this chapter, here is an illustrative catalogue of shenanigans.

Late in 2001, an ailing Kmart had reached its borrowing limits and was struggling to raise cash. They told their suppliers that a fault in their accounts payable system meant they were unable to issue any payments. Many suppliers were not convinced that the company, with sales of $36 bn per year, really had a systems problem. Several suppliers have chosen to sue them. Since then the company has restated its earnings position downwards to include several hundred million dollars of losses which surfaced when the retailer altered the way it chose to recognise certain supplier volume rebates. Clearly the previous method was rather over-optimistic.

Worldcom, second largest long-distance phone carrier in the US, misreported nearly $4 bn of expenses in 2001/2002. The company bypassed its auditors and recorded certain expenses as investments in the accounts. This had the effect of greatly improving their apparent cashflow and allowed them to show a profit instead of a loss for 2001.

The UK's Kwikfit vehicle repair chain boosted their apparent profits by failing to accrue for stock in the usual manner. They chose not to record money owed to suppliers in their accounts, despite having taken delivery of the associated goods. The business had been doing badly and its parent company were hoping to sell it soon. The discovery of accounting irregularities has helped depress the valuation to less than a third of its value three years ago.

UK electrical retailer Dixons has upset its shareholders in the way it has chosen to report its profits. Whilst the group have done nothing improper, the profit figure contains provisions and disposals of developed property. If these non-trading effects are removed, profits are down on the year instead of showing the healthy growth that a first glance would indicate.

Rite Aid, the US drugstore chain have been investigated by the SEC for accounting fraud. Four executives were indicted for conspiracy and multiple fraud; they were inflating reported earnings.

The previous chairman, finance director and buying director of UK DIY firm Wickes have all been charged with fraud. Prosecutors allege that they caused the business to operate two separate sets of documents for supplier negotiations: one set of letters reflected the real deals agreed with suppliers, a different set were shown to the auditors. Allegedly, the real deals aimed to push costs into later years in order to inflate profits by around £22 m in the short term. Five executives of the business were charged.

Suppliers under extreme pressure often prefer to have half a dozen pots of money in play rather than one. Negotiating is all about having room for compromise and manoeuvre, having options. Negotiations need not always centre on cost price reductions, when there are listing fees[1] and promotional support to discuss. Suppliers might pay for new fixtures, for store trials of new merchandising layouts or for customer research. They may be offered the chance to have their products displayed in prime space during promotions in exchange for a fee. You name it, a company somewhere has asked a supplier to pay for it.

In the bad old days, suppliers would also indulge in a certain amount of hospitality, they'd send the odd Christmas gift or occasionally make goodwill gestures, most of which modern sensibilities would instantly label as bribes. I've rarely come across any sign of these old practices, so I suspect it is well under control in most businesses. And the odd expenses-paid trip to see the rugby that I have noticed doesn't seem to buy much protection in return.

Buyers' instincts

Another side effect of the buyer's need to keep various deals 'up his sleeve' is that he is encouraged to construct a reputation based on instinct or gut feel.

The more the buyer-under-pressure agrees to fully document and formally analyse deals, the less likely he is to be able to squirrel away any emergency reserves. That means he'll be more likely to be caught out if the targets go up.

The more emphasis that's placed on having 'a feel' for commercial decisions, the easier it is to avoid filling in too much revealing paperwork. Detailed projections or analyses are a bit of a liability if they reveal everything. Buyers who have their reserves well hidden and who keep all their best ideas in their heads will be much better placed to pull off a miracle when the third quarter profits panic starts.

Because it helps in pulling off these miracles, the buyer who claims to use gut feel may well prove a lot more successful than his colleagues' plodding analytical approach. The more mystery the buyer surrounds their decision-making with – what Dan calls 'buyer's fog' – the better their survival chances. Eventually people start believing in it.

---

1   In a company keen to stamp out listing fees, one buyer told me they had instead to be classified as 'Supplier contributions – other'. The principle endured even though the name was outlawed.

Companies who put their buyers under these sorts of pressures create an approach I can only describe as sneaky. Clearly, this can't be right.

Personally, I think the emphasis many companies place on instinct is a dangerous thing. Granted, there may be instinctive decisions which pay off, that cautious analysis would have nipped in the bud. But that's no different from saying if you gamble you might win. That doesn't make gambling a good way to run a business. If it's based on 'instinct' not logic, it's a gamble.

In the companies I was describing, what looks like gambling is often only a smokescreen for logical, but clandestine, manoeuvring. But it still contributes to a culture of 'gut feel', something which is ripe for abuse. After all who can challenge any decision when it's based on a hunch?

I'm often amazed at the fact that senior managers in these businesses are comfortable with the idea of instinct. They accept that it is guiding important decisions in their business. Ask those same people to rely on astrology or employ psychics and they would rightly be dismissive, but an exception is made for gut feel.

Many businesses also face the problem of 'corporate amnesia'. Too much knowledge about how a business is run resides in the heads of a few key people – people who sometimes move on. As we will see in the next chapter, businesses should be evolving their processes continually and the first step towards that evolution is to get processes out in the open where we can see what they look like.

Even if commercial instinct[1] did exist, it undermines the business to employ it. If decision-making is made on a basis that can't be documented or explained, how can it be taught to others or refined? I'm not rubbishing the value of experience, I'm saying if experience has taught you lessons then *explain* them to others.

Those who do emphasise instinct are probably also aware that it's a useful survival tactic. It turns good decision-making into a magic trick. If magicians explained, "And as I pretend to reach into the top hat, I bring the rabbit up from under the table where it's been all along", people would soon lose interest in conjuring. Emphasising your unique and special abilities is both good showmanship and a good way of making sure you're not replaced on a whim. If people are wandering around saying, "How *does* he do it?" they're not about to give someone else your job.

---

1 Our most recent instincts developed on the plains of East Africa when we lived as hunter-gatherers. It's difficult to imagine how anything we evolved under those conditions could help us spot next Christmas's must-have soft toy.

New commercial team structure

Assuming all of these commercial teams out there are suffering all these problems and using all these unhealthy tactics, what can be done about the situation?

Chasing customers is hard, pressuring suppliers is easy and using resources from other departments is free. It's fairly obvious what that adds up to. Retailers who over-emphasise short-term margin gains need to change and the buying role needs to change too.

Short-term margin pressure keeps the focus on suppliers. They represent a large pool of funds, and unlike customers, companies can tell them what to do. Unfortunately, the current state of many companies' supplier relations is not much of a basis for sustainable improvements. So long as the situation is zero-sum, there's only so much to go round.

Is there a better way of working with suppliers, a more sustainable and profitable way?

That will be the focus of the remainder of the chapter. Let's take it on faith for a moment that there is a way and consider what could then be done about fixing up the commercial team structure.

It's been my belief for some time now that decisions about what stores sell have to be separated from the business of haggling with suppliers. The easiest way to do that is to give the tasks to different people.

In the chapter on finance, we will talk about job roles and the KPIs that go with them. To anticipate that discussion, one measure of a well-designed role is that it requires a sensible blend of personality traits. The tough negotiator needs to be kept separate from more team-oriented aspects of the role.

In the world of clothing retail, a buyer and a merchandiser (or what some companies call a 'selector') form a team and split responsibilities between them. This might be a sensible structure for general merchandise too (with a couple of enhancements). The buyer would find promising new products; the selector would decide which stores, if any, should stock them. The buyer would then secure the best deals.

The selector should be performance-assessed using a KPI that takes into account resources used, as well as margin. A return on space calculation, for instance, would be a good start. It makes hoarding space and proliferating SKU count unrewarding.

In a couple of companies, Dan and I have also recommended that the commercial teams be charged for the costs they create elsewhere in the business. These charges needn't be overly complex to administer or restrictive in their effects.

The commercial teams can still follow their entrepreneurial muse, but if they want to use more store labour, fill up more of the warehouse, or spend more money than they put in their original plan they are charged for it. The internal charges reflect the real cost to the business of those changes. If a spur of the moment deal still looks good to the commercial team when the relevant charges are deducted from the margin, then they'd go ahead.

The charges could be set each year, so that the commercial teams would merely consult a list of tariffs when considering a deal. The supporting departments would be bonused partly on their ability to keep their charges as small as possible.

In this way, commercial teams could be reasonably sure that a good deal for them was a good deal for the whole company. And since they don't have to ask permission, their freedom to act is not being compromised.

The combination of these two notions allows the commercial team to be entrepreneurial, but counts the true cost of its decisions, while leaving the rest of the business better able to support them.

Scalable commercial teams

When we talked about expansion I mentioned that splitting the buying role is a prerequisite for integration of a multi-brand retail group or efficient global sourcing. That's because the way the buying role is structured at the moment doesn't lend itself to working with products sourced by someone else under terms negotiated by someone else. Actually, 'doesn't lend itself to' is an understatement.

To use an example, one of the large UK retail groups[1] set up an office in Hong Kong to source products cheaply in the Far East. For the venture to really work, buyers in the various op-cos would have to let the Hong Kong office find and negotiate deals for certain lines. I've already described how margin pressure in some companies forces buyers to keep certain deals secret. Very few retailers operate commercial teams where there is so little pressure on the buyers that they can afford to let someone else manage their deals. The group I'm referring to was no exception.

---

1 I haven't used their name because I don't want to give the impression that they're any worse than most retailers. In many ways they are better than most, but they still suffer from some of the problems we've been talking about.

Similarly, another group noticed that the same products were being bought independently by several op-cos. It made more sense to negotiate a single deal for the whole group. The buyer from each op-co thought it was a great idea – provided they were the one to negotiate the group deal – otherwise they weren't so interested.

Given the amount of behind-the-scenes finessing buyers have to do, there's no way most of them can afford to share control. It won't help them in their job – though it might help the business – and it's not a good fit to the typical buying personality. If somehow, you've managed to recruit a buyer who has mastered the whole, impossibly long list of skills required for the role, can you really expect them to be good at relinquishing control too? At some stage we have to stop patching up problems by adding to the endless list of required skills and accept that the role needs a major overhaul.

If the person assembling a store range also arranges their own sourcing, the structure doesn't scale up very well to large organisations. Ranges need to vary by retail brand, perhaps by store type and maybe by region. More ranges require more range planners. If every range planner independently sources all his own products, duplication and inefficiency arise. But in many multi-brand retail groups that's pretty much the situation.

By separating sourcing from range planning, sourcing can be done at the global level, once; range planning can be done at the brand/region/store type level, as appropriate. Sourcing is unified and consolidated up to the group level, and range planning is diversified and devolved down as far as it needs to go. But if the person who negotiates the deal on a product also plans the ranges it appears in, either ranging or sourcing will be constrained – frequently both.

With a split role, when you add a new store type, you add range planners (selectors) but you keep sourcing as it is. If you open a Far East sourcing office, you add buyers, but no new selectors are required. Each task can be matched to current circumstances – no awkward compromise is required.

If the multi-brand retailers had that split structure, they could also begin to share their support functions across brands. A single, group-wide logistics infrastructure makes a lot more sense when you've got a single group-wide source of supply for each product.

The current buying role is so vital to modern retail that abolishing it seems unthinkable to many. But that's exactly why it has to go. Half the decisions in the business are made by an overworked, overstretched team. And the way the role is currently structured means there can actually be a conflict between keeping your job as a buyer and doing what's best for the business.

I'm sure you'll agree, that's enough about the buying role. Suffice it to say, the current structure can work well for a small business, but it doesn't scale up – and multiple retailing is all about scaling up.

Let's summarise the points about commercial team structure so that we can move on and look for an alternative.

- Margin pressure and rising targets force buyers to look for quick fixes.
- Pressuring suppliers for funds is the only option for a quick and easy margin fix.
- Adversarial negotiating encourages the supplier to offer rebates and deals.
- These solutions focus attention away from the customer and onto supplier deals.
- Concessions and rebates are short-termist and addictive.
- Current supplier relations don't offer a path to sustainable profit growth.

Collaborative commerce assembly point

Vertical integration of information

Welcome back if you've been away. This is the point you were going to skip to if you just wanted the overview. Let's just count everyone to make sure we're all here. Good.

We started out by imagining an individual product's supply thread and made the point that it formed a single logical process. For that process to operate efficiently, information would need to flow freely along the thread (which I likened to a telephone wire).

Then we looked at the functions performed at each stage in the supply chain and saw that each could be most efficiently handled by an independent and specialised business – a specialist retailer, a specialist supplier, a specialist logistics provider. For those who go down that route, specialisation helps each individual business become efficient internally; the independence enables them to work with each other in an efficient way. The 'invisible hand' Adam Smith spoke of takes care of matching supply to retail demand.[1]

We also looked at how the specialisation, the focusing in on core activities, had widened the divide between supplier and retailer. And we saw how short-term pressure on margin has turned relations across this divide adversarial. In some cases it has become a border across which skirmishes are fought.

The first casualty in this border war is information. Dan showed me a guide to negotiating recently in which the first recommendation was to tell your opposite number as little as possible. Anything your opponent knows about you can be used to predict your behaviour or to uncover your weaknesses. If someone knows what you want and what you will settle for, they have the upper hand in the bargaining.

---

1 Adam Smith was an incredible man, he more or less invented the idea of free markets being a good thing – an idea which can be summed up with the phrase, "leave it alone or it will never get better". He was also a keen inventor and managed to come up with a formula for invisibility, though he only ever managed to make one hand fully invisible. To this day people refer to Adam Smith's famous invisible hand when they want to remind each other of the importance of free markets.

At the outset we saw that the appeal of vertical integration is the efficient flow of information and the way in which it can be used to fine-tune the activities of each supply thread. Even though structural integration itself is generally unworkable, the benefits of free-flowing information are real enough. But those benefits can never be realised as part of a negotiating process that begins with a total news blackout.

We mentioned two specific kinds of information that would help a supply thread operate efficiently – instantaneous sales and stock information and longer-term customer feedback. The sales and stock information would be used to make predictions about future stock requirements – useful for keeping production in step with consumption. Customer feedback would guide innovation for the future.

That brings us up to date. Now let's think about how we could share information. Consider what would happen to the negotiating process if retailers shared their ordering forecasts with suppliers.

We saw that many multiple retailers are much larger than the majority of their suppliers. The retailer is better able to survive the loss of a particular supplier than the other way round. The retailer can hold this fact over the heads of small or medium-sized suppliers. Effectively, the retailer's negotiating position is based on its nonchalance, its readiness to walk away. It is better able to survive a breakdown in negotiating, so it can take bigger risks in its demands.

If the supplier knew exactly what stock the retailer needed to meet projected demand, the supplier's position would be enormously strengthened and the retailer's correspondingly weakened. The supplier would know when the retailer was bluffing and when they were desperate for stock.

The retailer who offered to share forecast information with a supplier would be voluntarily giving up most of their bargaining leverage – leverage which currently underpins the all-important short-term margin grabbing.

Secrecy is so important that it risks becoming more than a good negotiating ploy, it can become a way of life.

Forgive me for this little aside. I realise sniggering at your clients is probably the worst sin a consultant can commit (particularly in vanity consulting[1]) but some retailers have got so used to the principle of

---

1 Vanity consulting involves using consultants to tell you what you want to hear. The most common form is when you have an idea and you don't think your colleagues or shareholders will go for it if you present it yourself. You bring in impartial consultants who 'come up with' the idea and recommend it back to you. This can sometimes be done without the consultant's knowledge, if the idea is a good one.

A riddle

It certainly looks as though a cross-section of retailers genuinely believe wringing additional margin from their suppliers is a sustainable path to profit, rather than the short-term balloon-squeezing exercise we suggest here. Squeezing suppliers is so common that it's not even questioned as a source of profit by most investors. Using a little sleight of hand, there's a way to sneakily exploit that situation.

Consider the following hypothetical situation. A lacklustre retailer under new management negotiates some tough new supplier deals – there is nothing suspicious about that. The reduced cost price would show up as a sharp increase in profits and no-one would think it strange. If the retailer were promptly sold again, it would attract a premium because of its improved profits.

Companies are usually valued by projecting their profits forward a number of years. Because supplier-derived profits are not treated warily, any valuation of such a retailer would be based on the assumption of many more years of similar low cost prices.

Once the retailer changed hands, a change of board line-up would probably take place. If the new board were unable to hold cost prices down, the share price would fall and most people would conclude that the new board weren't as capable as their predecessors. The previous owners would make a handsome profit, with the new owners finding that the business had slumped some way back towards its previous lacklustre condition.

The sleight of hand was suggested by Dan. He wondered what would happen if a major investor were also a major supplier. They could inflate the retailer's profits, pre-sale, by allowing the retailer favourable buying terms. After they had made money on the sale, they could put cost prices back up. With a little ingenuity, their investment could be disguised.

To make this idea more exciting, Dan suggests reading the business section of the newspapers on the lookout for someone putting this scheme into practice.

secrecy, it has convinced them that every piece of information about their business is a nugget of gold. There is a certain black humour to a badly run company on the brink of disaster that considers information about how it operates to be priceless. It's as though they imagine people out there desperate to steal the secret of mismanagement.

At any rate, most retailers place so much importance on strong supplier negotiations that all relevant information is classified. Information sharing is not just rare, it's usually forbidden.

Stock buffers and lead times

The reason predictions of demand would be so useful further up the supply chain is that everything takes time. When retailers place an order, they often want the stock immediately. They can't usually have it immediately, but they'd like it and the supplier with the shortest lead times has an advantage. The supplier has two choices. First is to re-design their business to cut down manufacturing lead times – so that product can be quickly made to order. The second is to stockpile inventory in advance, so that it's ready to go when the order arrives. Orders are filled immediately from this buffer stock.

In practice buffer stock is used by all manner of businesses to bridge the gap between the organisation's capabilities (how quickly they can fill an order) and their customer's requirements (how quickly they *need* to fill an order).

Retailers do the same thing. They don't know exactly what next week's customer demand will be so they hold some extra stock just in case. If there are distributors involved, they too will tend to hold buffer stock. At the other end of the chain, the manufacturer's raw material suppliers have probably got some reserves of inventory as well.

In most businesses buffer stock is purely a mechanism for dealing with unpredictable demand, but it has a second effect in a retail business – it makes life more difficult for suppliers. By allowing the retailer to absorb unexpected customer demand, buffer stock makes the retailer's ordering patterns more difficult to predict.

We said that hiding stock and sales information from your suppliers strengthens your negotiating position. In order for a supplier to gauge a retailer's future stock requirements they need to know both customer sales and the retailer's inventory levels. It's not enough to know that customers are buying more unless you know how large a retailer's buffer stocks are. Increased customer demand doesn't imply increased ordering if the retailer is massively overstocked.

In some retailers, buffer stocks can go beyond their role as reserves of stock and become a tool for supplier negotiations. They mask customer demand from the supplier, whatever the buyer's intentions. But they can also free the buyer to chase discounts. For instance, if there's an attractive volume discount within reach, there's no need to wait for customers to buy more, hypothetically a buyer could just increase his buffer stocks. And a large stock buffer might well give him time to find a new supplier if he wanted to de-list the current one – a scary thought for the supplier.

Does this situation seem satisfactory? Piles of stock exist all along the supply chain to make up for the fact that no one shares information. Demand and supply are intentionally disconnected as a negotiating ploy. Reducing supplier's margins is seen by many as an important source of retail profit growth. How long can that go on? Supplier-squeezing is surely not a renewable resource. Turning up the pressure each year won't get away from the fact that there's only so much profit to go around in an adversarial supply chain.

The alternatives to the margin tug-of-war, such as increased supply chain efficiency, require slick information sharing – but that has been outlawed in the interests of keeping the pressure on. This strategy is running out of road.

Let's imagine for a moment that we had the opportunity to try a different approach – one based on information sharing – what would it look like?

The collaborative dividend

We saw how the structure of a vertically integrated supply chain was impractical, but its information flows – its nervous system – are appealing. Could we imagine a supply chain that had a physical structure composed of specialised, horizontally integrated businesses, but the nervous system of a single vertical organisation? A virtual supply chain. How would it work?

If a manufacturer were in possession of accurate demand forecasts they could plan their production so that it always remained within their 'efficiency zone'. They could also eliminate a lot of their buffer stocks. Costs would be lowered and capital freed up. We can call this financial improvement the collaborative dividend.

What does the retailer get? In exchange for providing this information, the retailer could be given a share of the benefits, a share of the collaborative dividend.

Better forecasting helps the supplier anticipate orders – which means shorter lead times and more reliability. That allows the retailer to lower buffer stocks, while at the same time increasing their stock availability.

For this scheme to work, the collaborative dividend we're talking about would need to be sizeable. But I've talked to a number of people who are sceptical that it would be worth all the effort. The response I give is to ask them to imagine a retailer placing orders without knowing *their own* stock or sales position. How efficient would their stock management be? What sort of improvement would you expect if you then provided the missing data? This sort of information can significantly lower costs and suppliers are in an analogous position.

At the moment, though, the very act of demanding that the supplier cut its prices drives the supplier's costs up, because the associated information blackout gets in the way of good forecasting. Profits could actually increase with the right information flows and those profits would be available for equitable redistribution.

But what is equitable? Wouldn't we replace a squabble over diminishing margin with a squabble over a growing margin? Well the first thing to understand is that if you're going to squabble, collaborative commerce is not for you. For the forecasts of demand to be useful to the supplier, the retailer has to be prepared to stand by them and the supplier has to believe them. The collaborative dividend can only exist in the first place if disputes can be eliminated.

One retailer I spoke to gave its suppliers forecasts, but they were not in any sense a commitment to buy. In fact, they weren't even generated by the same people who managed the supplier ordering. At best they were useless, at worse they could be used for deliberate misdirection. They were in danger of becoming another tool for supplier manipulation.

So it's worse than you thought. Not only are we talking about sharing information with suppliers, which at the moment is top secret, we are talking about making commitments to buy things you might not even want when the commitment comes due.

But if the retailer is free to deviate from their forecasts without penalty, then the forecasts aren't much use. Retailers would also have no incentive to invest a lot of effort in getting them right. If they have to commit to those forecasts, on the other hand, their accuracy suddenly becomes paramount.

Why would a retailer give up a strong negotiating position and then tie themselves into order commitments? The only satisfactory answer would be if it were in their best interests.

It may help to see it in that light if, instead of thinking about penalising the retailer for deviating from their forecasts, we think of it as rewarding them for conforming to them.

Suppliers can use a retailer's forecast to ensure stock will be available when the retailer needs it. The advance notice also allows the supplier to plan their manufacturing for peak efficiency. The lowest cost scenario for the supplier is when the retailer's orders exactly match their forecast. So why shouldn't that coincide with their cheapest prices? If the retailer deviates from the forecast, the supplier's costs go up, so why shouldn't their prices go up?

If the retailer helps the supplier lower their costs, they share the benefit. What's so difficult about that?

One sticking point is that the trust has to run both ways. Not only does the supplier have to trust the retailer's forecasts, the retailer has to trust the supplier's sharing of the profits. The compliance-to-forecast prices are the cheapest on offer, but how cheap is that? What if the supplier is holding something back in order to bolster their profits? How would the retailer know?

Why not break the ultimate rule in supplier negotiations and publish your real prices? The giant suppliers, like Procter and Gamble, use this sort of approach. If more suppliers let the world know what their deals were and refused to offer all the auxiliary back-door concessions and payments, the retailer wouldn't need to rely on trust. They could let competition and the free market keep everyone on their toes. If there are no discounts available for behind-the-scenes bargaining then why not make tariffs public?

The best supplier prices would be on offer to retailers who make the suppliers lives easier through collaboration. It's up to the retailer to pick a supplier to collaborate with, so the retailer can still shop around. It doesn't matter that retailers can't *force* the price down, because in a free market, competition takes care of price control. After all that's what keeps margins on the high street in check – the fact that customers can go elsewhere. The only exceptions are price cartels – deals conducted behind closed doors; in other words exactly the sort of thing we're trying to banish.

Ruling by transparency

A lot of work and a big change in attitudes is required before any of this could happen. A whole framework of co-operation needs to be in place to make collaboration safe.

If we look at other areas of society, we can see two important mechanisms that encourage trust. One is recourse; the other is reputation.

If people know that the courts are there to resolve disputes, trusting someone is less of a risk. Collaboration usually needs some mechanism for arbitration, resolution of disputes, redress. It needs a third party to which disagreements can be taken.

The other mechanism for keeping everything above board is the risk of damage to reputation. That doesn't sound like much of a deterrent, but think of the effort invested by businesses in sending happy messages of prosperity to shareholders, customer and potential employees. In a world where suppliers offer their best prices to retailers they can trust, a bad reputation would cost money.

As a general rule, short-term thinking is best done behind closed doors. Publicly-made decisions come under more scrutiny. Transparency of supplier relations would make information sharing possible and palatable. It would encourage trust and it will help with fix everyone's eyes on a rich future prize rather than a self-defeating short-term one.

And one final word on co-operation within the supply chain. I said a while back that we'd consider whether competition might sometimes be a better idea than co-operation. There is one situation in which it might help us move forwards. Consider what would happen if the supply chains of other businesses in other countries successfully adopted the collaborative policies outlined here. Imagine if you had to compete directly with factories who knew yesterday's sales and next year's ranges, lean and responsive supply chains and retailers whose suppliers were helping them work more efficiently.

If collaborative commerce becomes a reality, there's going to be a big advantage to going first.

What was that all about?

- The information-sharing aspect of vertical integration is attractive but the physical structure isn't practical.
- The best choice for physical structure has the drawback that it tends to make suppliers and retailers 'vertical competitors'.
- Short-term margin focus in retailers can cause short-termist decision-making in commercial teams.
- The structure of the buying role in many businesses makes this short-termism worse.
- Separating sourcing from range planning will take some pressure off the commercial team and facilitate global economies of scale.
- Openness and information sharing could provide an alternate supply-chain structure with sustainable profit growth.

CHAPTER 6

Finance

This journey

This chapter is about value – ways of measuring it, ways of generating it, even new places to look for it. Much of what we're going to talk about lies within the realm of existing financial practice – albeit of the state of the art variety. Once we've seen some of the sights along the way, we'll round things up by integrating the concepts we've covered here with the ideas from earlier chapters.

We get into rather dry areas on a couple of occasions, but I've tried to make sure you don't have to go too long without a flippant aside. Welcome to the last instalment.

Confessions of a finance wannabe

Can there be a more dissolute species of libertine on this Earth than the medical student? And yet there are few jobs that command more respect than doctors. Strange.

The same transformation seems to occur with accountancy. Trainee accountants are not heroes to their friends – it is not the hit with the opposite sex that playing guitar in a band seems to be. Yet the higher reaches of the bean-counting hierarchy seem to enjoy considerable cachet.

As a general rule among business thinkers, I think we all wish we knew a little more corporate finance. I don't mean we want to study it – heaven forbid. But it's like a serious work of literature or history; nobody looks forward to reading it, we just wish we already had.

My generation grew up in the era of the corporate raider and the asset-stripper – they weren't exactly philanthropists, but they freshened up the image of high finance and swept away the sense of a fusty, old-boy network. And when my peers were thinking about which careers to pursue, we couldn't help noticing that twenty-five-year-old junk bond traders[1] were

---

1   I'd fancied the idea of being a junk bond trader for some time before I found out what a bond was, and many years passed before I discovered what made some of them junk.

buying Porsches and moving in to loft apartments with good views of the city.

By the time I was out of my twenties, high finance seemed to have grown up a little as well. Venture capitalists with vision were spotting all the hot new technologies, injecting capital at the critical moment and rocketing them straight to explosive IPOs. And at the other end of the business scale, I remember being pretty impressed when I read about a couple of people[1] at Enron who realised they could make more money trading energy than generating it.

In the last few years, financial engineering has come to the world of retail and I've got a new piece of gee-whiz money-magic to gawp at. Whole Business Securitisation (WBS) is currently shaking things up and I'm even toying with the idea of starting a Guy Hands fan club.

WBS deals, with their references to mezzanine finance, asset-backing and securitised cashflows certainly give the impression of occurring high in the stratosphere of finance, but they are just the most exotically funded of a broader trend towards Buy-Out Funds.

Buy-Out Funds use their investor's money, leavened (or leveraged in the jargon) with money from bonds or securities, to buy up whole businesses. Various running repairs to the business free up enough cash to pay the interest on the bonds; the sale of the rejuvenated business provides the investor with significant rewards.

Glance at the prospectus for one of these funds and you'll often find the word 'contrarian' used to describe their outlook. This is a code word. It means 'we see further than the stock market does'. The aim of their buy-outs is to bring this hidden potential to light, to have it reflected in a valuation when they come to sell the company. By drawing together a pool of Private Equity (PE) capital, financiers are able to act on their contrarian insights. They are able to buy up and run a business. Hang on. Financiers running a business? That doesn't sound like a good idea, does it?

Finance at the helm

These deals are based on the novel belief that a team of finance people at the top can do a dramatically better job of running a company than its

---

1 I wonder what happened to them. Anyway, it's a salutary lesson to all of us never to encourage initiative in brilliant young employees.

incumbent management[1]. And yet far from being a tough sell, deals of this type are starting to look like a bandwagon for others to climb on.

So how could a financier and a few analysts be so sure they could make money from a retail business? Is this just a reincarnation of asset-stripping? Is it a sort of financial vote of no confidence, where the shaky long-term future of a business is scrapped in favour of a short-term payout?

Well, that's not how these deals work. For a start, the company usually retains its overall shape. It isn't a salvage operation that breaks the business down for spares; it's a restoration project – every stage of which is guided by the need to end up with a saleable business.

There are two ways to persuade someone to buy your business. First, you can sell it at less than a valuation suggests it's worth. Second, you can ask for full price but persuade the new owners that it has untapped potential. (Naturally, you mustn't add the value of that untapped potential into the asking price.)

These deals give every indication of being the second kind. They turn a bad company into a good one and leave the new owners scope to make it even better.

So, far from asset-stripping, a turnaround deal of this type is all about making enhancements – some of which actually take place and some of which are uncovered, but deliberately not implemented. The deal pays off in the relatively short-term – two or three years – but it's not at the expense of long-term profitability; it's because of it.

That doesn't fit very well with the stereotyped view of finance as a discipline based on bean-counting and disciplined spending. We don't expect vision, business transformation or an ability to unlock potential from a finance team. Those are supposedly jobs for the general manager, who isn't hindered by the blinkers of financial specialism. Why the role reversal?

I think the solution to this puzzle lies in the balance between the four strategic relationships in a business.

Tension

Recall my distrust of any characteristic or property which people consider a universal good. All attributes form a spectrum, and there's

---

1   The financiers will put in an operating board of retail managers, of course. It's a little like the traditional shareholder/ professional manager model, except in this scenario the shareholders call the directors in for a monthly meeting, grill them on progress and tell them how much money they are allowed to spend. And they don't wait for an AGM if they want to make a few line-up changes.

always a point marked 'too much' somewhere on it. That point is reached either because further progress takes more effort than it's worth – as it would if 'efficiency regardless of the cost' were your motto – or because the alternatives have some merits too.

An example of the latter case is customer-focus; you *can* have too much of it. People often act as though customer-focus is simply *out there*, disconnected from any other aspect of the business. 'Are you customer-facing, tick yes or no?' But in reality, it's a question of degree and more customer-facing means less of something else.

The alternatives to increased customer-focus aren't always bad things. In many businesses, a little more employee-focus might not be the end of the world.[1] Being supplier-focused (as last chapter's catalogue of criticism will have illustrated) is enjoying considerable behind-the-scenes popularity at the moment – particularly among businesses that would have you believe their only interest is their customers.

The remaining alternative is the fourth cardinal point on the relationship compass: shareholder-focus. Because the four relationships are rarely thought of as being on the same level as each other, shareholder-focus is not a term you'll often hear. A statement like 'committed to delivering shareholder value' is more common. But that doesn't make it less of a valid option.

The balance point

Take a look at the compass rose on the first page of the book. Imagine placing a dot somewhere between the four cardinal points, to indicate the priorities of your business. Each strategic relationship exerts a pull on the business, it makes demands of it, and each pulls it in a different direction. The dot represents the fulcrum at which they meet – let's call it the 'balance point'.

You can never completely eliminate the tension between the relationships. As you make concessions in one relationship, moving the business closer to one of the 'poles' (and complete alignment with that constituent), you lower the tension in that relationship – but at the same time you raise the tension in the other three.

---

1   As we mentioned in Chapter 4, in the UK John Lewis Partnership is co-owned by its employees and clearly states its determination to deal honestly with its suppliers and customers. Despite many people's scepticism, this approach has yet to lead to the company's demise.

For example, if you drop your prices you will make your customers happier, but your profits will fall, upsetting your shareholders. To repair the damage to shareholder interests you could push your suppliers for lower prices. If you want to keep your suppliers, customer *and* shareholders happy you need to lower costs and increase your efficiency. That means fewer people doing more work for less money – you're now squeezing your employees. Only increased efficiency can satisfy all four at once.

A balance point placed right at the centre of the rose, equidistant from each pole, would mean all four relationships have equal weight. That's probably not the case in your business, so where would your balance point be located?

It will depend on the priorities in your business. How often does customer satisfaction come before cost controls? What sort of sacrifices is your business prepared to make in the interests of employee morale? In what circumstances would you forego cost price improvements in the interests of supplier goodwill?

Consider the trade-off between these objectives and try to choose a balance point on the rose to represent the priorities of your company.

A triangle by any other name

The compass rose device is a similar idea to the cost-quality-time triangle of project management. (Except if you call it the cheapness-quality-speed triangle instead, the quantities vary in a consistent way to each other.) The idea is that there's a trade-off. If you try to make a project cheaper, for instance, you must either sacrifice speed or quality.

The Treacy model's use of a diagram to illustrate a trade-off is an even more direct ancestor of the relationship compass. It asks a business to prioritise its interest in operational excellence, customer intimacy, and product leadership – and points out that trying to do all three equally well is a costly way of ending up with a muddle.

In both cases the closer you come to one point of the triangle, the further away you find yourself from the others. The idea is the same with the compass rose.

Each option for balancing the tensions, each placement of the fulcrum, has specific advantages and distinct drawbacks. If the balance point is too far from the shareholder pole then the company could end up the target of a takeover. If it's too far from the customer pole, the sales will nose-dive – and so on.

Figuring out where your business's priorities lie can be difficult to do for several reasons. One is corporate split personality: there's no consistent, business-wide view on priorities. HR probably place employees pretty high in their ranking, whereas marketing might feel the same way about customers. The finance team probably have some strong views on financial partners and buyers might have a certain amount of evidence that suppliers loom large in the company's decision-making.

Secondly, a relationship can be intense but dysfunctional at the same time. Many businesses are strongly supplier-focused, but also strongly opposed to supplier collaboration. Just as many businesses place the shareholders' interests above all else, but at the same time communicate with them as little as possible.

And finally, working out the relative priorities is difficult because the quality and the scope of each relationship are different. Customers, for instance, don't really have a view on the internal structure of the business, whereas shareholders – with their focus on net margin – will have an interest in the firm's efficiency.

Viewed from one point of view, customers represent the firm's income, while suppliers and employees are its major costs. Shareholder's interests take in the relationship between the two. Shareholders will also have an interest in capital employed, unlike the other three constituents.

Each firm will choose to balance the tensions from the four relationships in a different way. Understanding the consequences of different choices will help us see how a finance-led turnaround can work. Turnaround deals effectively push the balance point sharply towards shareholder-focus. Whether that will constitute an improvement will depend on whether the balance-point has drifted a long way from the shareholder pole in the first place. Let's consider how reasserting the financial viewpoint can help.

Financial imaging

Several chapters ago I suggested that there were various ways to view a business, a little like there are various medical technologies for imaging a human body, and each is capable of distinguishing different features.

The corporate finance view of the business can be highly revealing. Imagine seeing your business not by normal light, but via the x-ray vision of investment analysis. The outward appearances of things become indistinct. The surface features we normally notice, the buildings, the people, are transparent. The luminous flows and pools of money are revealed within. Assets appear as stationary reservoirs of capital. The movement of products down the supply chain, seen this way, also reveals a river of funds flowing uphill, from the customers into the heart of the business. Here it branches and splits, fanning out into tributaries (like capillaries carrying blood) to reach all the various cost centres. On the other side of the business the river continues on, considerably diminished, towards the suppliers.

To the casual observer, retail businesses are broadly similar to one another with their stores, their staff, their warehouses stacked with product. Viewing the business with eyes sensitive only to financial wavelengths reveals that suitable targets for acquisition have a very different architecture to their healthy peers.

Full of capital

The capital employed by a business is of great interest to a financier, but it's almost invisible to the rest of us. Even if we squint to discern the money side of things, usually we only make out the revenues and expenditures that make up profit. Most of us aren't really aware of the balance sheet. Yet, underpinning the cashflows of a business are foundations built from fixed assets and capital.

To an acquisitive financier, capital employed is an important feature. There's a simple reason for that. Two businesses can have similar sales and profit levels but very different amounts of capital locked up in them. That raises the possibility that the business carrying the extra capital might not be using it efficiently. Maybe it only *needs* as much as its more frugal competitors. It's possible that the extra capital could be reclaimed.

You could liken this to a prospective buyer viewing several workshops with similar facilities, but noting that one has gold bars hidden under the floorboards.

But wouldn't a metaphorical cache of gold be included in the price of the business? Maybe not. Companies are usually valued on their projected earnings. For a viable business, any valuation will considerably exceed its net asset value. So long as it's a going concern, it will be worth more than the sum of its parts. The capital tied up in a business is irrelevant to most people because the only way to get at it is to shut the business down – which destroys much of the firm's value. The trick would be if you could extract that trapped capital without disrupting normal business operations.[1]

---

1   It's kind of like selling a kidney. You won't get many volunteers unless you can do it without killing the donor.

This is a benchmarking exercise, but done from the outside. You group businesses with similar organisational capabilities and then examine their use of capital. If you can see how to tune up a capital guzzler to run like its lean-burning neighbour, you have a possible candidate for a turnaround.

Hardening of the inventories

This sort of financial imaging is also useful for spotting what you might call circulation problems in the cashflow of a business. Just like clogged arteries, a business may find itself silting up from the inside.

Take the typical general merchandise retailer. They probably enjoy payment terms for goods that average about 45 days, with gross margin of around a third. That means if they can sell a product within 30 days of taking delivery of it, there is no working capital tied up in inventory – it's paid for itself by the time invoices are due.

Holding no more than a month's supply of any product doesn't sound unreasonable, does it? After all, lots of suppliers deliver every week and stores are resupplied every week. Even with a safety margin, why hold more than four week's stock?

A young person's guide to retail jargon (continued)

Stock turn is calculated as follows: figure out the current value of your inventory 'at retail'. That's to say, how much money would it make (after paying VAT) if you sold it all this minute. Now work out what your average daily sales (minus VAT) are. Divide the former by the latter. How many days would it take to sell your current inventory? That's your stock-turn period.

Stock cover is another way of stating the same thing. Your 'cover' is the number of days your stock would last if you didn't reorder anything.

Now work out the average cost of percentage goods as a percentage of the average sales price (minus VAT). (That's just one minus the average gross margin percentage) Multiply that by the stock turn period. You've just worked out the number of days it takes you to make enough money to pay your suppliers. If that number is larger than your agreed payment terms, you have negative cashflow and you need to allow some working capital to bridge the gap, if it's smaller you're actually generating capital from supplier credit.

And yet many retailers are drowning in slow-moving products with an average stock turn in excess of 90 days. It's not uncommon for the majority of a general merchandise retailer's products to sell fewer than one unit per store per week. Every store probably holds a case of each of these slow-movers, and there's another pallet-load sitting at the warehouse – and that might be true of thousands of products.

For a €1 bn a year retailer, every extra month of cover adds around €50 m to working capital requirements. That money *could* be used to open new stores, where it would generate additional revenue.

Imagine cutting the price on popular branded lines and de-listing the slow sellers. An operator might reason that the big brands have narrow enough margins already, without expanding their role in the range and selling them at a discount. Even allowing for the fact that volume will soar, there would probably be no net improvement in cash margin. To an operator there's no reason to try such a scheme.

A financier, on the other hand, might be just as interested in the cashflow improvement those changes would bring. Without adversely affecting margin, the much higher rates of sale would speed up the stock turn. The stock required for presentation purposes would become a much smaller fraction of the total.

For the sake of argument, let's imagine that a scheme like this would cut the average stock-turn period by a third. That would release a sizeable chunk of working capital. In our example retailer, it would probably be enough to pay the interest on the loan used to buy the business. With a trick like that up your sleeve you can get serious about planning an acquisition.

The top supermarkets tend to be very sharp in this area and are often very good at getting on-shelf quantities, pack sizes and rates of sale aligned and optimised (see display panel). Many other retailers aren't so skilful. The dynamics of most commercial teams work to drive up the SKU count, adding to the 'tail' of slow-moving products in the range and dragging down the average stock-turn (see Chapter 5).

A retailer with much poorer stock turn than its competitors, but with similar metrics in other areas, might find itself on the short list for the corporate equivalent of a coronary bypass – to be administered without consent by a turnaround team.

In many retailers, high capital requirements and slow cashflow go hand in hand. As the SKU count grows, more and more capital is tied up in stock and the lengthening 'tail' of slow-moving products drags down the stock turn. To a financier these problems are both highly visible and tantalisingly treatable.

Sales floor *versus* stockroom

One idea Dan and I have never managed to get a retailer to go for is keeping *two* stock balances for a store – one for the stockroom and one for the sales floor – and combining that with the use of security-sealed cases. If you have a few quiet moments and you haven't considered trying this, just think through a few of the possibilities. If you match case pack sizes to on-shelf quantities, the back room stock can mainly be composed of full cases with their warehouse security tape still sealed. Store stock-counts proceed very quickly in the stockroom – count the boxes and check the security tape – if the total comes out right, the stockroom's done. That's the sort of procedure that could form part of every store visit. The contents of a case are checked when it's opened as part of restocking the shelf. The stock is also transferred to the sales floor stock balance at the same time.

From head office, you'd be finally be able to get a true picture of presentation *versus* buffer stock. You'd be able to tell which stores were not keeping their shelves full and which merchandising layouts were prone to stock-outs. With head-office visibility of sealed back-room stock, you'd be able to cost-effectively uplift stock back to the RDC if required (makes closing stores or phasing out products very efficient). One final embellishment is to use unmarked cases, tagged with a delivery code. Store staff wouldn't need to know what was in any case while it was in the stockroom. Only when they request more of a product for shelf filling would the system instruct them which case to break open.

A business may have had a mountain of sluggish product for years, but with corrective action the excess stock will eventually sell through. After the underlying problems are resolved, the blockage in the supply chain will gradually clear itself[1]. And the remedy doesn't affect the foundations of the business. There is no need to change the store portfolio or the staff: the remedies can be applied in the decision-making process at head office.

---

1   It can be helped on its way with some major clearance activity. This is the supply chain equivalent of dynamiting an obstruction, but for very slow moving lines, selling at or below cost price is better than cluttering up the store for years to come.

When the markets step in

Although the finance-only view of the business we've been discussing reveals some of the important workings of a business, it doesn't tell the whole story. A financier without specialist retail skills is bound to miss many of the nuances and subtleties of running a portfolio of stores. The curious thing is that from time to time that's a *good* thing.

Where general financial considerations have become swamped by retail-specific concerns – like the need for range authority, or novelty, or excellence in customer service or whatever else – an unsympathetic hand on the tiller can be a boon.

Dan and I have spent considerable time with one major retailer whose brand, product, promotional and customer service initiatives were so numerous and complex that making a profit just wasn't possible. It was like trying to run twenty small businesses out of the same store. Individually, each one had its own plausible rationale, but taken together they required a vast cost-base that was dragging the business into the red. A financially-oriented team took over and turned a deaf ear to all the commercial arguments that favoured the status quo. They put simple profitability back in the driving seat. Improvement was pronounced and immediate.

Am I advocating some sort of bitter medicine for retail, where the only way to restore order is to declare a financial version of martial law? Not at all. The problems I'm outlining here are common to many retailers – it's one of the pitfalls of trying to keep your offer up to date. But a customer-driven offer, unchecked, can eventually nudge a business off its financial track and into the weeds. Once that happens, it sometimes takes a real jolt to get the company out of the mud.

The acquisition and turnaround deals I'm discussing here are one mechanism that the market has found for dealing with businesses that find themselves stuck. But if retailers learn to spot the signs, take remedial action and stay on track, they will never come to the attention of the turnaround teams in the first place.

Too busy to evolve

The previous chapter discussed many of the strategic and economic forces that shaped the current retail scene and the fact that they continue to exert pressure on businesses. In some cases, retailers have settled into an operating mode which is making further adaptation difficult. What was once a valuable innovation starts to become a liability, because circumstances have changed. It's up to each business to decide how it handles that situation.

The almost-predatory takeovers we've been discussing show that stagnation and a slow death is not the only fate that might await the business that fails to adapt. A lumbering behemoth that lags behind the herd can also become an attractive target to sharp-eyed money men.

Perhaps it's the fact that a company usually adapts and grows *at the same time* that makes this particular pitfall such a problem. In the early part of their lifecycle, retailers rush to reach national coverage. They are expanding their teams and adding new roles – sometimes whole new departments. Process and structure are fluid and, as modifications are made, any changes in the external environment are naturally factored in.

At some stage, retail businesses get over their growth spurt. A business finds that it's comfortably meeting demand for the first time and its priorities begin to shift. Consistency becomes not just a possibility, but an objective. And that's just as it should be. Efficiency and reliability come from refining and standardising processes. Businesses in rapid expansion accept that while they're riding the wave of booming sales there may not be time to worry about efficiency. As soon as calmer waters are reached, wise managers use the opportunity to put some stable structures in place.

What frequently gets forgotten is that sooner or later it all needs to change again. Businesses, at least in this respect, are like sharks – if they don't move forward they die.

That dilemma is often likened to the problem of changing a tyre on a moving vehicle. After you've consolidated your structure, how do you go back and change it? Alternatively, if we think of the business as a building, putting on a new roof is not too difficult, but replacing the foundations raises some interesting questions.

IT departments face this problem the whole time – the drive to improve, combined with the need for continuity – a revolution with no interruption in service.

What tends to happen is that the forces for change mould and squeeze the more malleable components of the business, until some solid feature or critical system is encountered and the process of change grinds to a halt. Updating your business is a little like varnishing a floor; sooner or later you need to paint the bit you're standing on.

As we've already discussed, current commercial team structure is one such impediment. Its creation enabled the national multiple retailer to be born and its continued importance keeps it at the heart of the business.

But its current form is holding back the next stage of retail growth – the efficient multi-brand, international retailer.

Sticking points, such as commercial team structure, are like obstructions in the path of a moving glacier. As the point of contact between unstoppable force and immoveable object, these obstructions become the focus of enormous pressure.

While none of the retail turnarounds I've been following have fully cracked the problem of commercial-team structure, they have managed to overcome a number of other common ailments. The arterial plaque of slow-moving product is something a turnaround team *can* tackle. That's where the deaf-ear and heavy-hand of a financier can be helpful in clearing the log-jam. The dyed-in-the-wool retail wisdom that justified the build-up of the range 'tail' cuts very little ice with a team who only care about cashflow, capital and profit.

But there have always been various corrective mechanisms that kick in when shareholders' expectations are not being met. The movement of the share price is a little like a ride in a hot air balloon – you can glide along as high above the ground as you like, but the first time you drop below the level of the treetops, the trip comes to an abrupt end. Acquisition, bankruptcy or a shareholder revolt will get you. PE turnarounds are just a taller tree than most. You don't have to descend as far before you hit trouble.

We've talked about what the turnaround teams see when they look at a troubled business. Let's think about the slightly less intense view of the shareholders.

Growth stocks

A word about shareholder expectations – it's worth noting that if share dividends were the whole story, there'd be little to say about a business's relationship with its shareholders. The whole thing could be handled in the annual report. But of course many investors buy stock because they think the price of it will go up, not just because they get an annual payout. When you factor that in, the whole character of the situation changes. Company performance is no longer a level playing field, because *expectations* about the share price start to play a part. Those expectations will be strongly influenced by the firm's relationship with its owners.

The power of expectations is the only explanation for something like the dot com boom. The only possible justification for buying massively overvalued stock is the conviction that the price will go even higher.

Unrestrained investment in Internet stocks reaffirmed the fact that current performance means almost nothing in some circumstances; it's expectations about the future that govern the share price. You don't need to be profitable *right now* to be considered a success. That's true of all equity-funded businesses because performance is only good if it's good *versus expectations* – and every business can have a hand in setting those expectations. That's where the relationship with the shareholders comes in.

To the equity markets, retail businesses must seem a little bit like overseas colonies from the bad old days of imperialism. The only contact they have with them is through their contributions to the central coffers, plus a few letters home. If the money dries up and the correspondence grows unreliable, eventually the markets send out a new set of managers to take over and run things properly. Viewed in this way one can see turnaround deals not just as a problem with the way businesses are run, but a problem in the way they communicate with their investors.

So what is it that shareholders want? Shareholders want their shares to be good investments. In the last decade or so, a lot of work has gone into bridging the gap between the role of shares as investment instruments and their function as ownership deeds of a business. New methodologies have arisen to tackle the conflict between the two roles. They help businesses make operational decisions directly aimed at improving the overall performance of the shares.

We'll just investigate in a little more detail how you run a business around these ideas of 'shareholder value'. If you're familiar with value-based management already, you might want to skip the next two sections.

Value added

Shareholder value is a pretty big subject. I'm going to squash it down to a few lines. It's just possible we might sacrifice a little fine detail in the process.

Shares are investments and the shares of most big companies are freely traded. The result of that trading is that expectations about the future of a company are constantly balanced against expectations about the future of the market(s).

If a particular share looks like it might offer a return that's out of line with similar alternatives, its price is adjusted to bring it into line. Effectively, what the market is doing is trying to make all investments equally good value for money.[1] The bargains will go up in price and the dogs will get cheaper until a consensus is reached that 'you get what you pay for'.[2] That's true not just for traded shares, but for other sources of funding like bonds.

Because the market is always adjusting its prices based on future expectations, it's possible to work out what those expectations are. From there, you can work out what return the market is expecting from an individual company's shares.

Companies interested in value-based management repeat that exercise for each source of funding their business uses (perhaps they've issued bonds as well as equity). By adding together the expectations for each type of funding, one can arrive at a figure for the total return expected from a business. That figure is called the Weighted Average Cost of Capital (WACC). If your business were a savings account, the WACC is the rate of interest savers are expecting you to pay.

Any investment your business makes that pays back less than the WACC is destroying value. Investors will have passed up other options on the basis that your shares offered a particular return. Failure to achieve that rate has cost them money.

From the company's point of view, investing funds in something that doesn't repay the WACC is like borrowing money at 8 per cent to invest in something that only pays 7.5 per cent. A value-based methodology helps companies understand that. The converse is that anything your company can do that has a higher return than the WACC is adding value.

That's the key to shareholder value. If you think of your business as being run entirely with money from loans then you need to make sure you can pay the interest on the loans with some left over. If your company makes less than the notional interest payments needed to fund it, it's wasting money.

Calculating the WACC is tricky. Figuring out the return your business is making is tricky. But in principle, all your business has to do is beat the WACC and all will be well.

---

1   It's worth mentioning that the market 'factors in' risk. It expects risky investments to pay higher returns. Or put another way a risky return will command a lower price than a certain one.

2   It might not be obvious why this happens. Speculative investors are constantly trying to get out of overvalued investments and into undervalued ones. The effect of that constant migration is that any obvious bargains are snapped up. What you're left with are investments that are equally good value, so far as anyone can tell.

Value-based management

The way I've described shareholder value, it's as a hurdle rate for investment decisions. Only projects that will beat the WACC should be approved. But how do you use a method like that to make day-to-day operational decisions that don't directly concern investment opportunities?

The answer is that value creation (or 'value added') becomes the top level KPI for the business. It's like a single read-out, a single gauge, that tells you how well the company is running. Any operational lever you can pull to make the needle rise more rapidly is in the best interests of the business. That's what value added *means*. In effect, you treat your business like it was one big capital project.

Various value-based approaches seek to uncover the link between more traditional measures and shareholder value. One popular approach links seven quantities, including measures like working capital requirements, sales growth and net profit,[1] in a way that illuminates their influence over value added. By managing the underlying quantities, the business can be sure it's managing value at the top level.

Relating to the shareholders

Value-based management helps businesses to take decisions that will keep their shareholders happy. That's great as far as it goes, but it's a little bit distant. After all, the shareholders aren't living on another planet. The company has various ways of communicating with them. As well as doing what the shareholders want, why not tell them that's what you're doing?

There are two common complaints I've heard directors make about shareholders. First, that they're short-termist and secondly that they are too sensitive to small pieces of (bad) news.

In other words, shareholders aren't interested in a company's longer term plans and they always assume the worst. In defence of shareholders I think most of the reason for that perception is poor communication.

The companies whose shares are traded in the equity markets aren't just retailers – there are, for instance, drug companies, oil companies and

---

1 Because these approaches are all about cashflow, they often seek to reverse the effects of various accounting policies. For instance, the profit figure used adds back any non-cash charges like depreciation, because regardless of the fact that capital expenditure may not hit the P&L all in one go, that money has been spent. Value added deals in 'real' cashflows not accounting charges.

energy utilities. Each of those sectors routinely invests billions in projects that won't pay off for many years. Developing a new drug, exploring for oil and building a power station are massive long-term investments. If the equity markets were short-termist, would they fund those companies?

It's not long-term investment they penalise; it's bad investment. Investments over the longer term are always riskier. It stands to reason if you have any doubts about a business, it's the major long-term investments you will be most anxious about. (We'll have more to say about short-termism towards the end of the chapter.)

Communication

But as regards communicating more, many businesses are uncomfortable sharing lots of detail with outsiders. We've already talked about the blanket of secrecy cast over supplier deals. Sharing too much information can jeopardise supplier deals, tip off competitors and make the shareholders jumpy – or so it's assumed.

In fact, the truth is that the *less* you hear, the more jumpy you get. The better a business becomes at controlling the flow of information, the more panic a piece of bad news will cause. After all, if the company could have hushed it up, they would have done so, right? Investors start to wonder if things are getting so bad that the company can't keep a lid on it any more.

The way to prevent volatile market reactions and fits of pessimism is not to get better at 'spinning' the news, but to open up a bit more.

One of the exciting possibilities of value-based management is that it can improve management relations with shareholders – to the benefit of both parties. First, the shareholders hear that their best interests are being used as the yardstick to check every decision in the business. Second, they are kept informed about progress. Mistakes that crop up when a company is obviously pursuing shareholder interests are less worrying to investors than problems that crop up when you don't know quite *what* they're up to.

The more informed the shareholders are, the more readily they'll understand the context of any problems and the less unnerved they are likely to be by setbacks. Of course, this is about preventing investors from over-reacting or jumping to wrong conclusions; it won't help if there really *are* serious problems on the horizon. It won't buy you time if you have a crisis you don't know how to fix, but then that's a dangerous path to set foot on in the first place.[1] On the other hand if you have a crisis *and* a plan for fixing it, a history of openness with the shareholders will improve your chances of being allowed time to work through it.

Better communication will also have an effect on the perceived short-termism of the markets. Investors will have a greater understanding, and therefore a greater faith, that funds are being invested in ways that link clearly and directly to their interests.

Unsurprisingly, in a book about strategic relationships, I'm going to suggest that the key to eliminating short-termism completely is better management of (you guessed it) strategic relationships. First we'll look at how value-based management tackles a running theme of this book – misaligned KPIs – then we'll add in strategic relationship management to round things off. If you've been standing in a book-store all this time, reading, the good news is that you can go home soon.

Process and its opposite

What's the opposite of process? I suppose it depends in what sense I mean 'opposite'. I'm thinking here in the sense of business ideas. I'm asking which business idea is at the other end of the spectrum from process?

There's a reasonable chance you've never considered it and if you have there's also a reasonable chance you think the answer might be 'chaos'. Well, there's plenty of evidence to suggest that chaos is a business practice, but I don't think we could claim it's a business *idea*.

I'd suggest that the answer is KPIs. I'm not just talking about bonusing a store manager on store sales, I'm also thinking of much more ingenious 'synthetic' measures of success. There are all sorts of composite calculations that go beyond basic accounting quantities and ratios.

Remember we just described the value added calculation as a single read-out that tells us whether our company is doing the right sorts of things or not. KPIs free us to experiment a little. If we find a way to get the needle on the value-added gauge to rise, we're doing something right.

If value added were really displayed on a read-out, it would probably be in the CEO's office. (Personally I think I'd make it a big, old-fashioned

---

1 The other side of the coin from concealing problems is over-promising on performance. It's perhaps better intentioned, but according to one retail luminary I spoke to, it's the cause of much suffering. Over-promising can sour relations with investors and bring a sense of desperation to operational decision-making. His recommendation was not to get carried away with those election speeches.

brass pressure gauge.) Now, what if everyone else in the business had their own personal gauges too? Instead of displaying value added for the whole business, they would just measure that employee's contribution to the total[1] – their own personal KPI. Employees would have the most important pre-requisite for empowerment: a way to tell when they're doing something right.

That's why process and KPIs are at opposite ends of a spectrum. At one extreme, process dominates and each employee is merely following a set of instructions. At the other end, there *are* no processes – anything that improves the KPIs is acceptable.

Apparently, cooking a McDonalds hamburger is all process. Every action is written down along with its timing; no room is left for variation. Someone has already worked out the best way to perform each step and the employee's job is to follow the approved process. Makes sense.

On the other hand, a highly empowered sales team personifies the KPI-led approach. Each salesman is free to think of imaginative new sales techniques. If it wins you sales, it's a good process.

When do we update?

Most retail businesses are an *ad hoc* mixture of process and KPI. Unfortunately, in many organisations neither one is updated as part of the normal running of the business.

Of the two approaches, KPIs are less rigidly tied to the *status quo*. When the environment changes, an organisation's behaviour needs to change with it. A business favouring KPIs is free to adapt to new conditions. They can continually look for new approaches to maximising their KPIs.

Of course, if business conditions change sufficiently, KPIs can run into trouble. If new factors arise that aren't correctly accounted for in the KPI, or employees start to behave in ways not foreseen when the measurements were devised,[2] KPIs can begin to mislead.

---

1   It might suit less gregarious managers. Instead of giving you an annual performance review, once a year they could send someone round to read your meter.

2   Dan told me about a quandary some store managers found themselves in. In a business where stores ordered their own stock, a new drive was putting them under pressure never to run out of any product. On the other hand, managers were being pushed equally hard to keep their stock levels low. Fast-moving products require a lot of stock, so what could they do? One manager realised that if you kept back one unit of each product in the stock room, the system never registered a stock-out and at the same time you didn't need to carry lots of inventory. Pretty soon, lots of managers were doing it. It's ingenious, but it's not the situation envisaged when the KPIs were devised.

Processes, in contrast, age rapidly. Any changes in external conditions can turn a process into a liability. In their favour, the lack of decision points in rigid processes means that they require fewer skills, they are efficient and they bring everyone up to the level of best practice. But if best practice changes because circumstances have changed, processes need to be redesigned. Many organisations don't have a process (a meta-process you might call it) to make sure that the redesign always occurs.

So process codifies appropriate behaviour, whereas KPIs help you to work it out for yourself. KPIs are more flexible in the face of change, but they do require the employee to show initiative and to devise their own versions of best practice. All the KPI can do is give feedback; it can't make suggestions.

Matching KPIs to roles

There are also problems with relying heavily on KPIs when job roles are fragmented. For instance when a single logical task is split between two people, it's a good idea to specify the details of any hand-offs. Consider delivering stock to a store. A delivery driver might be able to improve his efficiency by adapting his route to current traffic conditions and delays. On the other hand, stores might make more efficient use of staff, by accepting deliveries only at pre-arranged convenient times. In this example, unilateral innovation is a disruptive practice. Processes handle fragmented tasks better than KPIs.

Broadly speaking, the more you encourage employees to get creative, the more important it is to provide them with appropriate KPIs. The extensive problems we discussed around commercial team structure stem largely from the fact that buying performance is not properly aligned with company performance. In other words, it's possible to do something that looks like success to a buyer, but like a bad idea to the company as a whole. With correctly formulated KPIs, this wouldn't be the case.

What makes a good KPI? Well, let's start by saying that the scope of the job role should be the same as the scope of the KPI. It doesn't make sense to give someone control of a resource, but not measure how they use it. If you have the power to fill half the warehouse with product, for instance, shouldn't you be measured on how profitably you employ that space? Many businesses neither track this sort of activity with KPIs nor control it with processes.

Aligning KPIs

Implicit in matching role to KPI is the idea of aligning the KPIs of different roles. Properly aligned KPIs wouldn't push different job roles into conflict, because they'd measure success in a consistent way and at an appropriately high level.

To illustrate this point, be very cautious about the alignment between store KPIs and buying-team KPIs. Assuming your managers are allowed a certain amount of initiative in the running of their stores, badly chosen KPIs can lead them into unwitting conflict with the commercial teams. Many times, I've seen stores make decisions that boost their sales, but ultimately sacrifice cash margin. Of course stores aren't usually incentivised on or given information about gross margin, so it's hardly surprising. They are usually incentivised on sales.[1]

When correctly aligned, the KPIs for different roles don't conflict with each other, and all of them support the top-level KPI of value added.

In addition, it's important to make sure that the KPI and the success of the individual performing the role are properly linked. Granted, KPIs can never measure every aspect of a role, but it's still important to avoid double standards. Behaviour that drives down the KPI shouldn't be rewarded elsewhere, through approbation or promotion – the two must be synchronised. Equally, it's not fair to criticise behaviour that raises a KPI[2] (assuming it meets standards of ethics and professionalism).

You may think that I'm placing a lot of emphasis on KPIs and that the approach I'm talking about is too involved. But I don't see that we have a choice. Sales and profit *are* KPIs, they're just rather basic ones. If you give a store manager more money for hitting a sales target, you are tying

---

1   We've already discussed the converse, where buyers can cause problems for stores. One example comes from the fact that buyers' KPIs don't usually measure extra work they create for stores, so there is no incentive for buyers to 'batch up' changes to store merchandising. Because there are no penalties, each buyer can instruct stores to make changes as frequently as they wish. I have visited several companies where the visual merchandising has been completely undermined by the practice of dribbling new products out to stores each week. Because the real range never actually coincides with the planned layout, stores have to invent their own workable layouts each week. Thousands of people spend time redesigning something that has already been done once at head office.

2   I've encountered situations on a couple of occasions where companies 'hope' that employees will refrain from certain short-sighted activities, whilst acknowledging that they are more likely to get a bigger bonus if they go ahead.

KPIs to incentives. Sticking to basic KPIs[1] and refusing to link them to pay doesn't get away from the problem. It just means that your business isn't measuring success very well and isn't incentivising your staff very strongly to achieve it.

All we are really trying achieve with KPIs is to provide each employee with what you might call 'a commercial view' – an understanding of how their actions fit into the big picture. In other words, we want to give them the confidence to throw their weight behind a particular decision, secure in the knowledge that it will benefit the business as a whole.

It is worth mentioning that many roles and departments affect the fundamental financials in such a subtle and indirect way, that a close link to value added is probably not practical. Most of these teams will need to work through budgets and internal service level agreements (SLAs), which would be periodically realigned with the KPI hierarchy. So some roles would have a KPI with a 'live' link to value added, other roles would have a KPI that reflected performance *versus* SLA.

In modern, complex businesses[2] the only way to lessen the importance of KPIs is to place greater emphasis on process. Those devising the processes still need to cover much of the same ground as those who devise KPIs, but they need to go further and model the best way of optimising those KPIs. But keeping a business's processes efficient and up to date is a full-time job. It's only really practical for processes used by a large fraction of the workforce.[3]

The situation in many retailers is one of hit-and-miss updates. Occasional streamlining projects might be run to redesign a problem process, but it is often loss of effectiveness, not a lack of efficiency that prompts the initiative. A loss of efficiency, in itself, is often not enough to justify the effort and disruption.

Sometimes new processes simply evolve themselves, while most tend to gradually disintegrate. As parts of a process become outdated, they

---

1   That said, basic KPIs have the advantage that most people understand them. If you use complex 'synthetic' KPIs, base them on something people can grasp. In the supplier chapter we mentioned a system of simple internal charges that could be used to allow other departments access to scarce resources. People have no problem understanding that there may be a charge (even if it's only on paper) for using extra resources.

2   I say 'modern, complex businesses' to discount the third option, which is intuition or common sense. In a small business it's possible to see how your decisions affect the business. When you are one of thousands, guidelines (processes) or feedback (KPIs) are vital.

3   This is the franchise model, where all activities in a store or restaurant are committed to three-ring binders, ready to be replicated in thousands of outlets.

incorporate more and more flexibility and local decision-making – KPIs and 'personal judgement'[1] fill the gaps.

Triggers for change

Most process work, though, is bound up with an IT implementation these days. Either a new system forces a re-examination of processes or process redesign work is deferred until it can be combined with a software change. I have even encountered businesses where staff were so averse to new processes that managers had to go looking for a systems project to use as a vehicle for change.[2]

Slice it any way you want, most retailers would benefit enormously from a re-design of their processes and yet no business I've looked at tackles the problem systematically.

Unfortunately, many Business Process Re-engineering projects are nearly as bad as the disease they claim to cure.[3] The biggest of the three main problems with them is that they often boost efficiency at the cost of effectiveness. The old processes handled every eventuality inefficiently; the new processes handle *most* eventualities slickly and leave a few out completely.[4]

Second, BPR projects rarely take full advantage of the opportunity to review an organisation's capabilities. Making sure that low-level processes support the high-level description of the offer is vital. Unless strategy finds its way into process, it's just PR.

The third problem with BPR is that, frankly, people hate change. Your day job doesn't go away while the organisation is re-structuring, no matter how many consultants are brought in. Somehow employees need

---

1 Personal judgement is a great thing, but it's no substitute for knowing what's going on. Store staff are often told to exercise common sense, but they're rarely briefed on the full picture beforehand. As I recall, the difference between delegation and abdication is whether you give your chosen victim the tools to do the job or not.

2 And that's not the end of it either. Users often counter this ploy by insisting that the new system incorporate the old ways of working. The sub-text is, 'You can have your new system provided it's the same as the old one'.

3 Apart from the ones Dan and I ran, of course. They were great. Everyone said so.

4 Have you ever tried ordering bulky items, but specifying special delivery requirements? My brother had the same sofa delivered on half a dozen occasions. Sometimes it turned up in a van that wouldn't fit under the low bridge he'd warned them about at the end of his road; sometimes it came without the extra people he'd requested to carry it to his top-floor flat. The pre-computerised approach was inefficient, but at least the salesman could write a note on the order.

to assist in the redesign activity as well as coping with their normal workload. And for many people, their knowledge of the company's processes is one of their most important skills. Changing the business can invalidate that knowledge, and with it goes an important part of their status. For a little while, everyone is a trainee again. While humility may be good for the soul, it's hell for the ego.

A new role for finance

There are some things businesses could do to make these re-designs less disruptive. One piece of advice, in the words of dentists everywhere, is "don't leave it so long next time".

But how can a business make continual change a part of its routine operations? One good starting point might be to take advantage of a shift in the balance between finance and IT.

In what you might term 'the old days' a large part of the finance role was reporting – telling the business what had happened, counting the cost and quantifying the successes. Increasingly, management reporting is something for IT people to worry about.

Replenishment or merchandise systems already hold stock and sales data; back-office systems monitor discounts and shrinkage. It makes sense that management reporting is generated automatically from live operational data. Enterprise-wide systems are often capable of populating accounting ledgers directly and tracking variance to budget without manual intervention. Some businesses no longer need to reconcile their accounts with their operational records; the two use a single source of data.

Finance teams not only spend less time producing reports these days, they spend less time devising them. Many interactive reporting systems have graphical interfaces designed to let data-literate managers drag-and-drop their way through the creation of personalised reports.

If this new fangled bean-counting technology is starting to sound like it might do for finance what the spinning jenny did for the cottage textile industry, let me reassure you. I'm not suggesting that the role of finance is diminishing; I'm saying it's about to evolve.

The problem with the generalised value-based management methodologies we mentioned a while back is that the people who came up with them didn't know your business. They were forced to devise something that was one-size-fits-all. Somebody needs to custom-fit value-based management to the tasks that take place, and the decisions that are relevant, in *your* business. Who better to work on the link between management activity and underlying value drivers than the finance team?

In the future, I can imagine two versions of every business – the flesh-and-blood, bricks-and-mortar original and a second version, held in software: a financial simulation of the business which mirrors the real one. The model will hold all the distinctive financial features of your business and the connections between them. There will be hundreds of details like the typical costs of listing new products or recruiting a new employee, the shrinkage rates and the maturity profiles of new stores and lots more. Businesses will build up and maintain cost models of their own business, complete with a hierarchy of interlocking KPIs for running it.

As the model becomes more accurate, it will gradually grow from a reporting tool into a planning tool. It will become *predictive*, a way of asking 'what if?'. The model will evolve from a record of the business into a simulation of the business. It may even change the way businesses are designed, where the predictability of a process becomes just as much a factor in its design as its effectiveness or efficiency.

All in all, 'keeper of the model' is a much more strategic and commercial role for finance than reporting and it has the potential to add a lot more value. Finance analysts would spend their time trying to really understand the relationship between cause and effect in the business. They wouldn't, however, work by themselves.

KPIs will need to be devised for every role in the business (and SLAs for many). It makes sense that sometimes the creative process will work the other way round. Sometimes, we will take an important KPI and create a role to manage it. Because the process can work in either direction, finance will need to work closely with HR.

And while we're at it, a new role for HR

The hierarchy of KPIs needs to span the business, and all of them need to link eventually to value added at the top. Every business already contains another hierarchy, its management structure, which culminates with the CEO's role.

The hierarchies automatically touch at one point – where the CEO's role meets shareholder value – but they also need to meet everywhere else as well. Every role needs a KPI and every KPI needs to be someone's responsibility.

In this integrated future, the finance and HR teams would have a number of tasks in common. Both teams would regularly review the current structure, identifying any serious operating problems. In each case, the question would be "change the KPI or change the job?".

The goal would be to arrive at logical and simple KPIs and coherent and popular roles. Well-designed roles favour common personality types, can be filled from an existing (though possibly external) pool of candidates and contain a mix of tasks likely to give the incumbent a reasonable shot at job satisfaction. A well-designed KPI will be built from objectively measurable quantities and will link directly to value added; it will make intuitive sense and will accurately reflect the scope of the associated role.

Isn't the future too complicated?

Although the financial model I'm talking about probably sounds impossibly complex, that happens to be the direction business is heading in. If you abducted a retailer from the 1950s and brought him to the modern era, I think you'd get a similar reaction. Imagine showing him the algorithms used by a sales-reactive stock-replenishment system or explaining the principles of dynamic scheduling in distribution. To all intents and purposes, it would look to him pretty much like rocket science.[1]

As with a number of ideas you've encountered in this book, I'm not showing you a vision of next week, or even next year. The state of affairs I'm describing here is some distance off, but you will undoubtedly be able to see the signs of its approach already.

Value-based management methodologies and enterprise resource planning (ERP) systems are both gathering speed. They won't converge in the world of retail, but they will meet somewhere. When they do, they could create a scenario like the one described here – a self-documenting organisation that continually adapts to its environment, improves its own efficiency and actually makes itself easier to manage. By describing the idealised future, I'm hoping to tempt you a few steps along the path.

---

1 I've seen working systems for helping supermarkets site new stores which contain unbelievable amounts of traffic-flow, census and demographic information as well as the location of every set of traffic lights and every stop sign in the country. Complex? Yes – but worth it.

Trust issues in the stock market

Some pages back, as I was saddling up for a gallop through value-based management, I mentioned the perceived short-termism of the markets. I said that value-based management and open lines of communication would go a long way towards curing investor short-termism. Will the financial modelling and the KPI alignment I've been describing eliminate it completely?

Not quite. To get rid of investor short-termism completely, I think we would have to find a way to integrate strategic relationships into value-based management.[1] I'm going to describe, at least in general terms, what that union needs to achieve.

Managing the intangibles

What has market short-termism got to do with strategic relationships?

Well, think for a moment about how companies generally value prospective investments. It's usually done by forecasting all the future cashflows (both in and out), discounting them, and comparing the total to the capital invested. In other words we calculate a rate of return.

Where does that leave a business counting the cost of a 'no quibble' guarantee, for instance? That's one of those deals where you might issue refunds whether or not the customer can prove they're entitled. In fact, consider any gesture of customer goodwill. How do you value it?

What companies will normally do is *think* of it as an investment in customer relations, but *treat* it financially as an expense. Why? Because it's so darn difficult to account for it as an investment. When will it pay off and how much? Are there any assets to show for the investment?

In fact, customer relationships (in the form of brands) do occasionally get valued as intangible assets, but ironically it happens at one of the most perilous moments in their lifecycle: when they change hands. The first time a brand usually shows up on a balance sheet is when someone else buys it. These are normally product, not retail, brands so the change of ownership is less sensitive.

But retail brands, as we've been at pains to uncover, are surprisingly personal relationships between customer and company. Trying to transplant a new identity onto one end of the relationship is an inversion

---

1   Of course, I'm tempted to christen the resulting combination Value Added Relationship Management Integration, or VARMINT for short, but I've a feeling it might weaken my credibility.

of the usual medical situation: it's riskier the *healthier* the patient is. That's because a healthy brand is a healthy relationship; it feels real and personal. 'Personal' is just another way of saying that identity matters.

So accounting for retail brands only after the life-threatening surgery of a transplant can't be the best way of bringing their value to light.

At any rate, intangibles like brands are recognised (even by conservative accounting folk) as being worth sizeable sums of actual cash money. Considering their value, there's a lot we don't know about them.

Care and feeding of retail brands

For a start, it's probably wise to understand the mechanism by which the value gets into the brand in the first place. We want to be sure that our goodwill gestures and customer service initiatives, and so forth, are going where they're supposed to – that all that money we've spent is *really* building the brand.

From the point of view of the markets, companies are always investing in intangibles. Accounting standards recognise some of them – patents and trade names, for instance – others are *really* intangible like good employee relations. In fact, to distinguish the class of intangibles that exist completely beyond GAAP,[1] I'll call them invisible assets. A retail brand will be part legitimate intangibles (like the trademark) and part invisible.

To the markets, many of the intangible investments made by retailers look like gambling, only worse. Money vanishes into thin air and you don't even get a little slip for claiming your winnings later. There are no assets and nothing shows up on the balance sheet.

Money spent on things like customer goodwill looks remarkably like money just given away. When some of it turns up later as part of the valuation of the brand, everyone can breathe a sigh of relief that it wasn't all wasted. But you have to admit, it isn't quite as reassuring a way of spending money as building a power station.

Retailers know they need to build a relationship with the customer (even if they don't always express it in those terms) but the markets have trouble understanding the mechanism by which they achieve it. So do retailers.

The markets appear short-termist when they lose faith in those invisible investments. Even when things are going well, retailers spend money and investors just have to trust that it is still there, invisibly

---

1 Much like Gap (the clothing store) avoids high fashion and sticks to the classics (at least they did in their heyday), GAAP tries to do the same for accounting.

residing in customer loyalty, motivated employees or preferential deals. If backers lose faith in the business, they may start to question the existence of those invisible assets. They may begin to believe that the money is gone.

As I said a while back, it's not that the markets don't like investments with long-term pay-offs, it's that they don't like investments with no pay-offs.

When retail businesses seem to be doing a bad job of investing in relationships (the money goes in, but it never comes out), it's natural that the markets would become disenchanted. They might even feel they could do a better job of running things themselves. Knowledge of the intangibles is the only thing stopping a financier thinking they can manage a retail business. If it becomes obvious that the incumbent management has no idea how to manage those intangibles either, that barrier is removed.

That's where turnaround deals originate. The markets decide that if you're going to screw up the intangibles, you might as well do it under sound financial control. Or put another way, if your ability to back winners is limited, maybe it's time to give up gambling.

Invisible and fragile

So how could we go about reassuring the markets about intangible investment in relationships? Wouldn't the best way be to acknowledge them, to explain them and to develop a consistent approach to managing them?

The first step in that process would be to understand where the intangibles reside. What does it mean to say that we have invested in customer (or employee or supplier) relations? Where is that investment recorded?

Well, if you can remember all the way back to the customer chapter you'll already know the answer. We spent quite a lot of time understanding that customers judge our business. More than that, they keep something a little like a mental bank account open for us – recording the debits and credits of our interactions.

That is where the invisible assets live – in the minds of the customers. If we are spending that money and investing that effort wisely, it is being noted and acknowledged by the customers. It is building up a sense of familiarity, trust and maybe even obligation.

And you'll recall from the employee chapter, one important aspect of managing obligations is making sure both sides acknowledge each transaction. In the case of customers, that's about making sure that when you do something extra for them, they notice.

That's actually something marketing departments are very switched on about. You'll quite often see a company use a phrase like "As a valued customer we'd like to show you our appreciation ..." Of course, the mistake marketing departments always make is to exaggerate. That's all well and good if you're telling a story, but not if you're recording a transaction. It actually turns people off to do them a small favour and tell them it was a big deal.

But even allowing for marketing's destructive addiction to hyperbole,[1] the message is there: "Please note: we're doing you a favour". My phrasing might make it sound cynical, but I'm not criticising. There's nothing wrong with being explicit about obligations. We just have to avoid being heavy-handed or ungracious.

So we are not completely hopeless at paying into 'the relationship bank'. Our biggest failing is the accidental damage we do to these relationships once they're up and running. This came up in both the customer and employee chapters (the supplier relationship hasn't reached that stage yet). Without realising it we have a habit of sending some very damaging mixed messages. We intersperse our finest moments with gaffes that threaten to undo all the good work.

Whenever we misunderstand the nature of the relationship, we risk accidentally jettisoning it with the value we've built up still trapped inside. The brand-representation errors we make with our customers undermine their relationship with us. The lack of continuity in managing employees can erase any credit they've built up whenever they change bosses. In both cases, it's a little like a bank that periodically sends out notices saying, 'We have no record of your account'. Well that account is important; it's where a lot of the value in the business resides.

To bring shareholders and retailers together, we need to get better at managing all the repositories of value in the business – even the invisible ones inside relationships – and then we need to communicate that change.

The explosive growth of financial services in the last two decades has been characterised by new approaches to investment and new instruments for representing value. Retail needs to expand the definition of investment even further. We have to include those vital but invisible

---

1 Just to reiterate the point: marketing is more about making promises than it is about telling a good story. There is no retail offer so majestic or impressive that it can't be turned into an anti-climax by claiming it's better than it really is.

strategic relationships in our planning. We need to make them visible and find a way to bring them into the management fold. We need to extend the boundaries of our business to include *all* the things we do to create value – including the intangibles.

Many of the ideas we have covered in earlier chapters are quite abstract. Some of them paint a picture of the future and some of them you could start implementing tomorrow. But this chapter is where they become grounded in something concrete and fundamental – the valuation of your business.

What was that all about?

- Businesses can be run using a shareholder-oriented definition of success.
- The resulting 'value-based management' benefits both retailer and shareholder alike.
- The basis of value-based management is to link operational activities to a strategic measure of success.
- Providing all job roles with aligned KPIs would link every employee to the strategy.
- Currently, the value stored in relationships is invisible.
- Making it visible and learning to manage it will bring enormous benefits – not least a healthy relationship with investors.

Closing remarks

The overall journey

Well that's it. I hope everyone learned something, I know I did.

When we started planning this book, we envisaged it tackling retail at a much lower level – sort of a handbook for senior managers to follow. In the end, most of that content has found its way in here anyway, it just didn't feature as largely as originally expected.

Instead, we decided to go with the big ideas, while we had your attention – we hung all the detail on them.

So you've seen quite a lot about the *future* of retail and most importantly you've seen some new ways of looking at the old questions – how to keep customers happy, how to evoke loyalty from staff.

To the best of my knowledge this is the first time these new ways of thinking about retail brands and employee relations have been published anywhere. If you found them compelling, you can be the first to take a look at your business in this new light and see what it reveals.

Initially, I was concerned that ideas about managing strategic relationships were too far from the usual topics of retail discussion and they would fail to grab the average reader. But at the same time, I felt that if we don't have a chance to explore big, unusual, innovative ideas for retail then there's something wrong. Even if you came away unconvinced by what you read, I'd like to think that spending time with an opposing point of view at least helped you clarify your own thoughts.

As a career thinker, I have almost unlimited faith in people's ability to think their way through a problem when they try. Nothing happens without drive and enthusiasm, of course, but we've always had those. It's the new ideas that change things.

I worry that retailers don't spend enough time on the big picture and when they do it can get overtaken by the need to be confident and authoritative. Tackling big questions when we don't have the answers already is not something many people feel comfortable doing in front of an audience. So it becomes a matter for quiet, personal reflection or perhaps it gets crowded out completely.

Take a simple question. 'Should we put our resources behind a weak product to make it stronger or a strong product to make it even better?' I ask it from time to time of the people who control those resources, the promotional spend, the shelf space, the ads and signage. More often than not I get a look that tells me there just aren't enough hours in the day for a question like that. What with doing the job, there just isn't time to *theorise* about the job. Well, I don't want to turn retail into a debating society, but clarity of purpose is worth having. It greases the wheels all the way down the line through to implementation.

My greatest enemy in this crusade is of course open-plan offices. They are my Moriarty, thwarting me at every turn. I can't imagine a more effective method of jamming complex thought. Dan and I have both wondered when and where the modern manager is supposed to do her thinking. I'm afraid I have come to the conclusion that the only place for these activities is outside of work.

That's the other reason for the book being the way it is. If you're going to have to read about work in your leisure time I wanted it to be easy and funny. The chapter on finance contains ideas that I think would take a lot more out of you if you read them elsewhere. I wanted to get them across, but I wanted to do as much of the work at my end as I could.

The final thing I wanted to do was challenge. The chapter on suppliers contains a lot of things you can't say in a consulting project. Even if I wanted to say them, in the past I've usually been part of a team, and others would pay the price for my outspokenness if I offended the client. But in a book I can set the whole thing out – how we got to this point and why it's not the way to go forwards. The beauty is that you can throw the book down in disgust if you disagree. Very little harm is done. You might even have chuckled a couple of times before you felt the urge to burn the rest of it.

I hope you did look at things in a new way, you did have fun as you read, you were challenged. At the very least you know more about vampire bats than you did.

Index